UMCP

Foreign Policy Decision Making

About the Book and Author

An analysis of decision making and negotiation in international relations, this book offers a political-psychological model of the images that compose policymakers' world views. Dr. Cottam explores the limits these images impose on diplomatic adaptation to changes in the foreign policies of other states. She evaluates established models of political decision making and cognitive psychology, offering an alternative framework in which it is argued that policymakers organize the world psychologically in terms of images of seven ideal-typical types of states. Her survey research shows that particular attributes and behavioral expectations are found in association with each image and lead to identifiable patterns of information selection and policy formation. Proposing that diplomatic activity can be traced to and predicted from the image ascribed to a target state, this book contributes to the growing body of literature attempting to understand and explain the psychological basis of successes and failures in international policy formation and negotiations.

Martha Cottam is assistant professor of American foreign policy at the University of Denver's Graduate School of International Studies.

Foreign Policy Decision Making

The Influence of Cognition

Martha L. Cottam

Westview Press / Boulder and London

To Otto

Westview Special Studies in International Relations

This Westview softcover edition is printed on acid-free paper and bound in
softcovers that carry the highest rating of the National Association of State
Textbook Administrators, in consultation with the Association of American
Publishers and the Book Manufacturers' Institute.

Copyright © 1986 by Westview Press, Inc.

Published in 1986 in the United States of America by Westview Press, Inc.;
Frederick A. Praeger, Publisher; 5500 Central Avenue, Boulder, Colorado 80301

Library of Congress Cataloging-in-Publication Data
Cottam, Martha.
   Foreign policy decision making.
   (Westview special studies in international relations)
   Includes index.
   1. International relations--Research. I. Title.
II. Series.
JX1291.C65 1986   327'.072   86-13295
ISBN 0-8133-7246-1

Composition for this book was provided by the author.
This book was produced without formal editing by the publisher.

Printed and bound in the United States of America

The paper used in this publication meets the requirements
of the American National Standard for Permanence of Paper
for Printed Library Materials Z39.48-1984.

6   5   4   3   2   1

Contents

Tables

Acknowledgments

This book has benefitted from the valuable insights and comments of many people as it has evolved through numerous stages. Robert Jervis and Edward Gonzalez provided valuable criticisms and suggestions. Their guidance in the earliest stages of the project was crucial to its completion. Otwin Marenin and Richard Cottam have contributed important comments on various versions of the manuscript and unceasing intellectual and moral support. The numerous discussions I have had with them, and also with Richard Herrmann, concerning the theoretical issues discussed in this book have been particularly important. Ben Menke offered helpful suggestions concerning the survey while Kay Wolsborn kindly helped me sort out the results. I owe a great debt to a real scientist, Patricia Cottam, who reminded me at a very important moment that social scientists can be quite cavalier in their research and that results must be faced honestly. Asma Barlas and Chih-yu Shih provided much-appreciated assistance in preparing the manuscript for publication. Finally, I am grateful to my students who have bravely challenged my ideas and in the process contributed enormously to the development of those ideas.

Introduction

In 1978, dismayed by the souring of relations between the United States and Mexico, President Carter called
for a complete re-evaluation of United States policies toward Mexico. In the process the National Security Council
invited a Mexican official to express his personal view of
the historical and contemporary interaction between the two
countries. The official commented that:

> [W]ith the passage of time, especially since the oil
> expropriation in 1938, Mexico has acquired a certain
> confidence in her capacity to act internationally. The
> consistent relative independence of her foreign policy
> since then is, in itself, a powerful factor that will
> have its bearing in future relations with the United
> States.1

He argued that despite Mexico's unemployment and poverty,
Mexico did have self-confidence, a new powerful negotiating
tool (oil) and a determination to "increase the bonds of
solidarity with other developing countries..."2 The official
spoke at the height of the perceived promise in Mexico's oil
discoveries in the mid-1970's. As Mexico changed it sought a
more equal relationship with the United States. However, he
expressed no hope that the United States would adjust its
own policies to compliment Mexico's transformation:

> I discount -- and don't give any credit to -- any
> sudden newly discovered or rediscovered good will,
> sympathy or moral considerations on the part of the
> United States that could change its basic attitude
> towards Mexico. Its past history with us, its present-

1

2

day arrogance, selfishness and conservative mood will
not allow for change.3

Mexico is not the only country to complain bitterly
about the failure of the United States to recognize and
respond to change in its needs, demands and power. The
United States has been accused of failing to understand the
true nature of leftist movements in Nicaragua and El Salvador, and of interpreting them in outdated and irrelevant
Cold War terms. The United States and other highly industrialized countries have been accused of failing to understand and respond to the needs and demands of the Third
World for a New International Economic Order as well.

Why are policy makers slow to recognize and respond
to political change, particularly non-revolutionary change?
Why are there arguments among policy makers about the meaning of new issues and conflicts? Why do they disagree about
which negotiating positions will best serve the interests of
their own country? Do these puzzles reflect general patterns
of information processing which also affect other aspects of
international relations such as interpretations of diplomatic signals during a crisis, the conduct of intelligence
analysis and the planning of coherent and consistent policies?

One method of addressing these questions is to study
the perceptions of policy makers. An understanding of how
decision makers view the political world may lead to explanations of the difficulty they have in recognizing, agreeing
upon and responding to its transformations. As one scholar
put it, "[p]erceptions of the world and of other actors may
diverge from reality in patterns that we can detect and for
reasons that we can understand."4

This project is a study of the psychological processes involved in the recognition of non-revolutionary political change. The study has both a theoretical and empirical
purpose. The theoretical goal is to contribute to efforts in
political science to develop models for analyzing the effects of cognitive processes on political decision making.
The empirical goal is to develop and test hypotheses concerning the effects of cognitive patterns on policy makers'
ability to adapt to political change.

Several steps are involved in pursuing these goals.
First, some of the major cognitive approaches in political
science are reviewed. Second, a framework depicting policy
makers' images of the international world is developed and

supported with empirical evidence. The framework draws upon works in political science and psychology. Third, the effect of images on judgment is addressed with particular attention to the problems of adapting to change. Finally, hypotheses about the effects of images on adaptation to change are developed and tested in a case study of negotiations -- United States negotiations with Mexico in the area of energy trade from 1977 to 1979.

NOTES

1.   United   States,   National   Security   Council, Presidential Review Memorandum 41: Summary Report [1978]. This document is unpublished and was released to me by the National Security Council in 1982 under the Freedom of Information Act, p. 8.
2. Ibid., p. 2
3. Ibid., p. 3.
4. R.   Jervis,   Perception and   Misperception in International Politics (Princeton: Princeton University Press, 1976), p. 2.

1

The Decision Making Literature in International Relations: A Review of the Literature and New Directions

The decision making literature in international relations is vast. It can be divided crudely into studies of personality factors in decision making and studies of non-idiosyncratic psychological factors such as beliefs, values and cognition. The non-idiosyncratic group can be subdivided into those seeking to construct models and those studying the relevance of a variety of psychological approaches to a variety of decision making problems. There are two major cognitive models in the field, the Operational Code and Cognitive Maps. This chapter will examine the two dominant cognitive approaches and will then turn to new directions in theory and research including an introduction to the framework to be used throughout this study. First, however, a discussion of the non-idiosyncratic body of literature as a whole is necessary.

Robert Jervis suggests that decision making studies often suffer from three problems: they do not build upon earlier works; they do not use much psychology; and they do not link psychology and behavior.1 One might add to this list a common assumption that models exist when they do not (a result of the failure to link psychology and behavior) and a failure to utilize <u>appropriate</u> psychological theories. The last two problems have been particularly pervasive in studies of cognition and political decision making.

In a recent review and summary of the state of the art Alexander George optimistically lauded a "cognitive revolution" in psychology in the areas of "cognitive balance and dissonance theories, attribution theory, attitude theory, social learning theory and personality theory" that have moved them into a "common information-processing framework."2 These studies are said to have produced a paradigma-

5

tic shift from which studies of political decision making can benefit.3 Sadly, there is a negative side to developments in psychology and the political works that have drawn upon its models as well. First, cognitive balance and dissonance theories are increasingly criticized by psychologists and political scientists as theoretically unsound, untestable, and too simple to be of use in understanding complex decision-making.4

A second problem is that the "common information-processing framework" is elusive. Psychology has no common information processing framework nor has it had a resultant paradigmatic shift. Attribution theory, for example, has little relationship to "attitude theory" and even less to "personality theory" (if one can properly speak of personality "theory" rather than "theories"). In fact, social psychology is rent by theoretical fads and, like political scientists, psychologists often fail to use earlier works. Because there is no common information processing framework in psychology there also has been no paradigmatic shift. Jerome Bruner, for example, recently wrote, "I don't think we've had Big Bangs in psychology in the last 15 years..." 5

Partly because of these developments a third problem tends to afflict political works that draw upon psychology; a failure to utilize adequately old and new studies of cognition as a distinct psychological phenomenon. Cognitive psychology is not social psychology (although there may be some overlap as in Attribution Theory) and cognition is not the same as an attitude. Strictly speaking, cognition is:

> ...a collective term for the psychological processes involved in the acquisition, organization, and use of knowledge. Originally the work distinguished the rational from the emotional...and impulsive aspect of mental life. It passed out of currency, to be revived with the advent of COMPUTER SIMULATION of thought processes. The term is now used in COGNITIVE PSYCHOLOGY to refer to all the information processing activities of the brain, ranging from the analysis of immediate STIMULI to the organization of subjective experience. In contemporary terminology, cognition includes such processes and phenomena as PERCEPTION, memory, attention, PROBLEM-SOLVING, language, thinking, and imagery.6

Cognitive psychology, in turn, is:

A branch of PSYCHOLOGY defined partly by its subject matter, i.e., partly by its point of view. With respect to point of view, its main PRESUPPOSITION is that any interaction between an organism, and its ENVIRONMENT changes not only its overt behavior or physiological condition but also its knowledge of or information about the environment, and that this latter change may affect not only present response but also future orientation to the environment.7

Attitudes include both cognition and affect. Attitudes are a result of cognition and include "knowledge". Many psychologists argue that affect, or emotion, results from the appraisal of information. The organization of knowledge, the "cognitive screen", processes information.

There is a reason, therefore, to use what cognitive psychology has to offer, particularly if one is constructing a cognitive model of decision-making. Studies of policy makers' cognitive structures, how they understand, order, and simplify the world, may lead to an understanding of how information is processed and political events judged. These evaluations influence and interact with policy makers' values concerning how the world should be and result in policy preferences.

In short, there is a tendency to mix social psychological studies together to the neglect of many important cognitive approaches. This is not to say that the diverse theories in psychology have nothing to offer or that they should not be mentioned in the same study. Robert Jervis, for example draws upon social and cognitive psychology, studies of attitude change and other psychological works, in Perception and Misperception in International Politics. Jervis' purpose is to take a "broader and more eclectic" approach to the study of psychology and political decision-making in order to gain a "wider variety of insights and greater confidence in our explanations" by showing that psychological studies offer support.8 This is what he sets out to do and this is what he does. Jervis does not attempt to throw all of these theories into a psychological grab-bag and pronounce a psychological model. Jervis' study is one of the few exceptions, however, for too often political studies fail to utilize appropriate psychological literature and underestimate the importance of a careful examination of psychological concepts before attempting to transpose them

onto the political decision-making arena. One can apply
Jervis' comment that political decision making studies often
fail to use psychology to the cognitive studies in
particular.

The resistance to utilizing cognitive psychology
leads to a fourth problem in the literature and, as will be
seen, with Cognitive Maps and the Operational Code. Political scientists have accepted as interchangeable the notions
of "beliefs" and "cognitive systems," The idea that beliefs
form a (usually hierarchical) system is popular in social
psychology. In political works it is often unclear if
beliefs are cognition alone or attitudes. The unwillingness
to address this question is in part a result of relying upon
psychological literature that blurs the distinction between
cognition and attitudes or beliefs. This leads to very
serious theoretical problems. The object of cognitive
studies of international politics, particularly Cognitive
Maps, is to build models of policy makers' political world
views and to use these models to explain decisions. The main
purposes of models, according to Frohock, "are substantially
the same as those of any theory: stating lawful relationships between events; building upon a body of knowledge; and
so on. Further...a representational model must possess a
logical interrelationship among its concepts and empirical
propositions which are amenable to verification..."9 Blalock
points out that:

> Having selected a causal model, we then move in two
> directions. We attempt to think by means of the causal
> model and to make use of our causal assumptions to
> arrive at certain predictions that can be translated
> into testable hypotheses. At the same time, we at least
> imagine some operational procedures that can be used to
> test our conclusions. Our ideal in the first instance
> is some sort of deductive system of reasoning; in the
> second, it is the perfect experiment.10

Although the ambition of many political scientists
(especially Cognitive Mappers) is to build models of the
impact of cognition on political decision making, they often
lack the necessary psychological information to do so.
Because they do not separate beliefs and cognition they
cannot describe the cognitive elements of the political
world view, they cannot state the relationships between the
elements of the world view and they cannot produce testable
hypotheses about the effects of cognition on political

decision making. They do not have the necessary information
for a deductive system of reasoning. Having no hypotheses
testable in a variety of decision making events, the focus
shifts to the actors' situation-specific beliefs. This is a
serious problem in the literature but it is also a needless
one. This is not to say that beliefs and attitudes are
unimportant or that all studies of cognition and political
decision making are hopeless failures. The point is simply
that the appropriate body of psychology is often ignored
and the two major approaches in this area suffer as a
result. These issues are considered in detail below.

THE OPERATIONAL CODE

The Operational Code approach does attempt to
formulate a general, non-situation-specific, framework of
fundamental beliefs about politics and the political world.
Beliefs are seen as organized in a hierarchical system
and those specified in the Code are deemed central or
essentially unchangeable.11 Two types of beliefs are
important; philosophical and instrumental. Philosophical
beliefs are "fundamental assumptions" about political life.
Instrumental beliefs concern assumptions about how politics
should be approached, what kinds of behavior are
appropriate. 12 Several questions are asked about and
delineate policy makers' philosophical and instrumental
beliefs. They are:

Philosophical Beliefs

1. What is the "essential" nature of political life?
   Is the political universe essentially one of
   harmony or conflict? What is the fundamental
   character of one's political opponents?
2. What are the prospects for the eventual realization
   of one's fundamental political values and
   aspirations? Can one be optimistic or must one be
   pessimistic on this score; and in what respects the
   one and/or the other?
3. Is the political future predictable? In what sense
   and to what extent?
4. How much "control" or "mastery" can one have over
   historical development? What is one's role in

"moving" and "shaping" history in the desired direction?

5. What is the role of "chance" in human affairs and historical development?

Instrumental Beliefs

1. What is the best approach for selecting goals or objectives for political action?
2. How are the goals of action pursued most effectively?
3. How are the risks of political action calculated, controlled, and accepted?
4. What is the best "timing" of action to advance one's interests?
5. What is the utility and role of different means for advancing one's interests? 13

The Code is said to be part of a cognitive prism through which the world is structured and simplified. The answers to these particular questions are supposed to give the analyst the range of possible policy options that will be acceptable to the individual policy maker.14

Operational Codes have been constructed for a wide variety of leaders from the Bolsheviks to Frank Church, Lyndon Johnson, and Henry Kissinger. 15 The same set of questions informs each framework with occasional additions. Lately, efforts have been made to improve the concept of the Operational Code. Johnson, for example, tried to add a more dynamic element that makes the "working model" compatible with policy makers whose beliefs change and with variations in their activity levels.16 He does this by drawing a figure of the code with "at least five 'beliefs' dimensions and one 'energy' dimension along which the actor can be placed."17 He argues that the Operational Code should be viewed "in a three-tiered fashion: a cluster of beliefs illustrating legislative orientations toward domestic cons-tituency politics, a second cluster for domestic national politics, and a third for international politics."18

As a model of cognitive processes in political decision making, the Operational Code has the correct focus. The purpose of the Code is to use a set of beliefs that are politically important to all people to help the analyst understand how policy makers will respond to specific events. The Code is supposed to be the information processing structure that politicians use to help them organize and

simplify the complex political world. It has four general
problems.

One general difficulty with the approach is that the
term "beliefs" is not defined clearly and consistently.
Gunnar Sjoblom has argued that the Code refers to cognitive
beliefs, "beliefs that may be true or false, probable or
improbable..." and that it therefore excludes "ethical
beliefs, ideologies, etc."19 As important as Sjoblom's point
is, he is granting or assuming more coherence and utility in
the notion of cognitive beliefs than can actually be found
in the Code.One wonders whether the beliefs incorporated
into the philosophical and instrumental questions are knowledge alone or attitudes. Do the questions reveal a cognitive screen through which the policy-maker interprets events
or that screen plus his emotional response to past, present,
and future political circumstances? The difference is
important. If the questions reveal the policy maker's
cognitive world view, they will tell the analyst something
about how the individual will process information. If they
perform the other function they lead the analyst to findings
concerning policies the leader will strive for and 'motivated' biases in policy making.20 The adherents of the Code
do insist that cognition affects information processing but
they do not explain how this happens. This may be due to the
fact that they are not really concerned with cognition and
cognitive processes but with beliefs or attitudes. It is
difficult to construct a cognitive model when cognition and
cognitive processes are not the primary basis for that
model.

A second general problem with the Operational Code
is that no explanation is offered for the selection of these
particular beliefs. Why are these beliefs and not others the
"central" political beliefs? Further, the questions reveal
very little about the subject's assessment of other international actors. There is a question about the fundamental
character of the opponent but certainly there are many other
major international actors that are centrally important to a
policy maker. Why are his assessments of other actors neglected? The questions themselves reveal little about the
subject's expectations of the opponent's behavior. This must
be important in determining how policy makers understand the
political universe.

A third general problem with the framework is that
the beliefs revealed by the questions are vague and abstract
which makes a connection between the beliefs and behavior
difficult to achieve.21 This problem requires extensive

discussion. Analysts using the Code argue that a model should not be situation specific and that therefore one must not expect it to "provide a simple key to explanation and prediction."22 The questions that form the Operational Code lead to testable hypotheses only when situational and individual variables are added. Once the Operational Code questions have been answered for a particular policy maker one has a more precise picture of his or her beliefs and may be able to make behavioral predictions. This means that any Operational Code hypotheses are contingent upon the particular case and are not deduced from the theoretical strictures of the model. Hence, the Code is not a general theoretical model but remains a descriptive set of analytical categories.

This issue has not gone unnoticed by analysts using the Operational Code. Stephen Walker, for example, has addressed this particular issue in an article on Henry Kissinger's Operational Code. He notes that the originators of the Code and theorists who commented on the cognitive approach to foreign policy explanation have argued at times that it is not a useful endeavor to try to establish a link between the Code and behavior. He rejects this argument and instead emphasizes he need to connect explicitly the Code with foreign policy decision making behavior. However, he does not do this by providing a theoretical basis for the model itself. Instead, he sets out to "establish connections between Kissinger's operational code and American foreign policy behavior."23 In other words, he does not attempt to predict or explain using the model. Walker and Murphy tackle the issue of the relationship between the code and behavior in "The Utility of the Operational Code in Political Forecasting."24 In this article the authors also fail to reexamine the code itself -- the original ten questions -- and state very clearly that one must know the decision maker's beliefs before one can forecast or predict his behavior.25 The model is not revised and predictions of policy maker's behavior remain contingent upon one's ability to construct a detailed picture of the idiosyncractic beliefs of a single individual.

Alexander George has also recognized the need to connect the Operational Code construct with political behavior and addresses this problem in "The Casual Nexus between Cognitive Beliefs and Decision Making Behavior: The 'Operational Code' Belief Systems."26 Here he argues that the Operational Code beliefs "do not unilaterally determine [the] course of action" but that they should be important in the tasks of defining the situation and developing options.27 But his discussion of exactly how the Code beliefs will affect the definition of the situation remains suggestive. It will, he argues, affect the definition of the situation profoundly, enough to "eliminate from serious consideration certain policy options." 28 George focuses on the image of the opponent in particular and argues that the image may result in behavior such as the interpretation of ambiguous information as hostile, of latent conflicts as crises, and of situations in which the decision maker must interact with the opponent as dangerous. He also mentions a number of other behavioral patterns that could be associated with the Code beliefs such as the fourth and fifth philosophical beliefs. Policy choices are likely to be influenced by one's instrumental beliefs. "If [a policy maker] is an 'optimizer' rather than a 'satisficer' in his approach to goals selection... he is more likely to seek to develop and choose options that offer the prospect for greater payoffs." 29

Unfortunately, these are not hypotheses deduced from the psychological foundations of a political framework. They are examples of possible behavior, depending upon how the individual policy maker would answer the questions in the Operational Code. The specific case must provide the behavioral possibilities. The framework cannot do so. Further, the behavioral tendencies suggested are very sensible but are not associated with the psychological theory that also informed the framework itself. Instead, they appear to be intuitively based ideas. It is possible, of course, that one could conceivably develop typologies of ideal-typical Codes and suggest behavior patterns on that basis. But one would still be left with the other problems inherent in the Code itself such as those mentioned below.

Not surprisingly, the importance of constructing typologies has been tackled by Operational Code scholars and work is being done in this area. Holsti offers a sixfold typology. Walker has also been active in the effort to improve the Code by constructing typologies.30 These efforts, however, have resolved few of the Operational Code's problems.

Walker concisely presents Holsti's typology of six codes and attempts to boil the six down to four in "The Motivational Foundations of Political Belief Systems: A Re-Analysis of the Operational Code Construct." According to the author, Holsti:

...constructs a typology of six operational codes by first classifying an individual's beliefs regarding two fundamental aspects of political life...Second, he deduces a series of hypotheses about the other political beliefs which each type of individual ... is likely to possess. Third, he tests the validity of this typology of operational codes by applying it to the reinterpretation of several existing OPCODE studies by other scholars.31

The two questions asked are from the original ten code questions: What are the fundamental sources of conflict? (the answers being ˋhuman nature,' ˋattributes of nations' and ˋthe international system') and; What is the fundamental nature of the political universe? (the answers being ˋharmonious' or ˋconflictual'). A six cell matrix is created with each cell representing a code type with distinct combinations of answers to the questions. Several difficulties emerge immediately with this effort to typologize. First, Holsti's typology is validated by using the findings of people who have used the same operational code framework. Hence it is not surprising that he confirmed his hypotheses. This leads to a second problem: why those six types? One could very easily argue that the answer to the question "what is the fundamental nature of the political universe?" could include harmonious, conflictual and 'cyclical'. In that case, one could have nine types and one could probably confirm that third answer to the question by looking at previous operational code studies. In other words, there is a danger of the code becoming inbred, artificial and self-validating when its types are constructed in this manner.

The typology also suffers from the fact that it is based on the same questions that are the basis for the operational code. Hence, one may know a great deal about how type A views the political universe but that remains an exceptionally vague compilation of information. Intuition aside, it simply is not clear as to how the difference between type A's picture of the political universe ("Conflict is temporary; there is at least a latent harmony of interest") and type's B's picture ("Conflict is temporary; in a world of peaceful states there will be peace"); translates into different forms of behavior or what the theoretical basis for stating hypotheses about behavior would be.32

All of the above does not mean that one cannot

attempt to predict the behavior of individuals having one type of Operational Code, even given the vagueness of the beliefs asserted for each type. However, in the same sense that a typology is not a theory, a prediction is not an explanation. As was argued earlier, the questions in the Code are not clearly informed by cognitive psychology and the simple assertion that policy makers use a Code to screen reality does not constitute an explanation for their complex behavior. Similarly, the behavior of people falling into one or another type of Code is not automatically explained simply because they conform to a particular type. If the Code framework is not well-grounded in psychological theory, the types cannot be either. There should be a psychologically founded explanation for behavior both observed and predicted.

This issue has not escaped Walker in the article cited above. However, Walker's solution is not to investigate cognitive psychological findings but to assert that that information can be found in the pathbreaking work by Leites, George and Holsti.33 Instead of proceeding to incorporate a theory of cognition, Walker adds material from motivation studies in psychology. He begins with a call to the field to close the gaps between personality (that is, motivational) studies and cognitive approaches.34 It is then argued that Holsti's six types can be collapsed into four types (reinforcing the suggestion above that the types are quite artifical and can be expanded and contracted on the basis of intuition, correlation and self-validation rather than theoretical insight) and from there an effort is made to discuss the relationship between motivation, operational code beliefs, and foreign policy behavior. He asserts that "(a) motives account for variations in the development of beliefs systems; (b) belief systems account for the arousal of motives in decision making situations; (c) once aroused, the dominant motives reinforce the stability of the belief system against dissonant information..."35

The argument presented opens an enormous can of worms. First, the analyst mixes psychological theories together without defining motivation or beliefs and without developing concepts and findings from either theoretical orientation. Psychology has a levels of analysis condition in its theoretical constructs as does international relations and the same problems derive in mixing those theoretical levels. Nevertheless, Walker uses terms such as cognitive rigidity, cognitive dissonance, and cognitive consistency without defining them or even alluding to the fact that all three terms, and their accompanying research, have been, as mentioned above, enhanced, re-examined, and added to by further research and theory. He asserts that motivation (personality?) and cognition reinforce each other but to what end? There is no information in the argument concerning the exact effect of cognitive patterns on information processing so the assertion that motivation enters the picture and reinforces beliefs is not particularly insightful since one still does not know how beliefs affect behavior. In fact, this article basically replaces cognition with motivation since cognitive theories operate in absentia and more information is given concerning the impact of the power motive on behavior than the impact of cognitive processes on behavior. If one equates motivation studies with personality studies (as Walker apparently does in his first paragraph) then the Operational Code gradually becomes even more personality based (that is, idiosyncratic and situation/person specific) than ever before. The absence of a cognitive psychological theoretical base is replaced by a personality theoretical base. It also shows again the weakness of the original ten Operational Code questions in that Walker's discussion of the importance of power motivation could just as easily be incorporated into the ten questions as an additional "central belief."

The substitution of motivation analysis for cognitive theory and patterns is more obvious in Walker and Falkowski's "The Operational Codes of U.S. Presidents and Secretaries of State: Motivational Foundations and Behavioral Consequences." There is very little in the way of discussion of cognition in this article as well. Once again Festinger and cognitive dissonance is referred to but most of the emphasis is on motivation.[36] The authors acknowledge that "little work has been done to link operational code beliefs and political behavior, and the results have been somewhat uneven." [37] This article does not improve the situation. The "hypotheses" that are suggested are presented as speculations more than deductively developed hypotheses and, more importantly, they are based upon assumptions concerning the impact of motivation on behavior rather than cognitive processes.[38] One still learns nothing about the use of beliefs as screens for information processing, for predicting the actions of others (including states such as allies -- the concern of Operational Code construct still focuses on enemies), and the behavior that is produced as a result of these cognitive activities.

A final general problem with the Code is that it is most useful when applied to individuals. The earliest analysis using the Code was of groups, in particular, the Bolsheviks. There is no way of knowing whether the Bolsheviks should have been·treated as a unified group. It is possible that as a small revolutionary force they were of one mind. It is quite obvious, however, that American policy makers cannot be analyzed as a group, although group decision making is important. A framework that is capable of incorporating perceptual patterns and behavioral tendencies in groups of decision makers (through concepts such as the prevailing world view) would be more useful, particularly for analyzing the foreign policies of a state like the United States. This criticism of the Code is an old one but it is important and has not been adequately dealt with. Holsti argues that one cannot simply denounce studies of the individual and shift to studies of bureaucratic factors since that approach has not exactly fared well in producing great insight into international policies.39 This point, and others made by Holsti, are certainly valid. Nevertheless, the fundamental problem remains: The Operational Code is best suited to individuals. What is needed is a psychological model that can apply to single individuals or collections of individuals with similar world views (in which case they agree on policy) or conflicting world views (in which case one can understand the origins of policy disagreement).

In the long run the Operational Code is most useful as a guideline for describing some of the political beliefs of policy makers. Using the Code to generate testable hypotheses concerning political decision making remains problematic. It does not employ cognitive psychology beyond its founding assumption and it asks about a very small part of the policy makers' overall political world view.

COGNITIVE MAPS

A different cognitive approach to foreign policy decision making is Cognitive Mapping. Briefly, "[a] Cognitive Map is a way of representing belief structures related to a specific problem, and of making it possible to stimulate the thought processes that occur when the policy maker contemplates action in order to identify future developments."40 Cognitive Mapping is founded on the assumption that the thinking process is of primary

importance in political events. It is argued that political
events have no "meaning" apart from their interpretation.41
Decision makers bring "an interpretive" framework to their
experiences and they are constrained in policy making by
their beliefs.42 Beliefs reduce the variety of problems
identified and solutions posed for important issues.43

A major creator of the approach is Robert Axelrod. He
argues that a cognitive map is "a particular kind of mathe-
matical model of a person's belief system; in actual
practice, cognitive maps are derived from assertions of
beliefs."44 The maps are composed of two elements; concepts,
(which are variables), and causal beliefs, (which define the
relationships between the variables).45 Policy makers'
beliefs are reconstructed using any of a variety of methods
including analyses of documents, interviews, and questionnaires. Beliefs are placed in a diagram in which causal
beliefs form links with "concept variables" connected by
arrows. The parts of the map "interact rationally."46 The
links are given either a positive or negative valence which
depicts the nature of the causal relationship. A positive
causal relationship means "that changes occur in the same
direction, but not necessarily positively."47 Thus, a positive causal relationship can result in positive, negative,
or no change. For example, Axelrod points to statements by
British officials that "'the amount of security in Persia
augments the ability of the Persian government to maintain
order.'"48 He argues that:

> A word such as "augments" indicates a positive causal
> relationship between the cause variable and the effect
> variable. This means that an increase in the amount of
> security will cause an increase in the ability of the
> Persian government to maintain order. But it also means
> that a decrease in the amount of security will cause a
> decrease in the ability of the Persian government to
> maintain order. Thus a positive causal relationship
> means that changes occur in the same direction but not
> necessarily positively.49

If a causal relationship is negative there is an inverse
relationship between the variables.

A Cognitive Map is a representation of the beliefs
and concepts of policy makers. The next logical question is,
how does the map function during decisions? Bonham et al
explain the decision process and the use of the map in "A
Cognitive Model of Decision-Making: Application to Norwegian

Oil Policy." They argue that the decision process involves five steps; an early amplification of the situation in which the policy maker tries to fit new information in with his past experiences; a search for antecedents where the individual looks through his Cognitive Map for possible causes of the situation; a search for consequences; a search for policy alternatives which are "embedded in his or her explanation of the situation"; and a policy selection.50 The final step, selection of policy, is the point at which the analyst follows the "paths of the Cognitive Map from the policy options to the 'policy values' and calculates the policy options that will best satisfy a maximum number of values."51 Cognitive Maps have been used to study a variety of policy decision including the British Eastern Committee decisions concerning Persia, Norwegian oil policy, and Syrian intervention in Jordan as well as other cases.52

The Cognitive Map approach should be thought of as an interesting step forward in the use of cognitive psychology for political analysis. Although Axelrod basically ignores the psychological foundation for his argument, others have examined those issues.53 There are, however, several crucial problems with the approach. First, neither "beliefs" nor "concepts" are defined. The fact that beliefs have positive or negative valence may permit the reader to infer that they are affective and are attitudes. Trying to figure out the meaning of "concepts" is a different matter. Axelrod explains what a concept is through example, not definition: "A concept is something like 'the amount of security in Persia'; something that can take on different values, such as 'a great amount of security' or 'a small amount of security.'" 54 From his study of British decision-making concerning Persia in 1918 it appears that concepts are important issues associated with the policy problem and its possible resolution. His discussion of the term itself leaves the reader confused about its meaning but certain that a concept can have more that one value.

A second problem with the approach is its simplistic view of causality. Kinder and Weiss point out that "[c]ausality is defined rather coursely...: an increase in one variable results in an increase, a decrease, or no change in a given second variable. The strength of causal relationships is ignored; so are conditional and non monotonic relationships."55 One study actually discards paths found to be inconsistent with no justification.56 Inconsistent causal paths may be important in decision making and their rejection deserves explanation.

A third problem with the model is that the assessments of policy makers' beliefs relies exclusively on their written and/or oral statements. This means that the lexicographic procedures used to calculate policy preference may be done with insufficient or inaccurate data. Policy makers may not openly express some important beliefs either because they are publicly unacceptable or because they are so universally accepted that they need not be expressed. Further, some beliefs may be inordinately important for non-rational reasons but would not appear on the map as crucially important.

A final and very important criticism of this approach concerns is quality as a model. The Cognitive Map is not a model of decision making. It is a codebook for the analyst specifying how he or she should diagram beliefs and concepts. The map itself is not associated with generalizations or hypotheses about political decision making. One cannot explain political acts until a specific situation is analyzed. The map is not an outgrowth of a theory of decision making. One can create hypotheses about decision making only after the beliefs of policy makers involved in a particular act are assessed. Therefore, the approach has no predictive ability and can only explain with hindsight.

Aside from the technical problems with Cognitive Maps (such as undefined terms and questionable research methods) the greatest deficiency in the approach is that its stated purpose is much larger than the questions it asks in the end. The general goal of the approach is to understand how policy makers see the world and how this affects their decisions. This is a goal that demands the use of cognitive psychology. However, when cognitive mappers finally get down to asking the question upon which the model is built, the question is the old one: "What beliefs were important?" They begin with the assumption that decision makers bring an "interpretive framework" to their political experiences but they never develop a model of this political world view. With such a framework, non-situation-specific hypotheses concerning how policy makers interpret the political universe could be suggested and tested in specific situations.

Both Cognitive Maps and the Operational Code can be criticized for having a number of analytical shortcomings. This is not to say that they have contributed nothing to our understanding of political decision making or that it is easy to avoid these problems. The theorists in both areas have been crucial in advancing the general understanding of the limits in policy makers' abilities to process information perfectly and to make well-designed decisions. They have also been responsible for making the study of psychological characteristics of decision makers respectable in political science. Their success in opening the way to a new paradigmatic orientation is remarkable. Finally, both the Operational Code and the Cognitive Map approach, through their insights and limits, have pointed to the need for careful definition of terms; a comprehensive use of psychology; a firm link between psychology, political thinking and political behavior; and a willingness to suggest and test hypotheses derived from the psychological arguments. A number of recent works offer additional frameworks drawing more explicitly from cognitive psychology and related areas and that propose alternative models for explaining decision making in foreign policy. One in particular will be discussed below with support from some preliminary data.

NEW DIRECTIONS: INTRODUCTION TO THE FRAMEWORK

It has long been argued that policy makers employ images or categories of others in the inescapable propensity to organize, simplify, and understand the environment in which they make decision.57 These images are said to affect information processing and decision making. The most frequently discussed image is that of the enemy. It is argued here and in other works that this human tendency to form images of others not only extends far beyond the image of the enemy to many other identifiable images,[58] but that this psychological propensity and the resulting images and information processing patterns can be used to form an ideal-typical model of the psychological political world view of all decision makers. Two tasks are involved: the identification and description of the (ideal-typical) categories or images used to organize and simplify the international world and, based upon psychologists' findings concerning the effects of categories on information processing, the construction of testable hypotheses of political decision making.

There are a number of theoretical steps that are crucial to the examination of the images of the political world view. The first is the recognition that several forces contribute to judgments. For example, all people in any situation and regardless of the particular cognitive categories involved, are subject to perceptual distortions produced by the peculiar qualities of information. This source of bias, however, cannot explain enough about judgements to form the analytical basis of a model of decision making. The study of the characteristics of information leaves one with little understanding of how it will be used.

A more important theoretical step is the appropriate use of psychology. Psychology cannot be blindly applied to political analysis. The controls of the psychological laboratory will never be available for political research. Therefore, the findings of psychological studies cannot be expected to be duplicated in political analysis. What psychology does have to offer are very general guidelines for arguments about how people make political decisions. Although there should be a psychological justification for arguments about political decision making, the resulting model should be designed specifically for the analysis of political decision making.

Another important aspect of the appropriate use of psychology is the need to avoid uncritical borrowing of psychological theory. The criticism of political scientists' use of consistency theory has already been noted. Other political studies rely upon personality studies in psychology, including Freudian analysis, and ignore the opinion of many psychologists that personality factors account for a relatively small portion of behavior.59 Further, political scientists tend to pursue new fads in psychology like theoretical camp followers, gleefully applying one after another to political phenomenon. This contributes to the neglect of rigorous model building in the study of political decision making.

There are quite a few approaches to judgment in psychology that offer interesting findings concerning information processing and judgment problems involved in adapting to changing environmental conditions. Many of these approaches have been ignored by political science. This is partly due to the fact that some of these theories, such as Helson's Adaptation Level Theory, Parducci's Range Frequency Model, Volkmann's Rubber Band Model, and Anderson's work on weighted averages, are tested in experimental settings and have extremeley limited external validity. It is a long intellectual leap from findings about judgments and lengths of lines, sizes of squares, and weights of bags of sand to political judgments. However, cognitive and social psychologists, including Wyer, Upshaw, Asch, Allport, Bieri and, in particular, Rosch, have reduced the size of this chasm. It is from these areas of research that the analytical focus of this project will be drawn.60

The interpretation of cognitive organization and judgment developed by the theorists mentioned above does not rest upon the notion of heirarchically structured belief systems. Instead, the study of cognition and judgment evolved from Gestalt psychology. It concentrates upon the cognitive organization that the individual develops and uses to facilitate his or her interaction with the environment. Rather than viewing the individual as behaving in accordance with a fixed set of beliefs, the approach sees him or her as struggling to understand the environment and as having values that vary in importance and salience depending upon the context in which judgments take place. Judgments are seen as relative in all instances and context effects are taken into account. These studies promote a more holistic view of the human thinking process and the interaction between the individual and the environment.

The framework used in this project, to be described briefly below and in more detail in Chapters 2 and 4, consists of three parts. The first is a description of cognitive categories and the political world view. The second is a discussion of judgment processes involved in the interaction between the world view and incoming information. The third section addresses the impact of contextual effects upon the use of psychological categories and the interpretation of information.

Psychological Categories and the Political World View

The major assumption in this study is that policy makers have identifiable political world views and that they use these world views as a basis for making judgments. People organize their world by forming cognitive categories. A category is defined similarly by many psychologists. Zajonc's definition is "a class of events, objects, ideas or whatever. A given category invokes those attributes necessary for the identification of each member of the class to which the category refers."61 Categories and the attributes associated with them develop through experience. Rosch argues that there are two general principles involved in category formation. First, categories are formed to perform the function of providing the perceiver with a large amount of information about his environment with as little effort as possible. The individual needs categories that can make fine discriminations among stimuli but he also needs to have categories capable of reducing the differences among stimuli

to "behaviorally and cognitively usable proportions."[62] A
second principle is that categories must be suited to the
individual's particular interaction with his or her social
and physical worlds.[63] In other words, one is not born with
a full set of categories. Allport's summary of the purposes
served by psychological categories is perhaps the clearest
for the layman:

> The human mind must think with the aid of categories.
> ..Once formed, categories are the basis for normal
> prejudgment. We cannot possibly avoid this process.
> Orderly living depends upon it. [The process of catego-
> rization] forms large classes and clusters for guiding
> our daily adjustments. We spend most of our waking life
> calling upon preformed categories for this pur-
> pose...When we go to a physician with an ailment we
> expect him to behave in a certain way toward us. On
> these, and countless other occasions, we "type" a
> certain events, place it within a familiar rubric, and
> act accordingly. Sometimes we are mistaken...Yet our
> behavior was rational.It was based on high probability.
> Though we used the wrong category, we did the best we
> could.
>   What all this means is that our experience in life
> tends to form itself into clusters...and while we may
> call on the right cluster at the wrong time, or the
> wrong cluster at the right time, still the process in
> question dominates our entire mental life. A million
> events befall us every day. We cannot handle so many
> events. If we think of them at all, we type them.
>   Open-mindedness is considered to be a virtue. But,
> strictly speaking, it cannot occur. A new experience
> must be redacted into old categories. We cannot handle
> each event freshly in it own right. ...Bertrand Russell
> ...has summed up the matter in a phrase, "a mind per-
> petually open will be a mind perpetually vacant."[64]

Categories vary in complexity but have identifiable
internal characteristics. They are composed of attributes
associated with the perceived object, images of movements or
events, patterns of behavior associated with the object, and
response alternatives. The characteristics supply the perceiver with information concerning what is and what is not
included in the category. Although affect,that is, emotional
feeling, is associated with each category, the main
concern of this study is the cognitive organization itself.

One of the major and preliminary tasks of this study is to identify and describe the categories used by foreign policy makers. Using psychological research as a guideline and studies by political scientists on this general subject, it is suggested that policy makers use "type of state" categories. There are only two political studies that address the specific issue, but many other studies lend indirect aid.

Making Judgments: Using Categories

Beyond describing the political world view it is necessary to examine the judgment process or the use of cognitive categories. Psychological studies indicate that the judgment process involves two types of decisions. Nominal decisions must be made in which incoming information about an object is assessed to determine which category should be used in interpreting that information. Once the object has been associated with a category, a decision must be made as to where in that category the information belongs, that is, how typical a member of the category the object is. In technical terms, the perceiver uses an "implicit representation of a given stimulus dimension and will judge or 'measure' the value of further incoming stimuli in reference to the parameters of this...dimension."[65] In the judgment process, therefore, the individual makes an absolute, "nominal" judgment in which he or she decides upon category membership, and a relative, "ordinal" judgment in which the stimuli are placed in a position relative to other members of the category. For example, a person must decide if clouds on the horizon are bad weather clouds (nominal judgment) and if so whether they are vile enough to cause rain (the ordinal judgment). Similarly, a policy maker must decide if Cuba is an enemy (the nominal judgment) and if so whether it is as typical, and therefore as dangerous, as the Soviet Union (the ordinal judgment).

Nominal judgments are not difficult when the stimuli clearly hold most or all of the attributes, events, and response alternatives associated with the category. However, categories have boundaries and boundaries are often vague.[66] Some objects do not clearly and absolutely belong to a category. For example, if one organizes the inanimate world in part by using the category "furniture," it would not be clear if a large tree stump sitting in a friend's living room is part of that category or not. Judgments are made

more difficult by the fact that some objects are more typical of the category than others. World War II was a more
"typical" war than the war in Vietnam. Further, many
category boundaries are movable, that is, categories can be
expanded or reduced. For example, discrimination on the
basis of sex and race were once considered social issues but
are now clearly part of a category of political issues.
Women's suffrage was once a political issue and is no
longer. As the boundaries of categories change, judgments
become more difficult.

One of the most interesting aspects of the judgment
process occurs when judgments are made under circumstances
where in categories may no longer adequately structure the
environment. These are situations in which differences among
individuals and/or groups of individuals may be observed. It
is argued in the last half of this study that those who saw
Mexico as a classic example of a dependent country were
least able to recognize change in Mexico's foreign policy
after the discovery of vast quantities of petroleum in 1976.

Context Effects and Judgment

The third component of the framework involves the
interaction between the perceiver's world view and the
environment in which judgments are made. Among psychological
theories there are several competing interpretations of
contextual effects on judgments. Analysts closer to Gestalt
psychology argue that the context produces a change in the
meaning of incoming information. According to Solomon Asch,
for example, "[t]he single trait possesses the property of a
part in a whole. A change in a single trait may alter not
that aspect alone, but many others -- at times all...In the
process of mutual interaction the concrete character of each
trait is developed in accordance with the dynamic requirements set for it by the environment."67 This interpretation
leads to the argument that judgments are made not only on
the basis of the characteristics of the information or
person or object that is being judged, but on the basis of
those characteristics separately, their existence together,
and other environmental characteristics. Context effects
derive from the circumstances in which a judgment is made
and the peculiar combination of the judged object's qualities. This is why judgments are seen as perpetually relative
(even when they are nominal or absolute) and it is why one
can argue that this approach gives a more holistic view of

human thinking. In politics, it will be argued, context effects are most important in the establishment of perceptions of threat and/or opportunity associated with different types of states.

Because the context in which judgments are made affects the appearance of incoming information, it also affects the nominal and ordinal judgments of that information. There are several perceptual patterns that have been found to accompany this process and many point to sources of judgmental bias. These patterns will be discussed in the fourth chapter. For the moment, however, it is important to note that the difficulties experienced in making judgments are particularly strong when the incoming information should indicate a need for change in a category or in the categorization of an object, person, or state. Both situational context effects and the context created by characteristics of the judged object may produce a misleading aura preventing a required change.

The psychological framework developed in this project combines the patterns associated with the interaction between psychological categories, judgment patterns, and context effects and applies them to the political world view. In the first half of the study (Chapters 1-4) the framework is amplified and hypotheses linking the framework to behavior are presented. Chapter 2 contains a full discussion of categories and a description of political categories. In Chapter 3 the world view construct is supported with data from a survey administered to foreign policy makers. The fourth chapter links the categories with behavior. The judgment process is described, the effects of the political context are discussed, and hypotheses are formulated concerning the impact of the psychological world view on recognition of and response to environmental change.

The second half of this study is devoted to testing the hypotheses presented in Chapter 4. This is done through a detailed study of the negotiations between the United States and Mexico attempting to reach an agreement on the sale of natural gas. The case is an appropriate one for a variety of reasons. Mexico underwent a great deal of non-revolutionary change when great quantities of petroleum and natural gas were discovered in the early 1970's. It was thought that oil was Mexico's ticket to development and an equal relationship with the United States. Consequently, when six gas companies arranged to purchase natural gas from Mexico in 1976, Mexican officials demanded a high price. The importation of natural gas required U.S. governmental approval. Therefore, negotiations between the U.S. and Mexico on price arrangements began. The negotiations in 1977 failed to produce an agreement but did result in a troubling strain in U.S.- Mexico relations. Negotiations resumed in late 1978 and in 1979 an agreement was reached. During this period there were disagreements within the U.S. government as to the stance the United States should have taken on this issue and should take in the future. Policy makers have disagreed about the meaning of Mexico's actions, Mexico's future actions, and the interests of the United States. It will be argued that different perceptions or images of Mexico produced these disagreements and the strain in the relationship in late 1977. Further, it is argued that none of the traditional international relations theories (such as Realism, domestic interest group competition or bureaucratic politics) can explain the case. The case study data are from secondary and primary sources and a series of personal interviews with individuals involved in or close observers of the actual decision making process.

NOTES

1. R. Jervis, "Political Decision Making: Recent Contributions," Political Psychology 2 (1980): 86-101.
2. A George, Presidential Decisionmaking in Foreign Policy: The Effective Use of Information and Advice. (Boulder: Westview Press, 1980), p. 55-56.
3. Ibid., p. 56.
4. For a discussion of psychologists' objections see R. Wyer, Cognitive Organization and Change: An Information Processing Approach (Potomac, Maryland: Lawrence Erlbaum, Associates, 1974), Chapter 9. For a discussion of the use and misuse of these theories in political science see R. Jervis, Perception and Misperception in International Politics, p. 4-5.
5. J. Bruner, "Understanding Psychological Man," Psychology Today 16 (1982(: 42.
6. A Bullock and O. Stallybrass (eds.), The Harper Dictionary of Modern Thought (New York: Harper and Row, 1977), p. 109.
7. Ibid.
8. Jervis, Perception and Misperception, p. 6.
9. F.M. Frohock, The Nature of Political Inquiry (Home-

wood, Illinois: The Dorsey Press, 1967), p. 7.

10. H.M. Blalock, Jr., Causal Inferences in Nonexperimental Research (New York: W.W. Norton, 1964), p. 20.

11. D. Heradstveit and O. Narvesen, "Psychological Constraints on Decision-Making. A Discussion of Cognitive Approaches: Operational Code and Cognitive Map," Cooperation and Conflict 2 (1978): 79-80.

12. A. George, "The 'Operational Code' : A Neglected Approach to the Study of Political Leaders and Decision Making," International Studies Quarterly 13 (1969): 201-202.

13. Ibid., p. 201-205.

14. Ibid., p. 200.

15. See Leites, A Study of Bolshevism (Glencoe, Illinois: Free Press, 1953); L. Johnson, "Operational Codes and the Prediction of Leadership Behavior: Senator Frank Church at Midcareer," p. 89-109 in M. Hermann (ed.), A Psychological Examination of Political Leaders (New York: Free Press, 1977); S.G. Walker, "The Interface Between Beliefs and Behavior: Henry Kissinger's Operational Code and the Vietnam War," Journal of Conflict Resolution 21 (1977): 129-168; and C.S. Malone, "The Operational Code of Lyndon Baines Johnson," (Stanford: Stanford University Press, 1971).

16. See for example, L. Johnson, "Operational Codes."

17. Ibid., p. 89.

18. Ibid., p. 90.

19. G. Sjoblom, "Some Problems of the Operational Code Approach," in C. Jonsson (ed.), Cognitive Dynamics and International Politics. New York: St. Martin's Press, 1982, p. 47.

20. Robert Jervis defines motivated distortions of information as distortions that guide the perceiver to a goal, butress a decision or protect the person's ego. Unmotivated distortions are errors that the perceiver "would correct if he were aware of them." See R. Jervis, "Political Decision Making: Recent Contributions," p. 100.

21. See Sjoblom for a detailed critique, p. 60-64.

22. A. George, "The 'Operational Code,'" p. 200.

23. S.G. Walker, "The Interface Between Beliefs and Behavior," p. 137.

24. S.G. Walker, and T. Murphy, "The Utility of the Operational Code in Political Forecasting." Political Psychology 3 (1981-82): 24-60.

25. Ibid., p. 26, 32,29 and the cases p.40-45.

26. A. George, "The Causal Nexus Between Cognitive Beliefs and Decision Making Behavior: the "Operational Code" Belief System," in L. Falkowski (ed.), Psychological Models

30

in International Politics (Boulder: Westview Press, 1979).

27. Ibid., p. 101.

28. Ibid., p. 102.

29. Ibid., p. 103.

30. S.G. Walker, "The Motivational Foundations of Political Belief Systems: A Re-Analysis of the Operational Code Construct," International Studies Quarterly 27 (1983): 179-202.

31. Ibid., p. 181.

32. Ibid., p. 183.

33. Ibid., p. 179.

34. Ibid.

35. Ibid., p. 189.

36. S.G.Walker and L. Falkowski, "The Operational Codes of U.S. Presidents and Secretaries of States: Motivational Foundations and Behavioral Consequences, Political Psychology 5 (1984): 248.

37. Ibid., p. 246.

38. Ibid., p. 248.

39. O. Holsti, "The Operational Code Approach: Problems and Some Solutions." In C. Jonsson (ed.), Cognitive Dynamics and International Politics. New York: St. Martin's Press, 1982.

40. Heradsveit and Narvesen, p. 79.

41. M.G. Bonham, D. Heradsveit, O. Narvesen, and M.J. Shapiro, "A Cognitive Model of Decision-Making: Application to Norwegian Oil Policy," Cooperation and Conflict 2 (1978): 94.

42. Ibid., p. 94.

43. R. Axelrod, "The Analysis of Cognitive Maps," in R. Axelrod (ed.), The Structure of Decision (Princeton: Princeton University Press, 1976), p. 57.

44. Ibid., p. 56.

45. Ibid., p. 58.

46. Ibid., p. 56, 59.

47. Axelrod, p. 59.

48. Ibid.

49. Ibid.

50. Bonham et al., p. 95-96.

51. Ibid., p. 96.

52. See Ibid.; R. Axelrod, "Decision for Neoimperialism: The Deliberations of the British Eastern Committee in 1918," in R. Axelrod (ed.), The Structure of Decision (Princeton: Princeton University Press, 1976); and M.G. Bonham, "Explanation of the Unexpected: The Syrian Intervention in Jordan in 1970," inR. Axelrod (ed.), The Structure

31

of Decision (Princeton: University of Princeton Press, 1976).

53. Bonham et al.

54. R. Axelrod, "The Analysis of Cognitive Maps," in R. Axelrod (ed.), The Structure of Decision (Princeton: Princeton University Press, 1976), p. 59.

55. D.R. Kinder and J.A. Weiss, "In Lieu of Rationality: Psychological Perspectives on Foreign Policy Decision Making,Journal of Conflict Resolution 22 (1978): 713.

56. Bonham et al., p. 99.

57. See for example A. George, Presidential Decision-making in Foreign Policy; O. Holsti, "Cognitive Dynamics and Images of the Enemy," Journal of International Affairs 21 (1967); and R. Jervis, Perception and Misperception.

58. R. Cottam, Foreign Policy Motivation (Pittsburgh: University of Pittsburgh Press, 1977).

59. See L. Mischel, "Toward a Cognitive Social Learning Reconceptualization of Personality," Psychological Review 4 (1973): 252-278 for a discussion of the major criticisms of personality studies.

60. See R. Wyer, Cognitive Organization and Change: An Information Processing Approach; S.E. Asch, "Forming Impressions of Personality," Journal of Abnormal and Social Psychology 41 (1946): 258-290; J. Bieri, Clinical and Social Judgment: The Discrimination of Behavioral Information (New York: John Wiley and Sons, 1966); H.S.Upshaw, "Own Attitude as an Anchor in Equal Appearing Intervals," Journal of Abnormal and Social Psychology64 (1962): 85-96; and E. Rosch and B.Lloyd (eds.), Cognition and Categorization (Hillsdale, New Jersey: Lawrence Erlbaum Associates, 1978).

61. R.B. Zajonc, "Cognitive Theories of Social Psychology," in G. Lindzey and E. Aronson (eds.), The Handbook of Social Psychology, 2nd ed. (Reading, Massachusetts; Addison-Wesley, 1968), p. 332.

62. E. Rosch, "Principles of Categorization," in E. Rosch and B. Lloyd (eds.), Cognition and Categorization, p. 29.

63. Ibid.

64. G.Allport, The Nature of Prejudice (Garden City, New York: Doubleday, 1954), p. 19-20.

65. Bieri, p. 29.

66. G.A. Miller, "Practical and Lexical Knowledge," in E. Rosch and B. Lloyd (eds.),Cognition and Categorization, 308.

67. S.E. Asch, p. 284.

2

Psychological and Political
Categories: The Political World View

It has been argued that psychology has more to offer political science than cognitive balance and consistency theories and the premise that judgments are made on the basis of a hierarchy of beliefs. The goal of this chapter is to develop a framework depicting a political world view. Again, the major assumption is that people must organize and simplify the complex world. In the process they become predisposed to a certain psychological inertia in making judgments and to sluggishness in recognizing and responding to change. The chapter begins with a discussion of some of the important characteristics and functions of categories as noted by psychologists. It proceeds to an examination of political categories.

PSYCHOLOGICAL CATEGORIES

There are several important questions about psychological categories that should be considered: What are cognitive categories? What are their qualitative characteristics? How are they formed? What functions do they serve? Each of these questions will be considered by drawing upon the findings of psychological studies.

This is a field in psychology with a complicated history. It has involved the examination of judgments of physical objects by psychophysicists and has origins in Gestalt psychology. Research in this area today is carried on by cognitive and social psychologists and by the descendants of psychophysics. In fact, as Upshaw explains:

The traditional concern of the psychology of judgment

is with problems derived from psychophysics dealing
with the efficiency and accuracy of the human being as
an observer of environmental change. In the typical
psychophysical experiment a subject is presented a
series of stimuli which differ in terms of a specified
attribute. He is instructed to "judge" each stimulus,
which, in this context, may correspond to one of three
tasks. It may entail deciding which of a pair of stimuli has more of a particular property. On the other
hand, it may consist of the subject's sorting stimuli
into prescribed categories according to his perception
of the magnitude of each stimulus in terms of the
property. Finally, it may consist of the assignment of
the subject's own numbers to indicate perceived magni-
tude.1

The judged natural stimuli are frequently bags of sand
of differing weights, lines of differing lengths, and
squares of differing sizes. The subject's judgments of the
stimuli are then compared with the stimuli measurements on a
physical scale.2 Psychophysicists assume that individuals
use a hypothetical reference scale in making a judgment.
Thus:

[I]f a subject is asked to indicate his perception of a
set of stimuli in terms of some variable property, he
presumably complies by referring the stimuli to his
preexisting rule, thus incorporating the experimental
stimuli into his reference scale. Each judgment that he
makes may be assumed to reflect the location of the
appropriate stimulus on his reference scale.3

The categories used in the experimental reference scale are
equal appearing interval categories. It is assumed that one
can measure the sensory impact of the observed object on the
subject by comparing the actual physical value of the stimuli (for example, actual weight) with the expressed psychological values. Because the true psychological sensation
cannot be observed, it must be inferred from the responses
given on the experimental rating scale.
Some of the major theoretical arguments resulting from
these studies revolve around the events that take place
between the psychological recognition of the stimuli and the
judgmental evaluation of the stimuli. Many analysts argue
that the judgments are relative rather than absolute. Even
if the influence of all extraneous "noise" can be control-

led, the subject will still compare the stimulus with other stimuli in the series.4 The act of judging any stimulus involves both categorization and comparison. Judgments are categorical but are also influenced by the context in which they are made.

The difference between this approach to judgment and the cognitive consistency approach is explained by Upshaw:

> Consistent with the concept of the reference scale, the fundamental phenomena of judgment tend to be effects that pervade all of the judgments that a subject makes for a series of stimuli. Cognitive consistency phenomena, on the other hand, tend to be stimulus-specific, according to prevailing research traditions, if not according to theory.5

Because this approach to judgment calls attention to a series of stimuli and, because the context in which the stimuli is presented is assumed to affect judgment, the approach provides a basis for a more panoramic and comprehensive view of the process of making a judgment than does consistency theory.

There are many differences between judgments made in the psychophysical laboratory and social judgments. The psychophysicist's experiments use physical standards against which human judgments are evaluated. As Eiser and Stroebe note, this is one major area in which social judgment data cannot be compared to psychophysical judgments. Instead:

> In social judgments there is no "absolute" or "physical" measure that we can use of the position of any particular item or set of items along a given continuum. There is no way, therefore, in which we can relate the "psychological continuum" in terms of which the subject judges a series of stimuli to any underlying objective scale of measurement and the subjective scale used by the individual. All we can do is to compare the subjective scales of individuals with each other.6

The authors' point is that social judgments cannot be as precisely controlled and measured as can the judgments of physical objects. Nevertheless, it is not entirely correct to argue that there are no objective standards against which a social judgment can be compared. For example, if American policy makers used three categories to classify other states: `enemy,' `imperialist,' and `ally,' it might have been possible to find two Americans who differed in classifying Imperial Japan after Pearl Harbor as either an enemy or an imperialist. However, any American policy maker who classified Japan as an American ally at that time would be incorrect by any objective standard.

The judgment processes analyzed by psychophysicists have been studied in social judgment experiments as well. The findings of both areas of inquiry as to patterns of judgment will be discussed in a later chapter. At this point it is important to develop the concept of categories used in social judgments. The categories used in psychophysical experiments are very simple and are provided for the subject by the equal appearing interval scale. When social judgments are made the subject uses categories that he or she carries around to organize the real world.

CATEGORY CHARACTERISTICS

Categories have been defined in several similar ways. Zajonc defines a category as a "class of events, objects, ideas, or whatever."[7] Wyer argues that a category is a symbol representing internal or external stimuli in memory.[8] Rosch defines a category as "a number of objects that are considered equivalent."[9] Allport considers a category to be "an accessible cluster of associated ideas which as a whole has the property of guiding daily adjustments."[10] Again, the basic fundamental purpose of a category is to organize and simplify the environment. Categories must "provide maximum information with the least cognitive effort" and process incoming information for the perceiver so that it assumes a sensible, structured form rather than an arbitrary or random nature.[11]

The acquisition of natural categories used to facilitate survival in the social world is usually assumed to be culturally determined through socialization and through experience. Eleanor Rosch is a cognitive psychologist who has written extensively on the characteristics of psychological categories. She argues that they have both a vertical and horizontal dimension. "The vertical dimension concerns the inclusiveness of the category -- the dimension along which the terms collie, dog, mammal, animal and living thing vary."[12] Because the purpose of a category is to structure the world so that the perceiver can process information with maximum efficiency and minimum effort, Rosch argues that "the most basic level of categorization will be the most inclusive (abstract) level at which the categories can mirror the structure of attributes perceived in the world."13The horizontal dimension involves the differentiation of the categories "at the same level of inclusiveness -- the dimension on which dog, cat, bus, chair, and sofa vary."14 Along this dimension the ordering and processing functions are served through the representation of the category by a prototypical member. This notion, that categories are represented mainly by a prototypical member, stems from the Gestaltian assumption that there are ideal-typical perceptual stimuli that serve as perceptual anchoring points.15 Thus it is argued that categories are anchored by prototypes. The use of prototypes as examples against which incoming stimuli are compared when one is making a judgment is a controversial issue that will be discussed later. For the moment it is important to note that prototypical instances of a category contribute to the efficient ordering of the environment.

Through a series of experiments on the categorization of concrete objects, Rosch and others have speculated as to the level of abstraction at which the most basic categorical differentiations are made.16 Rosch argues that there are three different levels of abstraction at which categories are constructed. The highest level includes the less abstract categories. At the highest level, members of the category have few attributes in common. For example, the category "furniture" would incorporate objects so varied that the members of the category could have very different attributes. Some attributes would be shared but not enough for efficient cognitive distinctions between the category's members and other objects in the environment. For example, beds and chairs would be part of the category but share few attributes in common. The category permits little differentiation among the objects that may exist in one's home.

The second level of abstraction in category formation is "basic level" and is the most commonly used level for category formation. Categories at this level are the first to be used when the individual interprets incoming information. This level of abstraction divides the environment into "natural discontinuities" and therefore is the most cognitively efficient level of abstraction.17Finally, there are "subordinate" categories whose members share many attributes. The attributes overlap with those of other categories. For example, a category at this level of abstraction may be "kitchen chairs." Kitchen chairs share

many attributes with other kinds of chairs. The category is
not highly abstract.18

Basic level categories provide an ordering of the world
that promotes cognitively efficient information processing.
These categories group together objects with attributes
distinct from other objects yet similar to each other. For
example, the categories "dog" and "cat" organize the world
more efficiently for most people than for the more abstract
category "domesticated animal." They are also more efficient
than the less abstract categories "retriever" and "tabby."
Rosch argues that there are four "converging operational
definitions of the basic level of abstraction: attributes in
common, motor movements in common, objective similarity in
shape, and identifiability of averaged shapes." 19

Rosch's discussion of the basic level of abstraction
has important theoretical guidelines for the development of
ideal-typical political categories. One of the most important points is that the categories used most often have a
medium level of abstraction. This indicates that the categories used to organize the political world are not based
upon abstract interpretations of political ideology such as
"liberal democracy" as opposed to "social democracy" and
distinct from "fascism" and "communism." Although these
terms may be used in political speech, they are probably
code words rather than indicators of concepts upon which
categories are built. From a psychological standpoint one
should not expect to find that policy makers make distinctions between states and evaluate states on the basis of
an understanding of abstract ideological differences.
Rosch's findings also indicate that political categories are
not likely to be distinct in terms of simple non-abstract
indicators such as position on single issues, geography,
population size, or industrial or military capacity alone.
Theoretically, the psychological categories that form the
political world view should be basic level in degree of
abstraction.

Rosch points out that basic level categories are "ope-
rationally defined" by the attributes, movements, functions,
and shape of category members.19 Her discussion of the
operational definition of categories is based upon studies
of categorization of natural objects (trees, birds, colors,
etc.). Some of the defining characteristics of these categories are irrelevant in the political context. Motor movements and shape, for example, have no political equivalents
or importance. The notion that categories have descriptive
attributes of the members is important, however. Attributes

perceived as common to category members are also seen as correlated although there may be no reason for assuming the correlation. For example, wings and feathers are attributes of the category "bird" and are assumed to go together even though most people know of no particular reason for the wing-feather correlation. The tendency to assume correlations among attributes is a useful cognitive device providing the perceiver with a larger set of information about an object than he or she would have if all attributes had to be identified individually.20 Categories are more useful if they have more correlated attributes than unrelated attributes.

An important but relatively unexplored component of categories is the psychological "script." Scripts are recordings of events that remain in memory and serve as predictive aids. They provide the individual with a record upon which to base expectations of future events and outcomes. Scripts may be either episodic or categorical.21 In one preliminary study it was found that when subjects were asked to describe the events of every day as far back as they could remember they divided the day into similar units of events:

> There was considerable agreement on the kinds of units into which a day should be broken -- units such as making coffee, taking a shower, and going to statistics class. No one used much smaller units: That is, units such as picking up the toothpaste tube, squeezing toothpaste onto the brush, etc., never occurred. Nor did people use larger units such as "got myself out of the house in the morning" or "went to all my afternoon classes." 22

As the daily events became more remote in memory the size of units used to record events did not become larger and less specific. Instead, the subjects reported memory lapses.23 What the study indicates is that scripts and prototypical category members are closely associated. In two studies it was found that "prototypical category members are those than can play the role in events of members of that category."24 Thus, along with attributes, categories should contain event scripts and, of course, associated response alternatives.

In summary, categories are composed of attributes describing the members' important characteristics, a prototypical member, event scripts, and possible responses. The category informs the individual as to what a part of this environment looks like, the identity of the typical member, how it behaves, and how he or she can respond. When information is received and the stimuli categorized the individual knows quite a bit about it. The implications of the contents of the psychological category for political behavior will be discussed in detail in Chapter 4.

POLITICAL CATEGORIES

The studies discussed above can be used as guidelines for a framework depicting political categories. In this section the guidelines will be clarified. Based upon psychological and political studies, it is argued that at least seven categories organize the world for policy-makers. After the political categories have been developed the discussion will return to psychological studies in an examination of the functioning of psychological categories.

The first guideline suggested by psychological studies is that a framework depicting the categories that divide the political world should identify basic level categories. They must have a moderate degree of abstraction and conform to "natural" boundaries. Category members should share enough attributes so that they form a coherent unit distinct from other objects. The analytical task is to decide what the basic level of category formation is in perceptions of the political world. Images or categories distinguishing and grouping states in terms of official ideology is probably too abstract. Although policy makers frequently refer to ideological labels in describing states, these words are more indicative of code words than distinct categories since they are in fact so loosely and carelessly applied. The categorization of states on the basis of ideology requires an understanding of abstract principles such as conceptualizations of the preferred form of political organization for society and of utopian ideals. It may also result in the classification of the USSR and the People's Republic of China in the same category which does not constitute an efficient division of the political world.25 The first task in developing political categories, therefore, is to determine the basic level of abstraction at which the political world is divided and organized.

A second guideline offered by the psychological studies concerns the internal structure of categories. Political categories should have both a vertical and horizontal dimension. This means that they must separate the political environment from other parts of the policy maker's world. Therefore, the various political categories should share the same elements (such as military power, domestic political structure, etc.) that define the members as distinctly political. At the same time these categories have a horizontal dimension. The political world is not one giant category but is divided into several categories. Thus the particular characteristics and combinations of the attributes will differ within each category thereby forming unique units. Along with attributes, categories contain event scripts, response alternatives, and prototypical members. Therefore, one should expect political categories to inform the policy makers of important historical analogies, major issues, a range of possible behaviors, response alternatives and prototypical examples.

Basic Level Political Categories

There are several possible divisions of the international world. The most obvious division of the political environment is a division among states, although it is not likely to be based upon issue positions, geography, population, or other similar characteristics. If these characteristics are used to organize the environment the policy maker must have a great deal of factual information to make a classification of a state. This would be contrary to the purpose of a cognitive category: to provide the individual with a large amount of information once a classification has been made with a small amount of information. In addition, classifications made on the basis of issue positions or geography would lead to many overlaps among categories. These political qualities are not sufficiently abstract or important to produce mutually exclusive and useful categories. If one searches the political world for the most efficient and basic division it would appear to be a division among types of states. The category's attributes would inform the perceiver of the most important political characteristics of each type and of events and responses associated with each type of state. Then, with limited amounts of information, a given state can be classified, or categorized, as a particular type and the perceiver is supplied with a vast amount of information about that particular state as a result of its categorization.

There are several questions that immediately follow

this speculation: Is there any support in the political science literature for this argument? What are the types of states that divide the political environment and thus compose the political world view? The answer to the first question is that the literature offers some support for the argument, much of it indirect. The literature is limited by three major problems. First, most of the questions asked of policy makers are designed to discover what policy makers think (attitudes), not how they think (cognition). Attitude survey questions such as those undertaken by Russet and Hanson, Holsti and Rosenau, and Reychler reveal some very interesting and important patterns of elite attitudes but they were not designed to investigate how people think.26

A second problem is that political scientists themselves use categories with which to organize the world and they naturally disagree among themselves as to which image applies to which states. Hence, much energy is spent arguing about the analytical adequacy of different images of a particular country (for example, is the Soviet Union an imperialist or a passive antagonist?) leaving the study of the world view itself neglected. Nevertheless, the theoretical arguments and/or descriptive essays in the literature frequently point to and analyze political issues in terms of "types of states."

A final deficiency in the literature was discussed in the previous chapter. Many analysts stress the importance of discovering and working with the organization of policy makers' thoughts but ultimately fail to pursue the point. They limit themselves to beliefs associated with particular policy decisions rather than the interaction between the general world view and the specific situation. The analysts who do address the central theoretical issue will be discussed below.

In answering the second question posed above concerning the specific types of states that compose the world view, the literature is more helpful. Several articles and books will be used to provide a basis for the categories of the world view. The ideal-typical categories should be as close an approximation of reality as possible and theoretically sound. This requires that the categories be distinct and mutually exclusive. In the next section the literature will be surveyed to find evidence that "types of states" are the basis upon which the political world is divided psychologically and to find indications as to the particular types of states used.

TYPES OF STATES: EVIDENCE FROM THE LITERATURE

It was noted above that most of the attitudinal studies of foreign policy makers offer little evidence concerning world views. The questions usually asked of policy makers revolve around policy issues and general relationships between the United States and other countries. Nevertheless, some of the attitudinal studies do provide indirect information concerning policy makers' world views.

One of the more unusual attitudinal studies was done by R.B. Byers and David Leyton-Brown.27 In this study the authors questioned Canadian foreign policy elites about their interpretations of the international system. They asked the elites how they view the structure of the international system, the patterns of interaction within the system, and the causes of change and systemic instability.28 Most of the respondents saw the international system as composed of two or more blocs with only 5.6% arguing that the system is "too complex and fragmented to be identified with any systemic model."29 There were major disagreements concerning the actual structure of the system, with the highest percentage choosing a variant of the multipolar shape as the best description.30 Unfortunately, support for the argument that political observers use some "type of state" construct as a method of organizing the political world is limited in this article because the authors gave the respondents the organizational device of power blocs rather than permitting them to organize the environment freely. However, despite the fact that the interviewees were not permitted to choose their own organizational frameworks, only 5.6% rejected the idea of dividing the political system into units. This indicates that the concept was acceptable to most of the subjects.

There are other attitude studies that provide insights into cognitive organization and that point to an organization based on some conception of types of states. Russett and Hanson, in interviews with business elites, found significant numbers of respondents who have a realpolitik or balance of power view of international relations, demonstrating the central importance of nation-states in their world views.31 Luc Reyschler's interviews with diplomats show that they do not view a diminution of state integrity as important for the achievement of international peace but that they do see increased regional equality as an important factor.32 These examples are certainly not direct indications of a "type of state" view of the world but they do point out the importance placed upon configurations of states by political elites. Finally, Gerald Hopple has written an analysis of elite values in which he does not question his subjects on the organization of the political world but offers his own organization. He argues that there are four categories of states: Western, closed, unstable, and Third World.33 Hopple's categories are not distinct and mutually exclusive, (Third World and Western states may also be unstable and closed), but he does mention some interesting attributes that he regards as important determinants of state type including economic structure, capability, and governmental structure.34

Several additional works suggest more strongly a type of state organizing device. Ole Holsti has considered one aspect of this issue in a very interesting classic, "Cognitive Dynamics and Images of the Enemy." Holsti begins by arguing that individuals behave not only according to "objective" characteristics of a situation but also according to the meaning ascribed to it.35 Enemies, he argues, "are those who are defined as such, and if one acts upon that interpretation, it is more than likely that the original definition will be confirmed."36

In a discussion of decision-making, Holsti argues that an individual's belief system consists of several images containing knowledge of the past, present and future of the perceiver and his or her world.37 Images are the lenses through which information is filtered. They both help and hinder the individual as an information processor. They help by eliminating unimportant information from consideration. They hinder because they are stereotyped simplifications that can distort information. In addition the interaction of the images and new information is important.38

Most of Holsti's paper is devoted to a discussion of John Foster Dulles' image of the Soviet Union. Holsti does not attempt to develop the enemy image in the abstract, apart from the Dulles case, nor does he develop Dulles' enemy image in any other context than his view of the Soviet Union. Nevertheless, Holsti's study does offer some support for the argument that people use types of states to organize the political world.

A second relevant study is "The Effects of Thinking in Terms of Groups on Foreign Policy Perception: Foreign Service Officers and the Arab-Israeli Dispute, 1973." The author, Thomas O'Donnell, reports on research involving interviews with one hundred foreign service officers in 1973. He found several extremely interesting psychological patterns in questioning the officers, all of whom were Middle East specialists. The questions asked concerned only the Middle East dispute and O'Donnell did not investigate psychological world views as a whole. Nevertheless, he found that the Foreign Service Officers did group the twenty-one states involved in the Middle East dispute (excluding the United States) into seven to nine groups.39

O'Donnell also asked respondents to evaluate the states in terms of four attributes; effectiveness, flexibility, initiative and supportiveness of U.S. policy.40 O'Donnell found that there are differences in evaluation when states are considered separately rather than in groups. When subjects were asked to evaluate certain states in specific groups the states were seen as more similar in nature than they were when evaluated separately. For example, China and the USSR were evaluated in terms of overall foreign policy in the Middle East and in terms of the four foreign policy attributes in two different ways: First, they were judged separately and then they were evaluated as a single group. When subjects were asked to evaluate China and the USSR as a group the ratings of China became more similar to those of the USSR. The same result occurred when respondents were asked to judge France, Great Britain, and West Germany.41

Several implications can be drawn from this study. First, while the study did not focus on psychological categories, it does demonstrate empirically that policy-makers do categorize and that the act serves the need for cognitive efficiency. This is why China and the Soviet Union are seen as more similar when categorized together than when viewed separately. Second, the fact that perceptions of China became more similar to those of the USSR demonstrates the importance of categorical prototypes. The prototype is the "perfect" example of that type of state. Other states are evaluated in comparison to the prototype. The prototype reflects the most typical combination of attributes associated with a category. When a state is categorized it takes on the attributes associated with the category because the perceiver assumed these attributes naturally belong together. Hence differences between the prototype and other members become less apparent. Third, the study demonstrates the commonality of categories. The groups used to categorize these states were used by most of the respondents.

Finally, there is a growing body of literature that addresses the problem of the components of the political world view. Richard Cottam's Foreign Policy Motivation analyzes the perceptual world view as a whole rather than in a specific situation. The author proposes five world view categories but acknowledges that more are conceivable. The perceptual patterns in the model are images the perceiver has of another state. Five perceptual patterns are presented; enemy, allied, complex, imperial, and colonial.42 The patterns "appear in response to a perception of threat to or opportunity for something intensely valued which has relevance at the interstate level, most commonly the nation itself."43 Further, "these patterns correlate with two other aspects of the perceptual milieu -- perceived capability distance and perceived cultural distance."44

Each perceptual pattern is described in detail. The enemy pattern is one in which extreme threat is seen to emanate from a state similar in capability and culture to the perceiver's state. The complex image is evident when there is a very small amount of threat perceived to be associated with other states. The allied image is evoked when threat is perceived in the international arena. States seen as allies under those conditions are also seen as culturally equal to the perceiver's state. If the perception of cultural equality does not emerge, the imperial image is most likely to be the perceptual screen used by the perceiver. This pattern is one in which others are perceived as inferior in culture and capability and are associated by the perceiver with an opportunity to gain something advantageous. Finally, a colonial image is held of a state that is superior in capability and culture and from which threat or opportunity is seen to emanate.45

Each category, or pattern, has "several characteristics and standarized features which can serve as indicators."46 These include motivation (ranging from assumptions of simple to complex motivations on the part of others); capability (empirically measurable in terms of industrial potential, resource base, population, and military capability but also perceived in terms of national morale, quality of government, and the will to act); decision style (rational planning vs. ad hoc decision making); locus of decision making; and domestic forces interaction (that is, possible penalities to be faced by opponents of the prevailing view).47

The perceptual categories used in this project draw heavily from those developed in Foreign Policy Motivation. In each study it is argued that these perceptual images divide and organize international actors according to perceptions of types of states. The categories used in Foreign Policy Motivation satisfy the psychological conditions discussed earlier. They are basic level in that they are moderately abstract and cognitively efficient in their division of the political world. They are supported by indirect findings from studies mentioned above, by the author's own case studies of the British in Egypt, and by the empirical evidence in this and other projects. The "indicators" offered by the author are comprehensive category attributes. The study does not draw heavily from psychology, however, and a reading of the cognitive literature suggests some additions that can be made to the arguments presented in Foreign Policy Motivation.

A first possible addition would be the construction of separate analytical categories for "allies of the enemy" and "neutrals." The author argues that these images are equivalent perceptually to the enemy image. There may be a set of policy makers who do not use a neutral category in organizing the political world but the attributes and other aspects of the categories suggest that these additional categories should be cognitively distinct from each other and from the enemy image. The survey data discussed in the next chapter support this point to some extent. Second, research by cognitive psychologists indicates that in addition to attributes, categories have other elements such as event scripts. One could add ideal-typical event scripts to each image thus augmenting the model somewhat.

Finally, studies from cognitive psychology permit one to supplement and clarify Cottam's argument that perceptual patterns are invoked by the situational factors of threat and opportunity. The interaction between categories and situational factors is very complicated. As mentioned previously, cognitive psychologists have argued that perception of another person (or state) is influenced by the pre-existing image, the situation, and the interaction between the two. Thus situational factors interact with an image that existed before the specific event. Behavior in a particular situation is interpreted through the categorical screening device. Thus, while the situation clearly invokes the image, the image determines the definition given to the situation in the first place. The Soviet Union, for example, is seen as an "enemy" by most Americans before a specific problem arises. The enemy image of the USSR is not invoked by that event alone although the event may change the degree to which the USSR is seen as an enemy or heighten the salience of the category. In short, category and context combine psychologically but must be kept analytically distinct to avoid confusion.

The combination of category and context does produce

some confusion in <u>Foreign Policy Motivation</u> although it is easily deciferable. Cottam argues that the internal features of categories include perceptions of motivation, capability, decisional style, locus of decision making and domestic forces interaction.48 However, there are four other important elements, threat, opportunity, capability and cultural distance. The author argues that capability and cultural distance are part of the psychological milieu that is correlated with each perceptual pattern. At the same time he argues that additional ideal-typical perceptual patterns can be constructed through an analysis of the "various combinations of the four situational correlates, threat, opportunity, culture, and capability."49 It appears that situational factors define the categories yet categories are also said to contain the five elements of motivation, capability, decision style, locus of decision and domestic forces interaction. In addition, capability and cultural distance are part of a "psychological milieu" <u>and</u> they are situational factors. This is confusing, but the confusion arises more from a very rapid shift from discussion of category attributes, to context effects, to analytical tactics rather than from confusion in the argument itself. If one separates these three steps in the argument, one finds several important points.

First, the situational characteristics of threat, opportunity, capability and cultural distinctions do not define the categories. Rather, these elements are indicators for perceptual patterns. Certain patterns should appear when the analyst observes combinations of the elements. In other words, a particular <u>Gestalt</u> is created by the combination of these particular factors. The resulting perceptual milieu influences images of other states and will be important in influencing policy makers' behavior toward other states. It is argued below, however, that perceptions of cultual distinctions, capability differences, threat and opportunity are part of the ongoing, permanent category in which a state is classified as well as elements of the context in which interaction takes place. Because they are part of the image of another state before, during, and after an event, they influence the perception of the situation as it evolves. In the long run, people see what they expect to see and image determines what elements of the situation are striking. More will be said on these points in Chapter 4.

A recent book by Richard Herrmann, <u>Perceptions and Behavior in Soviet Foreign Policy</u>, further advances the development and employment of the concept of psychological

images. Herrmann argues that images are "indirect indicators
of perceptions" in that they are identifiable liguistic
pictures of other states from which perceptions can be
inferred.50 Perceptions of threat, opportunity, cultural
differences and capability differences are also used in this
study as "foreign policy concepts" that contribute to general perceptions of other states.51 Combinations of perceptions of these characteristics "interact as if in a system
and when combined into patterns act as models representing
integrated wholes."52 Herrmann draws from balance theory as
well as works in attribution theory and cognitive psychology
to present seven ideal-typical stereotypes or images organizing the international environment: enemy, barbarian,
degenerate, ally, dependent ally, child, and satellite.53

Perceptions and Behavior in Soviet Foreign Policy presents important ideas in the development of the concept of
images as an analytical device. It refines the stereotypes
associated with states perceived as equal in capability by
introducing the "degenerate" image. The "barbarian" image is
also an intriguing one, describing states seen as more
powerful in capability but culturally inferior. Further,
there is an explicit and challenging effort to associate
these images with specific policy preferences and patterns
of information interpretation. The study is supported by
careful empirical work on Soviet perceptions.

The categories used in this study reflect many of the
ideas of the analysts discussed above. The number of categories will be limited to seven because psychologists have
found that people prefer to use seven plus or minus two
categories when permitted to develop their own categories in
judgment experiments. Further, O'Donnell found that his
Foreign Service Officer subjects formed seven to nine categories when classifying states with no instructions from the
researcher.54 The use of seven categories, therefore, is
psychologically reasonable and does not result in a single
category for every state on earth.

The categories used here will be standardized and made
equivalent but distinct through variations among the attributes, response alternatives and event scripts. There will
be no defining criteria outside of the attributes, response
alternatives, and event scripts. As psychologists suggest,
the most theoretically satisfying method of constructing
categories is to compose a list of attributes, event
scripts, response alternatives, and prototypes and to
specify the categories that are possible given particular
combinations of these elements. The categories should be

distinct in the ideal-typical construct (exemplified by a prototypical example) but will be vague at the boundaries. They do not necessarily vary on each attribute but are distinct as combinations of all the category contents.

The categories used in this study are not designed to reflect only American thinking. All people must organize their environments. This means that policy makers in Kenya must organize the international arena just as Americans must. They will use the same type of state categories although the members of these categories may be different. The works by Richard Cottam and Richard Herrmann both demostrate the extend to which type of state images are used by policy makers and policy advocates world wide. Further, not all categories will be used all the time. For example, most Americans would not classify any state as a hegemonist (that is, a state clearly more powerful than their own country and aggressive in intentions), although some may see the Soviet Union as one rather than an enemy. Most Cubans, on the other hand, would need and use that category to organize their international environment: They would place the United States in that category. Individuals should use the same categories to organize the environment but may disagree about the classification of a particular state. As will be seen in the next chapter, images of Mexico held by American officials have differed: Some have seen Mexico as a neutral, while others have seen it as a dependent. Finally it is important to note that the technical relationship between the policy maker's state and another state may not be the same as his perception or image of that state. For example, the USSR and Great Britain were both formal allies of the United States during World War II but Roosevelt's perception and classification of the two were probably quite different. Similarly, the US is technically an ally of the states in Latin America but generally the image of those states is not equivalent to that of other technical allies such as Great Britain or West Germany.

Seven categories are used here including the enemy, hegemonist, dependent ally of the enemy, neutral, ally, dependent of the perceiver's state, and puppet of the perceiver's state. Each will be described and delineated through a discussion of the peculiar combinations of the attributes, event scripts, prototypes and response alternatives associated with the image. First, however, the attributes themselves must be described in detail. This means that all of the pieces of information one associates with a particular attribute should be presented. Each attribute is

quite complex. The list of attributes is not necessarily
complete in that it is possible that others may be included
in an image. However, the attributes that are discussed
below include major characteristics of states important in
the conduct of their international affairs. Ths list is
compiled in part from the attributes discussed by other
analysts. They include characteristics such as the type of
state's military capability, domestic political nature,
economy, culture, stance toward the perceiver's state,
flexibility in international bargaining, and general goals.
All of these are essential characteristics of states and
should contribute to perceptions of their general international position vis-a-vis the policy maker's state.

Attributes

   1. Military Capability. This attribute encompasses the
perceiver's understanding of the defensive and offensive
military potential of the other type of state; the extent of
governmental control over the military in the other type of
state; and the likelihood that that type of state will
resort to the use of military force. The importance of the
military capability attribute in perceptions of other states
has been discussed by Hopple and Cottam. The attribute can
be reduced to evaluations of the extent to which the other
is:

   a.   Superior, equal, or inferior in military strength to
        the perceiver's state.
   b.   Capable or incapable of using military force.

   2. Domestic Policy. Included in this attribute are
evaluations of the similarity in governmental structure and
functioning between the perceiver's state and other states;
the presence or absence of competing policy advocates in the
other state both within and outside of the governental
structure; and the effectiveness and efficiency of policy
implementation in the other type of state. These attributes
inform the perceiver of how communications between his state
and the other type of state are performed. They also
indicate whether the perceiver has a monolithic view of the
other state. The importance of this attribute was indicated
by Hopple and Cottam. O'Donnell pointed out the importance
of the effectiveness of policy making as an attribute. The
attribute can be reduced to the following qualities when

simplified:

    a. Governmental similarity;
    b. Presence or absence of competing policy advocates;
    c. Effective or ineffective policy implementation.

    3.   <u>Economic</u>   <u>Structure</u>. This attribute includes conceptions of the type of economy of the other state in terms of similarity to the perceiver's economy; the permeability of the other economy, that is, the extent to which other states can become involved in the domestic economy of that type of state; and the overall capacity and stability of the other economy (that is, industrial potential, agricultural self-sufficiency, the general growth rate and potential for growth). These attributes can be reduced to the following qualities:

    a. Stronger, equal, or weaker economy than the per-
       ceiver's;
    b. Permeable or impermeable economy.

    4.   <u>Culture.</u> This attribute is composed of the perceiver's sense of how similar another type of state is culturally to his own. This includes the perceiver's under-standing of differences in societal norms, the degree of the other type of state's national literacy, language differences, religious differences, the standard of living typical of this type of state, and the extent to which this type of state encourages cultural exchanges with others. The attribute reduces to evaluations of:

    a. Cultural superiority, equality, or inferiority.

    5.   <u>Supportivness.</u> O'Donnell introduced the importance of supportiveness of the perceiver's state's policy as an attribute. With each type of state the perceiver should have associated an understanding of how supportive states of each type are of his own state's policies.

    6.   <u>Flexibility.</u> This attribute was also introduced by O'Donnell. it is composed of the perceiver's sense of the willingness of policy-makers in the other nation to bargain, change tactics, and shift policy in response to new issues brought forth by other states. It reduces to evaluations of the other type of state in terms of whether it is:

a. Flexible, moderately flexible, or inflexible.

7. Goals. The final attribute includes the perceiver's interpretation of the extent to which the other type of state aggressively pursues its goals and the compatibility between that type of state's goals and his own state's goals. This attribute is indirectly derived from Cottam's discussion of motivation. These qualities reduce to evaluations of other as:

a. Aggressive or passive in pursuit of policy;
b. Compatible or incompatible in goals;

In addition to attributes, the psychological category appears to be composed of notions of behavioral response alternatives. In the policy-makers' experiences the response alternatives would consist of several policy and bargaining options. Each category, therefore, should have associated with it several potential bargaining recourses that vary in the extent to which they are applicable to each type of state and the extent to which they are likely to succeed.

Response Alternatives

1. Diplomatic Exchanges. The perceiver should have some understanding of whether or not diplomatic exchanges are possible with each type of state and in what ways. There should be a sense of whether only state-to-state bargaining is possible, whether non-governmental groups can be brought into the bargaining situation and be useful, and whether other states can be useful bargaining mediators. In a simplified form, the perceiver should have an understanding of whether:

a. Diplomatic exchanges on the state-to-state level are possible, useful and potentially successful;
b. Non-governmental groups are able to participate in bargaining and are likely to be influential;
c. Other states can be useful mediators in bargaining.

2. Military Force. Again, the perceiver must have some sense of the feasibility and utility of military force as an option in conflict situations with each type of state. Thus, in a simplified form, the perceiver should associate with each type of state an understanding of whether:

54

     a. Military force is an option and likely to succeed.

    3. Economic Force. Economic force is another potential response alternative about which the perceiver should have some impression associated with each type of state. Economic force can range from mild actions such as raising tariffs on particular items, to full scale coercion such as economic boycotts and blockades. In simplified form;

      a. Is economic force an option with this type of state and is it likely to succeed?

    4. Do Nothing. This option is not simply a last resort option available to the desperate. It also includes the perceiver's understanding of whether issues between his or her country and the other type of state will be resolved by simply disappearing if no response is made. Therefore, the individual can associate this option with each category as either a last resort or as a method of resolving disputed issues. As a last resort it is a possible alternative in any situation. As a method of resolving conflicts, however, it should be associated with only some types of states.

    5. Appeal to International Forums. This option may be seen as the most appropriate response to disputes with other types of states when a stronger response is either too dangerous or threatening to the long-run relations with the other state.

    Some cognitive psychologists have suggested that people may have event scripts associated with cognitive categories. For example, the simple natural category "bird" would have associated with it scripts of the object in flight. The script helps the individual identify and know something about birds. Political scientists have pointed to the importance of event scripts in influencing policy making. the scripts should be important in relation to the "lessons of history." Jervis, for example, argues that "[p]eople pay more attention to what has happened than to why it has happened."55 There are several types of event scripts that should be associated with the various types of states.

Event Scripts

    1. Instances of Aggression. The most obvious type of events that would form part of a cognitive category are events involving military aggression. The individual should

have recorded instances of military aggression by each type
of state toward the perceiver's state, a state similar to
the perceiver's state, an enemy of the perceiver, an ally of
the perceiver, and/or instances of aggression by the
perceiver's state against each type of state.

2. Government Stability. Another type of event that
would be an important characteristic associated with a type
of state consists of instances of governmental instability.
Some types of states may be heavily associated with coups,
palace revolts, revolutions, or frequent electoral contests.
Other types of states may be associated with continual
stability despite severe governmental crises.

3. Major Issues. Different types of states should also
vary in the extent to which they are associated with the
major issues of security and economic problems.

4. Analogies. A final event script would include applicable lessons drawn from history. In other words, a category
would describe a type of state that reminds the perceiver of
conditions present in highly salient historical situations.
For example, the historical analogies that are frequently
used by American policy-makers as analogies for current
events are Munich, Vietnam, and the Iranian hostage
crisis.56

Having described the attributes, responses, and event
scripts that should be associated with an image of a type of
state, it is now necessary to discuss the various combinations of these elements and they constitute each individual
category. This is done in the next chapter and is supported
with some preliminary survey data. Although the categories
are not completely different, the total combination of their
attributes, events scripts, associated response alternatives and prototypes show that they are psychologically
distinct.

CONCLUSION

The basic thrust of this chapter has been that type of
state images or categories are the natural, basic-level
psychological division of the political world. Categories
are composed of various attributes, events, behavioral
expectations and prototypical examples. The classification
of particular states in a category informs the individual
policy makers of many of the state's characteristics and
gives the policy makers a basis for predicting the state's
behavior. By understanding the category into which a state

has been placed, the analyst has insight into the assumptions the policy makers will make concerning the behavior of that state. The effects of such psychological predispositions on political action can then be studied in a variety of situations.

The categories described in the next chapter are in their ideal-typical form. It is argued later that although all people use the same categories they may differ in classifications of individual states or in the extent to which a state is seen as an ideal member of the category. Thus, some people see the USSR as a perfect example of an enemy and others disagree completely. Some people see Mexico as a dependent and others see it as a neutral.

NOTES

1. H. Upshaw, "Cognitive Consistency and the Psychology of Judgment," in R. Abelson (ed.), Theories of Cognitive Consistency: A Sourcebook (Chicago: Rand McNally, 1968), p. 211.

2. Ibid.

3. Ibid.

4. R.J. Eiser and W. Stroebe, Categorization and Social Judgment (New York: Academic Press, 1972), p. 7-10.

5. Upshaw, p. 213.

6. Eiser and Stroebe, p. 87-88.

7. R.B. Zajonc, "Cognitive Theories in Social Psychology," in G. Lindzey and E. Aronson (eds.), The Handbook of Social Psychology, 2nd ed. (Reading, Massachusetts: Addison-Wesley, 1968), p. 332.

8. R. Wyer, Cognitive Organization and Change: An Information Processing Approach (Potomac, Maryland: Lawrence Erlbaum Associates, 1974), p. 19.

9. E. Rosch, "Principles of Categorization," in E. Rosch and B. Lloyd (eds.), Cognition and Categorization (Hillsdale, New Jersey: Lawrence Erlbaum, 1978), p. 30.

10. G. Allport, The Nature of Prejudice, (Garden City, New Jersey: Doubleday, 1954), p. 166.

11. E. Rosch, "Principles of Categorization," p. 28.

12. Ibid., p. 30.

13. Ibid.

14. Ibid.

15. E. Rosch, "Cognitive Reference Points," Cognitive Pychology 7 (1975): 532.

16. Estimates of "levels of abstraction" were made as follows:

> Our claim concerning a basic level of abstraction can be formalized in terms of cue validity ... or in terms of the set theoretic representation of similarity provided by Tversky (1977...). Our validity is a probabilistic concept: the validity of a given cue 'x' as a predictor of category 'y.' The conditional probability of 'x'/'y' increases as the frequency with which cue 'x' is associated with category 'y' increases and decreases as the frequency with which cue 'x' is associated with categories other than 'y' increases ... The cue validity of an entire category may be defined as the summation of the cue validities for that category of each of the attributes of the category. A category with high cue validity is, by definition, more differentiated from other categories than one of lower cue validity. E. Rosch, "Principles of Categorization," p. 30-31.

17. Ibid., p. 31.

18. Ibid.

19. Ibid., p. 35.

20. Ibid., p. 43 and in E. Rosch, "Universals and Cultural Specifics in Human Categorization," in R. Brislin, S. Bochner, and W. Lonner (eds.), Cross-Cultural Perspectives on Learning (New York: Halstead Press, 1975), p. 198-199.

21. R. Wyer and D.E. Carlston, Social Cognition, Inference, and Attribution (Hillsdale, New Jersey: Lawrence Erlbaum, 1979), p. 30.

22. Rosch, "Principles of Categorization," p. 44.

23. Ibid., p. 45.

24. Ibid., p. 45

25. There is some very indirect evidence available to indicate that ideological distinctions are not natural divisions among states. B. Russett and L. Hanson (Interest and Ideology: The Foreign Policy Beliefs of American Businessmen [San Francisco: W.H. Freeman, 1975]) found ideology to be a secondary reason for hypothetical interventions in their study of business elite attitudes on foreign policy. The ideological distinctions in their book were crude, lumping "ideologies" such as "totalitarianism" and "communism" together using only the most obvious

58

ideological opponent (communism) as a possible physical opponent. Even with rough indicators such as these the possibility of ideological threat did not prompt a majority of businessmen or military officers to advocate intervention.

26. Ibid., p. 7; O.R. Holsti and J.N. Rosenau, "The Meaning of Vietnam: Belief Systems of American Leaders," International Journal 32 (1977): 452-474; and L. Reychler, Patterns of Diplomatic Thinking: A Cross-National Study of Structural and Social Psychological Determinants (New York: Praeger, 1979).

27. R. B. Byers and D. Leyton-Brown, "Canadian Elite Images of the International System,"International Journal 32 (1977):608-639.

28. Ibid., p. 608.

29. Ibid., p. 614.

30. Ibid., Table 1, p. 613.

31. Russett and Hanson, p. 123-130.

32. Reyschler, p. 136-153.

33. G. Hopple, "Elite Values and Foreign Policy Analysis: Preliminary Findings," in L.S. Falkowski (ed.), Psychological Models in International Politics (Boulder: Westview Press, 1979).

34. Ibid., p. 224-225.

35. O.R. Holsti, "Cognitive Dynamics and Images of the Enemy," Journal of International Affairs 21 (1967): 16.

36. Ibid.

37. Ibid.

38. Ibid., p. 18-19.

39. O'Donnell, "The Effects of Thinking in Terms of Groups on Foreign Policy Perceptions: Foreign Service Officers and the Arab-Israeli Dispute, 1973," Paper presented at the 21st Convention of the International Studies Association, Los Angeles, California, 19-23 March, 1980, p. 3.

40. Ibid., p. 7.

41. Ibid., p. 9-16.

42. R. Cottam, Foreign Policy Motivation (Pittsburgh: University of Pittsburgh Press, 1977), p. 62-64.

43. Ibid., p. 63.

44. Ibid.

45. Ibid., p. 64-74.

46. Ibid., p. 64.

47. Ibid.

48. Ibid., p. 63.

49. Ibid.

50. R. Herrmann, Perceptions and Behavior in Soviet Foreign Policy, Pittsburgh: University of Pittsburgh Press, 1985, p. 31.

51. Ibid.

52. Ibid., p. 32.

53. Ibid.

54. O'Donnell, "The Effects of Thinking in Groups" and G.A. Miller, "The Magical Number Seven, Plus or Minus Two," Psychological Review 63 (1956): 81-97.

55. R. Jervis., Perception and Misperception p. 228.

56. Ibid., p. 270.

3

Political World View Categories:
Some Empirical Evidence

Both psychological and political analyses suggest the utility of the world view concept for decision making studies. In an effort to develop the individual images more fully and to find some more solid empirical evidence of their existence, a survey was distributed to government officials during the summer of 1981. The survey was designed to gather information concerning policy makers' organization of the political world and the images in their world views.

The survey was mailed to officials in the Department of State, Department of Energy, the United States International Communications Agency (now the United States Information Agency), and the Agency for International Development. A pool of over 1,000 potential respondents was compiled. All members were of middle or higher Government Service (GS) or Foreign Service (FS) rank.1 The selection of individuals who had foreign policy expertise was an important criterion for the International Communications Agency and the Department of Energy. Individuals who held the positions of "research analyst" or "communications specialist" were selected from the International Communications Agency. These positions require constant attention to foreign events. Respondents in these positions were thus assumed to be knowledgeable in international affairs and American foreign policy. The Department of Energy sample was selected from the International Affairs division of the agency. The names of 500 people were randomly selected from the pool to receive surveys. Three hundred surveys were sent to the State Department, 73 to the Department of Energy, 52 to the Agency for international Development, and 65 went to members of the International Communications Agency. Fifty-one were returned in usable conditions. As with any survey, caution must be used in evaluating the significance of the results. The results of this survey are offered as a contribution to the material used to lay the foundation for the psychological framework. They data are not taken as conclusive support for the argument, merely as additional evidence.2

Most of the survey respondents were male (82.4%) members of the State Department (66.7%) and between the ages of 30 and 50 years (65%). The respondents tended to be of high rank: Approximately 73% of the FS respondents were of ranks 3 to 1, the highest rank possible. Seventy-six percent of the GS respondents were of ranks 13 to 15. The most common specialty was political affairs. Finally, most respondents considered themselves "Moderate/Middle of the Road" in political orientation (49%). The next most common political orientation was Liberal (29.4%).

The first two survey questions gave the respondents the opportunity to organize the international environment with as little interference from the analyst as possible. In question 1 respondents were asked to organize nineteen states into groups according to similarities in general international policies. This gave the respondents little guidance with the hope that they would construct categories that reflected their own world views. With the exception of Mexico, the nineteen states were chosen arbitrarily. Mexico was placed on the list so that some information could be accumulated for the last part of this study. An effort was made to include at least some states from major geographical areas of the world. The list included Brazil, Canada, China, Czechoslovakia, El Salvador, France, Great Britain, Guatemala, India, Mexico, Nigeria, North Korea, Poland, South Africa, South Korea, Switzerland, USSR, West Germany, and Yugoslavia. The states were listed alphabetically to avoid leading respondents in any way.

Respondents were asked to form groups of these nineteen states in order to test the assumption that the political world is organized into type-of-state categories. It was expected that the emergent groups would resemble six of the seven type-of-state categories discussed briefly in Chapter 2. The hegemonist category was not expected to appear since, as will be argued below, it is a category of little relevance for most Americans.

In question 2 the respondents were asked to group the same nineteen states according to overall policies toward the United States. The purpose of this question was twofold: first, it was designed to explore the possibility that a change in the judgment context would produce the same categories but variations in the membership of those categories. If the question produced completely different groups the validity of the type-of-state category framework would have to be questioned. A second purpose for this question was to examine judgments of states in terms of overall policies toward the United States. It was thought that this may give a more accurate picture of the operating world views of the respondents than the first question. Evaluations of other states in terms of overall policies toward the United States would at least be more meaningful to respondents than evaluations in terms of general international policies.

The third question asked respondents to label the groups they created in questions 1 and 2. It was designed to see if respondents chose labels for their groups that indicated some "type-of-state" classification.

The results of the first three questions were generally supportive of the categories suggested in Chapter 2. Table 1 shows the percent of respondents who matched each country with each other country. A standard was set wherein at least 50% of the respondents had to match two countries together before they could be considered part of a group. Several groups emerge.

The one-to-one matches show a clear association by the respondents of the Atlantic Alliance, an ally category. France, West Germany, Great Britain, and Canada are all placed together by over 80% of the respondents. The groups formed by the Soviet Union and its allies, the enemy and dependent ally of the enemy groups, are less striking but quite evident. Another group appears and is composed of Brazil, Mexico, India, and, marginally, Yugoslavia.

Guatemala may also be part of that group. This group appears to be composed of neutrals or members of the nonaligned movement. Switzerland is not part of this group. In fact, it is placed in a group by itself by 35% of the respondents. It is placed with the Allies by about 45% of the respondents. China is grouped alone by 41% of the respondents and Yugoslavia is by another 33%. South Africa is also isolated.

At first glance three of the six expected groups emerge. Two more groups emerge when the surveys are examined in more detail than the one-to-one matchings of Table 1. El Salvador and Guatemala are very highly associated.They are matched by 78% of the respondents. This presents a puzzle. Note that in Table 1 El Salvador is not highly associated with Brazil, Mexico, India, or Nigeria. Guatemala is more closely associated with Brazil but is not grouped with Mexico, Nigeria,

TABLE 1: States Arranged in Groups According to Foreign Policy Similarity (% of respondents)

	Brazil	Mexico	Nigeria	India	Yugoslavia	El Salvador	Guatemala	Canada	France	Great Britain	West Germany	Switzerland	South Korea	South Africa	Czechoslovakia	North Korea	Poland	USSR	China
Brazil	10																		
Mexico	65	8																	
Nigeria	49	67	14																
India	39	53	61	14															
Yugoslavia	0	35	49	53	16														
El Salvador	47	39	16	18	14	14													
Guatemala	51	41	18	18	16	78	10												
Canada	12	8	6	2	0	4	4	6											
France	12	10	6	2	2	4	6	80	14										
Great Britain	12	12	4	4	2	6	6	90	80	4									
West Germany	12	12	4	4	2	6	6	84	84	90	6								
Switzerland	12	12	14	18	10	4	4	43	41	47	47	35							
South Korea	35	22	22	14	12	26	31	24	24	22	20	10	39						
South Africa	10	10	8	6	6	10	10	22	26	26	22	26	14	57					
Czechoslovakia	0	2	4	4	16	2	2	0	0	0	2	0	2	0	8				
North Korea	2	4	6	8	16	2	4	0	0	4	4	0	2	2	58	14			
Poland	4	2	4	6	26	2	2	0	0	4	4	0	4	2	75	59	10		
USSR	0	0	2	6	12	0	0	0	0	0	0	0	4	0	79	68	65	14	
China	4	4	8	12	33	6	8	0	0	0	2	10	12	6	20	12	22	12	41

or India by 50% of the respondents. The question arises as to whether or not El Salvador and Guatemala form a distinct (possibly dependent) group.

The answer to this question requires a detailed examination of how El Salvador and Guatemala are grouped. An interesting pattern emerges. The two are not grouped together by 9 respondents (18%). They are grouped with the Atlantic Alliance by 2 people (4%). They are grouped with the major non-aligned or neutral nations by 12 respondents (24%). Another 16 (31%) group them alone together or with South Korea. The final 12 respondents (24%) place Guatemala and El Salvador in a group with Mexico and/or Brazil. The latter is particularly interesting. While the other groups formed by respondents are usually given labels such as "pro-US," "anti-US," "sympathetic," and so on, six of the respondents who constructed this category labeled it "Latin America." It was labeled "Latin American non-communist" by two others and "dependent" or "client state" by two more (two respondents gave the group no label).

The fact that the group is the only geographically titled group that emerged and the fact that it received other labels such as "dependent" and "client state" seems to indicate that at a minimum Latin America has a special connotation for the respondents. It is possible that this special connotation involves some US sphere of influence association or, in terms of this study, the notion that Latin America is composed of United States client states, that is, dependents. In any case, the Monroe Doctrine lives on.

As a whole, El Salvador and Guatemala are seen as part of a separate group by 37, or 73% of the respondents. Only 14 (28%) place the two in the neutral or ally category. Although seven (14%) label the group in which they place El Salvador and Guatemala "dependent" their association indicates the presence of some category similar to the dependent category discussed in more detail below. The patterns that emerged also indicate that a portion of the respondents place Brazil and Mexico in a non-aligned or neutral category and another portion place them in a dependent category.

The lower association of the USSR with its allies in comparison with the association among the Atlantic Alliance states prompted a detailed examination of the surveys in search of a dependent ally of the enemy category. It was discovered that 23 of the respondents, 45%, did separate some of the USSR's allies into a different group. The states included in dependent allies of the USSR groups varied. For

example, excluding the USSR, 3 respondents grouped Poland
with Czechoslovakia; 3 combined Poland, Czechoslovakia and
North Korea; 4 grouped Poland and China together; 3 combined
North Korea with China; 4 left Czechoslovakia in a group by
itself; 5 did the same thing with Poland; and 8 placed North
Korea in a solitary group. A pattern did emerge indicating
that the Soviet Union and its allies are not seen as composing a complete group by all people. However, respondents
differed in which allies they chose to separate from the
USSR. As shown below, this category grew in responses to the
second question.

In summary, the results for the first question indicated that five of the six expected categories did emerge.
The puppet category did not emerge clearly. Two of the five
categories were fuzzy, the dependent of the perceiver's
state and the dependent ally of the enemy. It is not surprising or particularly disappointing to find this fuzziness.
Psychologists argue that categories vary greatly in quality
and that some will be less clear-cut than others.

The responses to question 2 produced exactly the patterns expected.The groups that emerged in the first question
re-emerged with some shifts in the categorization of
specific states. The second question asked respondents to
group states according to overall policies toward the United
States. The results for the one-to-one matches are shown in
Table 2.

The ally category emerged very clearly in the results
for question 2. Each state of the Atlantic Alliance was
associated with each other state by over 65% of the respondents. There was some change in evaluations of France: Only
69% grouped France with Canada in this question compared to
80% of the responses to question 1. The percent of respondents grouping France with West Germany and Great Britain
also fell slightly. Although France remained firmly in the
ally category, its association with non-aligned nations
grew. To some extent the association of all of the allies
with the non-aligned states grew because some respondents
created massive pro- and anti-US groups. In addition, some
of the non-aligned countries, Brazil in particular, were
moved into the ally category. However, France's association
with the non-aligned neutrals is stronger than that of any
of the other allies. France's grouping with Brazil, Mexico,
Nigeria and India shot up by 18%, 16%, 16%, and 12%
respectively. The biggest change for both Great Britain and
France was in their association with Brazil. This is
probably more attributable to revised judgments of Brazil

TABLE 2: States Grouped According to Policies Toward the United States (% of respondents)

	Brazil	Mexico	Nigeria	India	Yugoslavia	El Salvador	Guatemala	Canada	France	Great Britain	West Germany	Switzerland	South Korea	South Africa	Czechoslovakia	North Korea	Poland	USSR	China
Brazil	10																		
Mexico	63	12																	
Nigeria	57	61	14																
India	41	39	47	20															
Yugoslavia	28	28	37	37	22														
El Salvador	43	35	24	24	22	12													
Guatemala	45	41	29	29	18	75	12												
Canada	29	18	12	6	2	18	18	8											
France	29	26	22	14	10	18	16	69	8										
Great Britain	28	16	14	8	4	20	18	88	75	6									
West Germany	28	14	12	29	4	20	16	82	77	88	10								
Switzerland	24	20	26	22	14	16	16	43	41	47	49	29							
South Korea	31	12	18	10	8	37	28	55	43	55	55	29	18						
South Africa	29	20	20	10	14	28	20	28	22	28	28	28	28	39					
Czechoslovakia	2	4	2	8	18	2	4	0	0	0	0	0	2	0	0				
North Korea	0	2	2	8	8	0	0	0	3	0	0	0	3	0	75	16			
Poland	6	6	8	12	29	2	2	0	4	0	0	4	2	9	65	49	16		
USSR	2	2	2	10	10	2	0	0	2	0	2	0	2	2	82	82	53	4	
China	26	22	31	24	39	22	20	12	18	14	16	18	18	18	18	16	29	10	22

than to different judgments of Britain and France. Another interesting aspect of the ally classifications was the growth in the percent of respondents grouping South Korea with the Atlantic Alliance countries. The association of South Korea and France rose by 20%, with Canada by 31%, the Great Britain, 33% and with West Germany, 35%. South Korea is matched with all countries of the Atlantic Alliance except France by over 50% of the respondents. The association with these countries was not higher than 24% in the first question.

The Soviet alliance system also re-emerged but with a change in the strength of associations between the USSR and its allies. The respondents grouping the USSR with each of the three major allies remained above 50%. In fact, the respondents combining the USSR with Czechoslovakia and North Korea increased by 4% and 16% respectively. However, the number placing the Soviet Union with Poland fell by 12%. Poland's association with Czechoslovakia and North Korea also fell. When the questionnaires are examined in detail, one can see that the respondents who separate the Soviet Union from some of its allies rose to 27, that is 53%. Of those, 24 put Poland in a group without the USSR. (The surveys were taken before martial law was imposed but after the emergence of Solidarity. Thus they must have been influenced by recent events in Poland but not by some of the more dramatic responses by the government.) The responses to question 2 show in general that in terms of policy toward the United States there is less distinction between the USSR and Czechoslovakia and North Korea but more of a difference between the Soviet Union and Poland.

Then non-aligned or neutral group retained its essence in the responses to this question. Some change in individual state groupings did emerge. Yugoslavia's pairing with Mexico, Nigeria, and India slipped but its association with Brazil increased by 28%. India's association with Mexico and Nigeria also decreased. The combinations of El Salvador, Brazil, and Guatemala, and Brazil and Mexico, fell slightly. El Salvador and Guatemala were grouped with India and Nigeria more often than in responses to question 1. The two countries remained highly combined together. As in question 1, a close examination of the placements of El Salvador and Guatemala proves interesting. This time they are not grouped together by 11 respondents, up 4%. They are both grouped with the Atlantic Allies by 12%. They are grouped alone together (or with South Korea) by 22%, down 10%. They are placed in a general Latin American group by 6 respondents, two of whom labeled the group "client state" or "dependent."

The results for the marginal group formed by Guatemala and El Salvador are interesting, particularly when combined with the change in associations for South Korea. There seems to be some tendency to place countries that are "dependent" into a group of strong allies when judgments are made concerning policies toward the United States alone. South Korea, as was mentioned earlier, joined the Atlantic Alliance for over 50% of the respondents. However, it was grouped with El Salvador and Guatemala by 3 respondents and was placed in a category labeled "client state" along with Brazil and Mexico by one. In general, respondents were more divided between placing Guatemala and El Salvador with the neutrals, Atlantic allies, and a dependent category.

In summary, the same three strong groups emerged in the results for question 2. The two fuzzy groups also re-emerged with somewhat greater clarity. The puppet type did not show up as a separate group.The classifications of some countries do shift with the changed context. In general, respondents appear to be more divided over classifications than they were in responses to question 1.

Question 3 asked the respondents to label the groups they had created in questions 1 and 2. The labels varied in precise terminology and did not completely match the groups derived from the responses to the first two questions. Nevertheless, the labels attached to the groups are basically reflective of the stance of these countries toward the United States. Below are some of the labels:

Ally: Western powers; Allies; friendly; pro-US; Atlantic Alliance; NATO and surrogate; Ally/independent ally; reformers; western-oriented; OECD; pro-western; western industrialized allies.

Enemy: Eastern bloc; hostile; adversary; generally anti-US; a case apart; communist bloc; repressive left-wing; xenophobic; authoritarian; aggressive communist; anti-US communist regimes; key rival; Warsaw Pact; competitors/adversaries; communist confrontational; anti-western.

Dependent of the US: Dependent; dependent on US; economic/political dependency; limited US dependent; client state; pro-US autocratic regimes; basket cases; non-starters; US dependents; Third World right wing.

Dependent Ally of the Enemy: Pro-US communist regimes; rabidly anti-US; communist allies independent from Moscow; non-aggressive politically; pseudo-hostile; pseudo-friendly; 'independent' Eastern Europe; moderate Soviet dominated; dependent ally of the USSR; Russian orbit; Communist non-confrontational; cooperative communist.

Neutral: Truly non-aligned; neutral; politically wary; friendly but cautious; dependent neutral/independent neutral; neither pro- nor anti-US; status quo powers; developing countries with 3rd world orientation; LDCs concerned with developmental issues; favor some degree of change in international economic order;classical neutral moderate; non-aligned, radical non-aligned; G-77; developing.

Questions 4 and 5 (see questionnaire) were designed to gather further support for the argument that people classify states according to some "type of state" criteria rather than some other distinguishing method. Question 4 sought to do this by asking respondents to rate a series of international actors according to importance in shaping international issues. The list of actors included multinational corporations, United Nations agencies, individual state governments, economic cartels, regional organizations, international judicial agencies and terrorist groups. Respondents were asked to rate each actor on a scale from 1 to 7 with 1 labeled "unimportant" and 7 labeled "important." It was believed that the most important of these international actors would also be most useful in serving as a standard for organizing the political world. The results are shown in Table 3. Individual state governments have the highest number of "important" ratings. Fifty percent of the respondents gave individual state governments the highest possible mark. A total of 92% gave individual state governments a score of 5 or above. The next most important international actor was the economic cartel. A total of only 10% gave the actor a 7 but 92% gave it a rating of 5,6,or 7. The third most important actor was the multinational corporation. The least significant actors were international judicial agencies and UN agencies.

TABLE 3

Relative Influence of Seven International Actors in   Shaping
International Issues (% of respondents)

Actor	Unimportant 1	2	3	4	5	Important 6	7	N
Multinational Corporations	0	10	29	26	26	8	2	50
United Nations Agencies	3	24	40	20	10	0	0	50
Individual State Governments	2	2	2	2	14	27	51	49
Economic Cartels	0	2	0	6	50	32	10	50
Regional Organizations	4	16	22	30	18	10	0	50
International Judicial Agencies	36	34	16	10	4	0	0	50
Terrorist Groups	6	24	18	24	28	0	0	50

Question 5 asked respondents to select, in order of
usefulness, four methods of distinguishing one state from
another. The respondents were also given the opportunity to
add a distinguishing criterion if they wished. They were
supposed to rank the criterion from 1 to 5 in order of
importance with 1 being most useful. The results are given
in Table 4. The responses were difficult to evaluate because
some respondents listed several criteria as equally important. Table 4 shows that "states distinguished by their
general policies toward the US" was the method chosen most
often as being most useful. The second most popular first
choice was "states distinguished by their ideological stance." It was expected that "states distinguished by their

general policies toward the US" would be chosen as most useful. The results support the assumption that this is the criterion that would serve most efficiently as a basis for forming political categories.

TABLE 4

Relative Ranking of Five Ways of Distinguishing One State From Another
(% of respondents)

Distinction Criteria	Most Useful 1	2	3	4	Least Useful 5	N
States distinguished by regional position such as geographic location	11	26	32	28	4	47
States distinguished by their general policies toward the US such as Enemy, Ally, Neutral, Dependent, etc.	49	17	26	6	2	47
States distinguished by ideological stance such as fascism, Christian democracy, liberal democracy, etc.	24	30	17	22	7	46
States distinguished by size	4	22	16	36	22	45

Questions 6 through 17 were designed to test the category attributes. The questions forced the respondents to use the seven categories "enemy," "ally," "hegemonist," "dependent," "puppet," "dependent ally of the enemy," and "neutral." What the responses indicate, therefore, is whether or not the category names make sense to the respondents and whether or not the attributes expected to belong to these categories are actually associated with them. Twelve questions were developed in which respondents had to assess the extent to which each type of state has each attribute. Responses were registered on a seven point rating scale (see attached questionnaire). In interpreting the scale, means 1.0 through 3.0 are considered low, 3.1 through 5.0, medium, and 5.1 through 7.0 high. The results are presented in Table 5.

TABLE 5

Attributes for Seven Types of States (M= mean; SD= standard deviation; N= number of respondents)

Attribute	Enemy	Hegemonist	Dependent ally of an enemy	Neutral	Ally	Dependent of USA	Puppet of USA
1. Military strength compared to USA (inferior = 1, equal = 4, superior = 7)	M = 4.2 SD = 1.3 N = 42	M = 3.5 SD = 1.4 N = 39	M = 2.1 SD = 1.1 N = 39	M = 1.6 SD = 0.9 N = 40	M = 3.1 SD = 1.0 N = 41	M = 1.9 SD = 1.0 N = 41	M = 1.7 SD = 1.2 N = 36
2. Willingness to use military force (very unwilling = 1, moderately willing = 4, very willing = 7)	M = 4.9 SD = 1.5 N = 42	M = 4.6 SD = 1.7 N = 38	M = 3.7 SD = 1.7 N = 42	M = 1.5 SD = 1.4 N = 43	M = 3.1 SD = 1.4 N = 40	M = 3.2 SD = 1.6 N = 41	M = 3.2 SD = 1.6 N = 35
3. Similarity to US in form of government (very dissimilar = 1, moderately similar = 4; very similar = 7)	M = 1.2 SD = 0.4 N = 42	M = 1.6 SD = 1.1 N = 38	M = 1.7 SD = 0.9 N = 42	M = 4.3 SD = 1.2 N = 41	M = 6.0 SD = 0.9 N = 41	M = 4.5 SD = 1.1 N = 41	M = 3.8 SD = 1.2 N = 35
4. Domestic groups actively attempting to influence foreign policy (absent = 1, moderately active = 4, present and very active = 7)	M = 2.1 SD = 1.5 N = 43	M = 2.3 SD = 1.4 N = 38	M = 2.2 SD = 1.3 N = 43	M = 4.9 SD = 1.7 N = 43	M = 6.1 SD = 1.3 N = 43	M = 4.9 SD = 1.4 N = 43	M = 3.8 SD = 1.7 N = 37
5. Effectiveness in policy implementation (very effective = 1, moderately effective = 4, ineffective = 7)	M = 2.9 SD = 1.5 N = 41	M = 3.3 SD = 1.5 N = 37	M = 4.7 SD = 1.7 N = 41	M = 4.0 SD = 1.6 N = 40	M = 3.0 SD = 1.2 N = 39	M = 4.7 SD = 1.4 N = 39	M = 5.1 SD = 1.2 N = 35
6. Economic strength in comparison to the US (superior = 1, equal = 4, inferior = 7)	M = 5.3 SD = 1.1 N = 42	M = 5.7 SD = 1.0 N = 38	M = 6.3 SD = 0.8 N = 41	M = 4.9 SD = 1.7 N = 40	M = 4.0 SD = 1.1 N = 42	M = 5.6 SD = 1.1 N = 42	M = 6.2 SD = 1.0 N = 35
7. Economic penetration permitting economic interaction with other states (highly penetrable = 1, moderately penetrable = 4, impenetrable = 7)	M = 5.7 SD = 1.3 N = 41	M = 5.7 SD = 0.9 N = 37	M = 5.7 SD = 1.3 N = 40	M = 3.3 SD = 1.5 N = 41	M = 2.2 SD = 1.2 N = 41	M = 2.3 SD = 1.2 N = 42	M = 2.5 SD = 1.6 N = 36
8. Culture in comparison to USA (less advanced = 1; equal = 4, more advanced = 7)	M = 3.1 SD = 1.3 N = 41	M = 3.3 SD = 1.3 N = 36	M = 3.0 SD = 1.2 N = 39	M = 4.0 SD = 1.0 N = 40	M = 4.7 SD = 1.3 N = 41	M = 3.3 SD = 0.8 N = 40	M = 2.9 SD = 1.0 N = 34
9. Degree of support for international policies of US (highly supportive = 1, moderately supportive = 4, completely supportive = 7)	M = 6.6 SD = 1.1 N = 42	M = 5.8 SD = 1.4 N = 39	M = 6.3 SD = 1.1 N = 43	M = 4.5 SD = 1.1 N = 43	M = 2.1 SD = 0.8 N = 41	M = 2.1 SD = 0.9 N = 43	M = 1.6 SD = 0.9 N = 37
10. Flexibility in bargaining (inflexible = 1, moderately flexible = 4, highly flexible = 7)	M = 2.3 SD = 1.4 N = 43	M = 2.6 SD = 1.4 N = 39	M = 2.5 SD = 1.2 N = 42	M = 4.4 SD = 1.3 N = 42	M = 5.1 SD = 1.2 N = 42	M = 4.4 SD = 1.4 N = 43	M = 4.0 SD = 1.8 N = 37
11. Degree of determination and will in pursuing international goals (vigorous = 1, moderate = 4, passive = 7)	M = 1.6 SD = 0.7 N = 42	M = 1.9 SD = 1.2 N = 38	M = 4.0 SD = 1.8 N = 42	M = 4.2 SD = 1.4 N = 41	M = 3.0 SD = 1.2 N = 41	M = 4.6 SD = 1.4 N = 42	M = 5.4 SD = 1.2 N = 36
12. Compatibility of goals with US international goals (high = 1, moderate = 4, incompatible = 7)	M = 6.8 SD = 0.5 N = 43	M = 6.2 SD = 1.2 N = 37	M = 6.2 SD = 0.8 N = 43	M = 3.8 SD = 0.8 N = 43	M = 1.7 SD = 0.7 N = 42	M = 2.4 SD = 1.1 N = 43	M = 2.5 SD = 1.4 N = 36

ENEMY

The image of the enemy should be one it which this type of state is seen as militarily equal to the perceiver's state and willing to use its military capabilities. In terms of domestic political structure the enemy should be assumed to be quite dissimilar to the perceiver's state and lacking in competing policy advocates dissenting from the prevailing elite's position. Further, the leadership should be seen as monolithic and capable of careful orchestration of devious plots.3 The type would be seen as having an economic capacity essentially equal to the perceiver's that is also stable although impermeable. Culturally, in terms of technical sophistication, literacy, etc., the type should be seen as equal to the perceiver's state, although its values will be distained. The image is one of a state that is unsupportive of the goals and policies of the perceiver's state, inflexible in policy formation and implementation, and aggressive in pursuit of its goals.

The response alternatives associated with the image were expected to include diplomatic exchanges as an important response but one assumed to offer little in terms of fundamentally altering the behavior of the enemy image. The use of military force would also be associated with the image as would the use of economic force (sanctions or boycotts). Doing nothing is a response alternative not expected to be associated with the image: responding to the actions of a state given the enemy image is presumed to be seen as essential. Appealing to international circles was a response expected to be found in association with the category. Finally, it was expected that the image would be associated with event scripts including instances of aggressive behavior, security issues (including economic issues seen in terms of security implications), and historical analogies comparing current actions to those of Hitler and other historical enemies.

Questions 6 and 7 (1 and 2 in Table 5) asked the respondents to evaluate the enemy in terms of "military strength compared to the US" and "willingness to use military force." As expected, the enemy's military strength was seen as equal to that of the United States, that is, the perceiver's state. The mean rating of the enemy's military strength was 4.2. Point `4' on the scale was labeled "equal." The mean rating of the enemy in "willingness to use military force" was 4.9, slightly higher than moderate.

As mentioned above, it was expected that the enemy

image would be one of a state with a very different form of government in comparison to the perceiver's, a government with few competing policy advocates and efficient in policy implementation. These attributes were expected because the enemy should be seen as monolithic, permitting no recognition of variety or difference of opinion. The results for the questions exploring the association of these attributes with the enemy image were also supportive of the expectations. The mean rating of the enemy in "similarity in form of government to the US" was 1.2 where 1 on the scale was labeled "very dissimilar." The mean rating for "domestic group activity" was 2.1 where 1 on the scale was labeled "absent." Finally, the mean rating for "effectiveness in policy implementation" was 2.9, where 1 on the scale was labeled "very effective."

The results for questions concerning the economic attributes associated with this image were moderately supportive of expectations. The mean rating for economic strength was 5.3 with `4' labeled "equal" on the scale. The enemy was therefore given an overall rating of slightly lower economic strength than expected. This is not surprising given the fact that most respondents were apparently using the USSR as the ideal-typical enemy (as can be seen from results of other questions discussed below). The enemy's economic penetrability was about what was expected, perhaps slightly lower than desired. The mean rating is 5.7 which is within the realm of impenetrable on the scale but at the low end.

It was expected that the enemy would be seen as essentially equal culturally to the perceiver's state. Asking respondents to compare the cultural sophistication of other types of states to their own is risky at best. The question was included in the survey with great trepidation and the expectation that the respondents would not answer frankly even if they felt strongly about differences in cultural sophistication between their country and the types of states they evaluated. Therefore, it was surprising to find a mean rating of 3.1 on the low end of equal. The standard deviation shows that there were individuals who gave the enemy a very low rating as well as those who gave it an equal rating.

The last four questions all had results supportive of expectations. It was assumed that the enemy type would be seen as very unsupportive of United States policies, inflexible in international bargaining, vigorous in pursuit of international goals, and having goals incompatible with

those of the United States. The means for these four questions were exactly as expected. The enemy type was rated as
completely unsupportive of the United States, basically
inflexible, vigorously determined in pursuit of goals, and
incompatible with the United States as far as foreign policy
goals are concerned.

As a whole, the results for enemy attributes supported
the theoretical expectations.

HEGEMONIST

The hegemonist type did not fare well in this series of
questions. This type of state should have been seen as one
that is more powerful than the perceiver's state, essentially an imperialist. Since most Americans cannot conceive
of a state so powerful, and since there really is no example
of such a state for Americans (with the exception of those
who see the Soviet Union this way), it is not a great disap-
pointment to find results that were confused and unsupportive. An additional problem was evident from comments in the
margins of the surveys indicating that some respondents
apparently did not know what the word "hegemonist" means.
(The term was used to avoid all of the connotations associated with the term "imperialist.")

In the abstract, it was assumed that the hegemonist
image is one of a state that is superior to the perceiver's
state in most attributes. It should be more powerful militarily and economically and willing to use its economic and
military strength against the perceiver's state. It should
also be a type of state dissimilar to the perceiver's in
domestic structure but highly effective in policy implementation. It should be perceived as more advanced culturally,
as essentially unsupportive of the perceiver's state's policies, inflexible in bargaining, and aggressive in pursuit of
its goals. This is, in fact, the way people from the Third
World often describe the United States. It is clearly an
image that is part of their world view.

Response alternatives of a particular variety should
also be associated with this image. Diplomatic exchanges
should be perceived as important but as providing little
likelihood of achieving the perceiver's goals. Non-governmental groups may also be involved in the bargaining but
again with little likelihood of success. The use of military force against a hegemonist would also be expected to be
doomed to failure as would efforts to hurt the hegemonist

economically. Doing nothing in response to actions by the
hegemonist should be an alternative associated with the
image, as would appealing to international circles. Finally, the event scripts expected to be associated with the
image are events of overt or covert imperialist aggression.

The results for the hegemonist attribute questions were
strange. The mean rating showed that the hegemonist was
perceived by respondents to be slightly inferior to the
United States in strength and less than moderately willing
to use military force. Both results were not supportive of
predictions. The hegemonist was expected to be seen as
dissimilar in form of government, lacking in competing policy
advocates, and effective in policy implementation. The first
two expectations were supported with mean ratings of 1.6 and
2.3, respectively, where the first points on the scales were
"very dissimilar" and "absent." The hegemonist was seen as
slightly less effective than expected, with a mean rating of
3.3. This is in the "moderately effective" classification
rather than the "effective" end of the scale.

The results for question 11, a comparison of the economic strength of the hegemonist with the United States, did
not conform to expectations. It was argued that the
hegemonist would be seen as superior to the perceiver's
state economically. The mean rating showed an evaluation of
the hegemonist as less than equal to the United States in
economic strength. It was also assumed that the type could
be seen as economically permeable but that the perceiver's
state would not be able to take advantage of this attribute.
The responses for this question rated the economic
permeability of this type of state as 5.7, on the
impenetrable side of the scale.

The ideal-typical hegemonist should be seen as culturally superior to the perceiver's state. The mean cultural
comparison was 3.3 or slightly less than equal. The last
four attributes did have results conforming to expectations.
The hegemonist should have been seen as relatively lacking
in support for the United States. The mean rating for the
support question was 5.8, on the unsupportive end of the
scale. It was expected that the hegemonist would be seen as
inflexible. The results conformed to this expectation with a
mean rating of 2.6. The hegemonist was perceived as vigorous
in pursuit of goals and as having goals incompatible with
those of the United States.

Interestingly, the attributes ascribed to the hegemonist by these respondents were almost exactly those of the
enemy. Yet, if one glances at responses to questions asking

for examples of an hegemonist's behavior, the acts are those of hegemonic powers. The respondents can, apparently, recognize the acts of such a power. (One respondent even mentioned the United States as a hegemonist.) If this is a category used by others and not by Americans, it may account for some difficulty Americans have in understanding others' perceptions of the US as omnipotent.

DEPENDENT ALLY OF THE ENEMY

The attributes ascribed to the dependent ally of the enemy type were generally supportive of expectations and produce more information concerning distinctions made between this image and that of the enemy. It was expected that the image would be of a state that is inferior militarily to the perceiver's state but always potentially equal due to its relationship with the enemy. It is not an image of a state that is willing to use military force. The domestic polity of this type of state should be seen as dissimilar to the perceiver's and inefficient in policy implementations. The economy was expected to be perceived as weak and relatively impermeable. Perceptions of culture were expected to result in inferior evaluations. The type of state should be assumed to be unsupportive of the policies of the perceiver's state and inflexible in policy formation. The dependent ally of the enemy should be assumed to be passive in pursuit of its own goals.

A number of possible response alternatives should be associated with this type of state. Diplomatic exchanges would be included but given the influence of the enemy, direct diplomatic interaction with the enemy's dependent should not generally be associated with effective efforts to alter its behavior. Military force would clearly be an option but its use would be associated with some kind of reaction by the enemy. Economic coercion would also be associated with the type of state as would be appealing to international circles. The event scripts associated with this particular image should include acts of aggression, possibly by this type of state against others. Major issues associated with the image should include security issues.

The attributes ascribed to this image by respondents were generally supportive of expectations. The first two attributes, "military strength compared to the US" and "willingness to use military force," are important in the extent to which they help differentiate between the enemy

associated with this type of state. Diplomatic exchanges
would be included but given the influence of the enemy,
direct diplomatic interaction with the enemy's dependent
should not generally be associated with effective efforts to
alter its behavior. Military force would clearly be an
option but its use would be associated with some kind of
reaction by the enemy. Economic coercion would also be
associated with the type of state as would be appealing to
international circles. The event scripts associated with
this particular image should include acts of aggression,
possibly by this type of state against others. Major issues
associated with the image should include security issues.

The attributes ascribed to this image by respondents
were generally supportive of expectations. The first two
attributes, "military strength compared to the US" and
"willingness to use military force," are important in the
extent to which they help differentiate between the enemy
and the dependent of the enemy images. It was assumed that
the dependent type would be seen as militarily weaker than
with some kind of reaction by the enemy. Economic coercion
would also be associated with the type of state as would
appealing to international circles. The event scripts associated with this particular image should include acts of
aggression, possibly by this type of state against others.
Major issues associated with the image should include security issues.

The attributes ascribed to this image by respondents
were generally supportive of expectations. The first two
attributes, "military strength compared to the US" and
"willingness to use military force," are important in the
extent to which they help differentiate between the enemy
and the dependent of the enemy images. It was assumed that
the dependent type would be seen as militarily weaker that
the United States despite its military affiliation with the
enemy. In fact, the mean response for this attribute was 2.1
with 1 on the scale being "inferior." The enemy, in contrast, was given a 4.2 mean rating. The difference is enough
to indicate that there is a distinction made between the
enemy and its ally in military strength. The dependent ally
of the enemy was also seen as less willing than the enemy to
use military force and, as expected, not completely unwilling to use military force. The mean was 3.7, in the middle
of the scale.

Domestic policy advocates were seen as essentially
absent in the dependent ally of the enemy type. However, it
was seen as only moderately effective in policy implementa-

tion with a mean rating of 4.7, less effective than the enemy. As expected, the dependent ally of the enemy was perceived as weaker economically than the United States. The mean rating here was 6.3, very close to the inferior extreme. This result was a much weaker rating than the enemy received.

The dependent ally of the enemy was evaluated culturally as less than equal to the United States. As expected, it was seen as unsupportive of the international policies of the United States. The mean score on this question was 6.3 with 7 being "completely unsupportive." The type was rated as inflexible. The question concerning the degree of determination in pursuing international goals gave further evidence that there is some distinction made between the dependent ally of the enemy and the enemy itself. The mean score for the dependent was 4.0 which is moderate while the enemy's score was 1.6. Finally, the dependent ally of the enemy was seen as having goals that are incompatible with those of the United States.

NEUTRAL

The results for the attributes ascribed to the neutral conformed to those expected. It was assumed that the neutral would be seen as militarily inferior to the United States and, because of the historical association of neutrality with Switzerland, unwilling to use military force. (For those who do not associate neutrality with Switzerland's passifism, the image may be of states willing to use military force.) Both expectations were confirmed. The mean rating for military strength was 1.8, where 1 was "inferior." The mean rating for willingness to use military force was also very low.

It was also assumed that neutrals would be seen as nonthreatening but not consistenty or completely friendly. Because neutrals are non-threatening, policy makers should see competing policy advocates as part of the neutral's domestic arena. However, the neutral should not be seen as completely similar to the perceiver's state. A neutral is not an ally and does not involve the perceptions of assured support and compatibility that produce perceptions of similarity. The results revealed that the respondents rated the neutral as moderately similar to the USA and as having moderately active competing policy advocates. It was argued that the neutral should be seen as relatively similar to the perceiver's state in economic characteristics, including strength and penetrability. The results show that the neutral is indeed rated as economically equal to the United States. The mean rating was 4.9 which is only slightly on the inferior side of equal. This is an interesting result. It does seem to point to the importance of lack of threat in producing assumptions of similarity. Actually, when one considers the possible "neutrals" in the world today, not one approaches the USA in terms of economic strength, yet the respondents gave the neutral a score of near equality. The neutral was also seen as moderately penetrable.

It was assumed that the neutral would probably be seen as culturally equal to the United States and this was born out in the results. Its support for the policies of the perceiver's state was expected to be only moderate since it would not threaten the perceiver's state but would not help either. In fact, its rating for supportiveness was moderate, 4.5. It was also assumed that the neutral would be assigned an attribute of no more than moderate flexibility. It is flexible in the sense that it does not strictly adhere to any "camp" but inflexible in its neutrality. The respondents gave it a mean rating of 4.4 on this attibute. It was also expected to receive only moderate ratings in determination in pursuing international goals and compatibility of those goals with the perceiver's state. These expectations were also fulfilled with mean scores of 4.2 and 3.8 respectively.

Additional theoretical expectations about the response alternatives and event scripts associated with the image were developed. It was assumed that diplomatic exchanges Lith neutrals would clearly be important components of the category. Non-governmental participants in bargaining with neutrals are conceivable and potentially effective. The use of military force, however, should not be closely associated with this category nor should the use of extremely coercive economic sanctions. However, economic pressure would clearly be associated with the category as a bargaining tool. Doing nothing in response to a neutral's actions or appealing to international circles for support should also be responses associated with the image. Americans should not include event scripts of aggressive behavior by the neutral in the image. The governments of neutrals should be associated with stability, economic issues and security issues such as arms control. Alliance issues should not, of course, be associated with the image. It was expected that the prototypical example of a neutral for the Americans responding to the questionnaire would be Switzerland. A discussion of the findings regarding these characteristics of the image will be provided later.

ALLY

In the ideal-typical extreme, the ally type was expected to be perceived as similar to the respondents' state in military strength, willingness to use military force, domestic structure and economic strength. It was also expected to be seen as a type of state in which policy advocates compete openly and a state that is economically open and penetrable. The results were as expected. The military strength mean rating for the ally was 3.1, within the equal range. Given the military inferiority of present-day allies of the USA, the score of 3.1 is amazingly close to the perfectly equal score of 4. The ally was expected to be perceived as equal to the perceiver's state in willingness to use military force. The results gave the ally a mean score of 3.1, within the moderate range.

Because people assume that those they like are similar to themselves, it was argued that allies should be seen as very similar to the United States in form of government. The mean score was 6.0 where 7 was labeled "very similar." The results, therefore, showed that the respondents did assume that allies are similar in form of government with their own state. The assumption that allies are perceived as friendly and non-monolithic was also expected to result in the respondents giving a high score to the presence of competing policy advocates. The mean score for this question was 6.1. The 7 on the response scale represented competing and active policy advocates. The ally type was not given as high a score in effectiveness in policy implementation as expected, however. On the other hand, it was assumed that the type would be seen as cultually equal and it was, with a mean of 4.7, slightly toward the "more advanced" end of the scale.

Several other attributes were also ascribed to the image as expected. The ally type was seen as supportive of the United States and flexible. It was expected that it would be seen as equal to the USA in vigorous pursuit of goals. The means score for this attribute was 3. Finally, the type should have been seen as pursuing goals that are highly compatible with those of the United States. This expectation was fulfilled with a mean score of 1.7.

In terms of response alternatives and event scripts, several expectations were developed. It was assumed that diplomatic exchanges would be highly associated with the category, and that neither military force nor economic force would be acceptable as response alternatives. Doing nothing in response to bilateral issues with the ideal-typical ally should not be closely associated with the category. The perceiver would presumably wish to maintain good relations with an ally and would need to negotiate issues in order to do so. The event scripts in the category should include instances in which an ally came to the aid of the perceiver's state. Major issues would include security issues foremost and economic issues secondarily. Finally, for an American it was expected that Great Britain would be seen as the ideal-typical example of an ally. Again, the results to questions exploring these issues will be presented later.

DEPENDENT OF THE USA

The dependent category had few unexpected results. It was hypothesized that the dependent would be seen as militarily inferior to the United States. The overall mean was 1.9, on the inferior end of the scale. The dependent was expected to be associated with little willingness to use military force. The mean score for this attribute was 3.2, on the unwilling end of "moderate." The type was not expected to be seen as extremely similar to the United States in form of government. It was believed that the dependent may be seen as dissimilar to the perceiver's state but that perceptions may vary since the type will not be seen as monolithic. In fact, the type was associated with moderate similarity to the United States in form of government. This in itself is interesting since the respondents mentioned countries such as Israel, South Korea, and El Salvador as perfect examples of a dependent. These states are neither similar to the US nor similar to each other in form of government (although, Israel, of course, is democratic). The indication is that, true to psychological patterns, people assume greater similarity between themselves and those who are friendly than may actually be the case. It was hypothesized that respondents would also perceive competing policy advocates as present in the dependent type of state. The results indicated a perception of moderate activity. Policy implementation was expected to be perceived as ineffective and inefficient. The responses to this question, however, resulted in a mean score of 4.7 which is moderately effective.

As expected, the dependent state was seen as economically inferior to the United States. The overall mean score was 5.6 which is on the inferior end of the scale but slightly closer to equal than expected. It was assumed that this type of state would be seen as economically penetrable. The responses had a mean of 2.3 on the highly penetrable end of the scale, but not dramatically so.

It was argued from a theoretical standpoint that dependents of the United States would be seen as culturally inferior, or less advanced. Frank responses, however, were not expected from respondents. Nevertheless, the mean for the question was 3.3, on the less advanced side of equal. The result may, of course, reflect open responses, in which case the dependent is seen as more culturally advanced than expected. The type should have been associated with policies highly supportive of the United States. The mean in this case was 2.1, highly supportive. Only limited flexibility was expected in perceptions of this type and the mean score was 4.4, in the moderately flexible portion. It was assumed that the dependent would be perceived as essentially passive in pursuit of its international goals. In fact, it was seen as moderately active. Finally, it was assumed that the goals of the dependent type would be perceived as compatible with those of the United States and they were.

Deviations from expectations for this type were moderate. Additional data discussed later explored the response alternatives and event scripts in the category. Briefly, it was expected that response alternatives would include diplomatic exchanges, the use of military force, the use of economic force, doing nothing, and appealing to international circles. The use of military force, however, was assumed to be associated with possible severe consequences in terms of reactions of other states and heightened nationalism. The use of economic force should be perceived as offering good success rates. Instances of aggression should be associated with this type of state. The instances, however, would consist of cases in which the dependent has aggressed against other states, not the perceiver's. The governments of dependent states may be associated with internal instability. Major issues would include economic matters and loyalty to alliances. The prototype of the dependent state for Americans could be South Korea, possibly Mexico, or the Philippines.

PUPPET

The final type of state explored is the puppet. Despite the fact that this type did not emerge as a distinct group in the first series of questions, the results from the attribute questions essentially conformed to expectations. In the abstract it was expected that this type would be seen as militarily inferior to the United States, moderately willing to use military force, similar to the perceiver's state in terms of domestic structure but perceived as having few competing policy advocates within the polity. The governments of states perceived with the puppet image were expected to be associated with inefficient policy implementation. Most of these expectations were upheld. Militarily the image was of a state that is vastly inferior to the United States (a mean of 1.7) and slightly less than moderately willing to use military force (3.2). In domestic structure it was seen as moderately similar to the United States with a mean of 3.8 and with a moderate association of pressure groups (3.8). The effectiveness of policy implementation score was 5.1, just barely on the ineffective side of the scale.

Another expected attribute was inferiority to the USA economically and high economic penetrability. These expectations were supported in the results. It was also assumed that the people of the puppet state would be seen as less advanced culturally. The responses for this question had a mean of 2.8, on the less advanced side of the scale. Again, the willingness of respondents to answer this question with any response other than an automatic "equal" is surprising.

In international behavior, the puppet type was expected to be associated with support for the United States, flexibility, relative vigor in pursuit of its goals, and compatible goals. The results confirmed the first expectation. Puppets were associated with great support for the international policies of the United States. The type was seen as only moderately flexible in international bargaining with a mean of 4.0. The responses to the question on "degree of determination in pursuing international goals" were not supportive of expectations. In fact, the mean was 5.4, on the passive side of moderately determined in pursuing goals. The final attribute was supportive of expectations. The mean score for goal compatibility was 2.5.

The responses for this category and the dependent category are quite similar. The puppet type is seen as slightly more willing to follow the United States line as can be inferred from its score on the question concerning support for US policies. It is also seen as more passive than the dependent type. The results for other questions suggest that the puppet type is either an historical category or that puppets are classified with allies. More will be said on this point later. Additional questions explored response alternatives and events scripts. Basically, it was assumed that the responses associated with puppets would include diplomatic exchanges and economic force in addition to doing nothing and appealing to international circles. It was assumed that the perceiver would be fully cognizant of the asymmetrical nature of the relationship in terms of dependence and needs. The puppet would be assumed to be unlikely to resist pressure from the perceiver's state; hence military force would not be associated with the category for the puppet would be assumed to buckle in to diplomatic or economic pressure long before the use of military force would be considered. The puppet's weakness and compliance should dominate perceptions of response alternatives. Event scripts associated with the category were expected to include governmental instability within the puppet, and economic issues with alliance issues secondary. Instances of aggression would be associated with the category if the perceiver's state had come to the rescue of a puppet state militarily in recent history.

Question 18 (see attached survey) was designed to gather data concerning categorical prototypes. It asked respondents to give a perfect example of each type of state and permitted open-ended responses. The results for this question demonstrate both the variation in quality of the various categories, (some are much stronger and more well-defined than others), and the peculiar nature of the puppet image. A rather large set of choices emerged for some categories, including the puppet category. In other cases, such as the ally and enemy images, respondents tended to select the same states as perfect examples of the type of state. In Table 6 below the selections are displayed but states selected by fewer than 10% of the respondents are not shown in the table.

As the table shows, the USSR was the unqualified winner for the perfect example of the enemy. Nazi Germany followed in second place but with only 14% of the respondents selecting it. As usual, the hegemonist category is confused. The

USSR was most often chosen as the perfect example of this type of state with the People's Republic of China second. It is difficult to interpret this response particularly when compared to the selections of enemies. One cannot determine if the respondents were thinking of the hegemonist vis-a-vis their own state (the US) or in general. From the perspective of Afghanistanis and Vietnamese, for example, the USSR and PRC respectively could easily be deemed perfect examples of

TABLE 6

Perfect Examples of Each Type of State (10% of respondents or more)

Category	Choice	% of respondents	N
Enemy	USSR	66	33
	Nazi Germany	14	7
Hegemonist	USSR	47	20
	PRC	16	7
Dependent Ally	Czechoslovakia	20	10
of the Enemy	East Germany	14	7
	Cuba	14	7
	Bulgaria	14	7
	Poland	10	5
Neutral	Switzerland	56	28
	India	13	6
Ally	Great Britain	62	31
	West Germany	10	5
	Canada	10	5
Dependent of	South Korea	21	10
USA	Israel	19	9
	El Salvador	13	6
	Philippines	11	5
Puppet of the	South Korea	29	11
USA	South Vietnam	24	9
	El Salvador	13	5
	Puerto Rico	13	5

hegemonists. Both are overwhelmingly powerful and are seen as very aggressive. For an American, however, the USSR would fit the enemy category. The fact that China was never mentioned as a perfect example of an enemy may indicate that these responses to the hegemonist question did reflect an evaluation of these states in general, rather than vis-a-vis the US. In addition, the fact that one respondent mentioned the USA as his perfect example of a hegemonist would support that interpretation.

Responses to the question requesting perfect examples of the dependent ally of the enemy reflect the vague boundaries of that category. No single state stood out as the overwhelming favorite example for respondents. Czechoslovakia was chosen most often, by 20% of the respondents. East Germany, Bulgaria, and Cuba were tied for second place with 14% of the respondents selecting them. Only three respondents mentioned a country from World War II (Italy, not shown above).

The results for the perfect example of a neutral were interesting. Fifty-six percent of the respondents chose Switzerland as the best example. The next most popular example was India, followed by less than 10% for Sweden and Yugoslavia. These results were interesting because Switzerland was not grouped with either India or Yugoslavia in the first two questions. Nevertheless, they all appear here as perfect examples. This suggests several things: First, Switzerland is the ideal-typical example of a neutral for a majority of the respondent. Second, the non-aligned nations are probably part of the same category but farther away from the ideal extreme. Third, the neutral category is not strictly neutral for all respondents.

Switzerland was, after all, grouped with the Atlantic Alliance by around 40% of the respondents yet is selected by over 50% as a perfect example of a neutral. It therefore appears that while countries such as the Third World non-aligned are part of the category, they are not often thought of as perfect examples. A perfect example of a neutral is one that is more closely associated with the respondents' allies than with other neutrals. Thus, although the neutral category exists and is distinct, it does not really reflect true neutrality but opposition to the opponents of the United States. Not all respondents feel this way, of course, since some do select Third World neutrals as perfect examples of the category.

The replies to the question asking for perfect examples of an ally were exactly what one would expect. Great Britain

was the strong first choice and was followed by logical
alternatives. The responses for the dependent ally of the US
and the puppet of the US are more complex. The responses for
the puppet category show the historical nature of that
image.   South · Korea was listed most often as a perfect
example followed closely by South Vietnam. El Salvador and
Puerto Rico came as the next most popular choices. It is
important to note that only 38 of the respondents actually
chose to give an example of a puppet; some declining because
they could not think of any examples. A most intriguing
aspect of these results was that South Korea was the most
frequently mentioned puppet but was placed with the Atlantic
Alliance by over 50% of the respondents when grouped according to policies toward the United States. This prompts
two questions: are puppets incorporated into the ally category? Does this explain why the puppet category did not
appear earlier? To explore these questions, all of the
responses listing South Korea, El Salvador, or Guatemala as
perfect examples of a puppet were re-examined to see if they
also placed these countries with the Atlantic Alliance in
question 2. A total of 18 respondents, 47%, chose South
Korea, El Salvador, or Guatemala as their perfect examples
of a puppet. Of these, 8, or 46%, placed their choice with
the Atlantic Alliance in response to question 2. Three
respondents, 17%, placed the choice in a "Latin America"
group. Three more placed the puppet choice with the non-
aligned Third World. Four placed the choice alone in a group
by itself. Unfortunately, only three of the countries chosen
as perfect examples of a puppet were on the list in question
2. In general, those who chose one of the three as their
examples of a puppet placed them with the Atlantic Alliance.
If these results are not meaningless, then puppets must be
thought of as as reliable as allies and as having behavioral
similarities. It is possible, of course, that the category
is only an historical one. Nevertheless, the strange pattern
of classifying puppets with allies is noteworthy.

   The selections of perfect examples of a dependent of
the USA adds more information. El Salvador and South Korea
are cited by 13 and 21% as perfect examples. None of those
who used one of these two as the perfect example of a
puppet also used it as a perfect example of a dependent.
Thus, there may be a distinction between dependent and
puppet after all. As can be seen, other choices for this
category were Israel and the Philippines.

   These results are interesting in several ways. First,
they demonstrate the less concrete quality of the dependent

of the United States and dependent ally of the enemy categories. Responses for these categories were more varied with more states being chosen as perfect examples and less agreement among respondents. As was mentioned above, the neutral category has some peculiar qualities which become even more evident in the responses to questions 19-25. Finally, there are very few examples from World War II. Respondents were told in the instructions that they chould choose current or historical examples but they generally stuck to examples from the Vietnam era to the present.

The results for questions 19-25 provide some of the most interesting information from the questionnaire. In these questions respondents were asked to rate each of a list of eleven countries on a scale from 1 to 7 as examples of an enemy, ally, neutral, dependent of the US, puppet of the US, dependent ally of the enemy, and hegemonist. The numbers 1 and 7 on the scales were labeled either "perfect" or "terrible" examples. The labels were switched back and forth for each succeeding question to prevent response bias. The countries chosen were the Soviet Union, China, Poland, Cuba, Great Britain, Canada, West Germany, Guatemala, Mexico, India, and Switzerland. These countries were chosen to give the respondents a wide variety of countries and to provide potential perfect and terrible examples for each type of state. Mexico was included because of its importance for the second half of this study.

The results for question 19 rated the eleven countries as examples of an enemy. The results are in Table 7.

TABLE 7
Ratings of 11 Countries as Examples of an Enemy (%)

Country	Terrible example					Perfect example			
	1	2	3	4	5	6	7	Mean	N
S. Union	2	0	0	0	12	16	69	6.5	49
China	2	13	31	21	19	15	0	3.9	48
Poland	2	10	29	17	29	13	0	4.0	48
Cuba	0	4	2	0	15	44	35	6.0	48
G. Britain	96	0	2	0	0	2	0	1.1	49
Canada	81	13	2	2	2	0	0	1.3	48
W. Germany	78	21	0	0	0	2	0	1.3	50
Guatemala	31	33	24	9	2	0	0	2.2	45
Mexico	14	39	33	14	0	0	0	2.5	49

(Continued)

TABLE 7 (Continued)
Ratings of 11 Countries as Examples of an Enemy (%)

Country	Terrible example					Perfect example			
	1	2	3	4	5	6	7	Mean	N
India	11	23	32	21	11	2	0	3.0	47
Switzerland	59	14	14	8	4	0	0	1.8	49

The Soviet Union was rated a perfect example by 69% of the respondents with a mean score of 6.5. The scores for China were also impressive. China clearly was not seen as an enemy. Poland is seen as distinct on the scale with a mean score of 4.0. Cuba, on the other hand, is seen as quite like the Soviet Union with a mean score of 6.0. The western allies were all very low on the scale toward the terrible example side. Interestingly, Mexico and India were slightly higher toward the perfect example side than the Atlantic Allies. This would seem to indicate that some measure of threat is associated with neutrals and it confirms that neutrals may not be seen as enemies but they certainly are not allies either.

Table 8 gives the results of ratings of the eleven countries as examples of hegemonists. The labels for the ends of the scale were switched so that 1 is the perfect example rating and 7 is the terrible example rating.

TABLE 8
Ratings of 11 Countries as Examples of a Hegemonist (%)

Country	Perfect example					Terrible example			
	1	2	3	4	5	6	7	Mean	N
S. Union	63	30	0	0	0	0	7	1.7	46
China	14	23	23	21	5	9	5	3.3	43
Poland	5	2	5	7	9	28	44	5.7	43
Cuba	7	36	27	5	5	9	11	3.4	44
G. Britain	5	5	2	12	10	31	36	5.5	42
Canada	7	0	0	7	2	23	61	6.1	44
W. Germany	5	5	7	7	12	16	49	5.6	43
Guatemala	5	0	0	12	10	31	43	5.9	42
Mexico	5	2	0	17	2	33	41	5.7	42

(Continued)

92

TABLE 8 (Continued)
Ratings of 11 Countries as Examples of a Hegemonist (%)

Country	Perfect example						Terrible example		
	1	2	3	4	5	6	7	Mean	N
India	3	8	15	32	23	21	8	4.5	39
Switzerland	7	0	0	5	2	9	77	6.3	44

Once more the Soviet Union is given the highest rating as a perfect example. China is second with a mean score of 3.3. Cuba is a close third with a mean score of 3.4. Poland once again appears to be seen quite differently than the Soviet Union. Its mean score is 5.7. The western allies were seen as poor examples of a hegemonist but these ratings were not as poor as their scores were when they were judged as examples of enemies. This may reflect the respondents' knowledge of their historical records. Mexico has a similar mean rating of 5.7 which could not be explained as a reflection of knowledge of Mexico's past.

Table 9 gives the results for each of the eleven countries as examples of an ally.

TABLE 9
Ratings of 11 Countries as Examples of an Ally (%)

Country	Terrible example					Perfect example			
	1	2	3	4	5	6	7	Mean	N
S. Union	96	4	0	0	0	0	0	1.0	48
China	4	23	30	26	13	4	0	3.3	47
Poland	9	36	42	9	4	0	0	2.6	45
Cuba	85	13	2	0	0	0	0	1.2	46
G.Britain	0	0	0	0	0	18	82	6.8	50
Canada	0	0	0	2	6	33	59	6.5	49
W. Germany	0	0	0	0	6	44	50	6.4	50
Guatemala	2	11	20	16	31	13	7	4.3	45
Mexico	2	0	19	36	32	11	0	4.3	47
India	4	26	35	24	9	2	0	3.1	46
Switzerland	0	11	6	26	30	23	4	4.6	47

These results indicate once again that the respondents understood the question. The Soviet Union is rated a terrible example by 96% of the respondents. Its mean rating is 1.0 China is seen as less of a bad example than the USSR but is still not even in the middle of the scale. Its mean rating is 3.3. Poland is also treated as a poor example of an ally with a mean rating of 2.6. The Atlantic Allies, on the other hand, get perfect ratings. Great Britain and Canada have the highest scores. Their mean ratings are 6.8 and 6.5, respectively. West Germany's mean score is only a bit lower than Canada's. The most interesting results are the scores for India, Mexico, and Switzerland. Here the distinction between ally and neutral clearly emerges. All of these countries have ratings around the middle of the scale, much lower than the ratings for the Atlantic Alliance. India's score is particularly low, with a mean of only 3.1. Switzerland and Mexico are both slightly higher than the middle of the scale in mean score. Guatemala's score is also around the middle of the scale indicating that it too is not close to a perfect example of an ally.

Table 10 gives the results for the respondents' ratings of the same countries as examples of a neutral. The Soviet Union and its allies all have scores well toward the terrible example side of the scale, as does China. Interestingly, Great Britain, West Germany and Canada also have scores close to the terrible extreme. Guatemala's score is low (terrible) with a mean of 2.8. The cases of Mexico, India, and Switzerland are most important. Switzerland is very clearly seen as a nearly perfect example of a neutral. Nearly 62% of the respondents gave Switzerland a perfect example score. Its mean rating was 6.2, very close to the 7 extreme. The scores for Mexico and India are not as high, but higher than than for any of the other countries on the list. India's mean score was 4.5, above the middle of the scale on the perfect example side. Mexico's mean

TABLE 10
Ratings of 11 Countries as a Neutral (%)

Country	Terrible example					Perfect example			
	1	2	3	4	5	6	7	Mean	N
S. Union	100	0	0	0	0	0	0	1.0	46
China	49	21	19	9	2	0	0	1.9	47
Poland	36	47	16	2	0	0	0	1.8	45
Cuba	83	15	2	0	0	0	0	1.2	47

(Continued)

TABLE 10 (continued)
Ratings of 11 Countries as a Neutral (%)

Country	Terrible example					Perfect example			
	1	2	3	4	5	6	7	Mean	N
G. Britain	67	13	11	7	0	2	0	1.7	45
Canada	49	9	18	13	9	2	0	2.3	45
W.Germany	56	18	11	7	7	2	0	2.0	45
Guatemala	25	21	23	16	14	2	0	2.8	44
Mexico	4	9	21	21	28	11	6	4.2	47
India	4	6	15	23	19	21	11	4.5	47
Switzerland	2	2	2	6	4	21	62	6.1	47

rating was 4.2, also slightly above the middle of the scale on the perfect side. Switzerland and India both receive substantially higher scores as examples of neutrals than as examples of allies. Mexico, however, does not. Mexico's mean scores are almost exactly the same although none of the respondents give Mexico a 7 as an example of an ally and 6.4% give Mexico a 7 as an example of a neutral. An explanation for this must wait until the results of the ratings for the dependent ally of the United States have been evaluated.

Table 11 presents the results for the ratings of all eleven states as examples of dependents of the United States. A score of 1

TABLE 11

Ratings of 11 Countries as Dependents of the USA (%)

Country	Perfect example					Terrible example			
	1	2	3	4	5	6	7	Mean	N
Soviet Union	9	0	0	0	0	5	86	6.4	44
China	0	2	2	13	24	33	24	5.6	45
Poland	0	2	2	5	33	37	21	5.6	43
Cuba	0	0	0	0	2	14	84	6.8	43
G. Britain	0	9	44	17	15	7	9	3.9	46
Canada	0	16	31	22	20	7	4	3.8	45

(Continued)

TABLE 11 (Continued)
Ratings of 11 Countries as Dependents of the USA (%)

Country	Perfect example 1	2	3	4	5	Terrible example 6	7	Mean	N
W. Germany	0	2	29	31	18	16	4	4.3	45
Guatemala	28	21	17	11	6	11	6	3.0	47
Mexico	2	20	16	18	27	9	9	4.1	45
India	0	0	14	16	23	21	27	5.3	44
Switzerland	0	2	7	23	16	33	19	5.3	43

is that of the perfect example, 7 the terrible example. Fortunately, the USSR, China, Poland, and Cuba all received terrible example ratings. The mean scores for Great Britain and Canada, however, are below the middle of the scale and toward the perfect example end. This must reflect their military dependence upon the United States. Guatemala has the mean score closest to the perfect example end of the scale, a score of 3.0. This is only slightly below the middle of the scale. Mexico, India, and Switzerland are between the communist countries and the Atlantic Alliance. The difference in the means for Canada and Great Britain is very small. These results do seem to point again to the distinctive quality of the three neutral or non-aligned nations. They are seen as slighly more independent of the US than the Atlantic Allies. Most interesting is the ratng for Mexico. As in its scores on the ally and neutral scales, Mexico's mean is around the middle of the scale. In fact, 38% see Mexico as a good example of a dependent with a score of 3 or below on the scale. Another 45% see Mexico as a relatively poor example of a dependent.

Because Mexico has relatively equal means on the scales for ally, neutral, and dependent, and because it is only slightly toward the terrible example side of the dependent scale, the question arises as to whether or not there are three distinct groups of people who see Mexico as belonging to one or the other categories. A closer examination of the surveys yields more information. Of all respondents, only one rated Mexico as as a good an example of an Ally as it was an example of a dependent. Only one rated Mexico as as good an example of a neutral as it was an example of a dependent. Seven respondents gave Mexico the same rating as an example of an ally and a neutral, but four of the seven gave Mexico a much stronger score as a dependent than as either a neutral or an ally. Therefore, only four respondents failed to distinguish Mexico as a better example of one type of state than the other types. It is possible to argue that the respondents who answered these questions fall into three groups: those who saw Mexico as a good example of an ally; those who saw its as a good example of a dependent; and those who saw it as a good example of a neutral. The smallest group is the one composed of people who saw Mexico as a relatively good example of a dependent. The mean for Mexico as a dependent is slightly toward the terrible side of the scale. However, 22% of the respondents gave Mexico a score of 1 or 2 . Only 11% gave Mexico the equivalent score as an example of an ally. The division in image of Mexico is understandable if one reflects upon the events preceding the year the survey was taken, 1981. Mexico had undergone rapid financial and political transformations during the preceding six years and had not yet reached the financial crisis it fell victim to in 1982. Consequently, images of Mexico would naturally be fluctuating within governmental circles.

Table 12 gives the results of the ratings of the eleven states as examples of a puppet.

TABLE 12
Ratings of 11 Countries as Puppets of the USA (%)

Country	Terrible example					Perfect example		Mean	N
	1	2	3	4	5	6	7		
Soviet Union	98	2	0	0	0	0	0	1.0	45
China	70	16	7	2	5	0	0	1.6	43
Poland	68	25	5	3	0	0	0	1.4	40
Cuba	93	7	0	0	0	0	0	1.1	44
G. Britain	51	23	12	5	5	5	0	2.0	43
Canada	48	25	9	7	9	2	0	2.1	44
W. Germany	49	28	9	2	12	0	0	2.0	43
Guatemala	29	18	13	7	9	9	16	3.4	45
Mexico	47	21	7	19	5	2	0	2.2	43
India	62	26	5	7	0	0	0	1.6	42
Switzer- land	60	24	12	5	0	0	0	1.6	42

With the exception of Guatemala, all countries have a mean
score of 2.3 or less (with 1 labeled "terrible example" on
the scale). Although more people saw Guatemala as a bad
example of a puppet, a quarter of the respondents gave it a
6 or a 7, the perfect example rating. This shows the importance of image in determining evaluations of a state for
Guatemala by 1977 had already shown how strongly it would
resist US pressures to change internal policies when it
rejected Carter's efforts to tie human rights performance
there to military aid from the US.

Table 13 displays the results for the eleven countries
rated as examples of a dependent ally of the enemy.

TABLE 13

Ratings of 11 Countries as Dependent Allies of an Enemy (%)

Country	Perfect example					Terrible example			
	1	2	3	4	5	6	7	Mean	N
Soviet Union	5	0	0	2	0	2	91	6.6	42
China	0	2	4	2	4	20	67	6.4	45
Poland	25	27	29	15	2	2	0	2.5	48
Cuba	85	13	2	0	0	0	0	1.2	47
G. Britain	2	0	0	0	2	11	84	6.7	45
Canada	0	0	0	0	0	14	86	6.9	43
W. Germany	0	0	0	0	0	21	80	6.8	44
Guatemala	0	2	2	10	10	24	52	6.1	42
Mexico	0	0	2	5	12	16	65	6.4	43
India	0	2	26	21	15	13	23	4.8	47
Switzer-land	0	0	0	2	11	14	73	6.6	44

There are several aspects of this table worth noting. First,
Poland and Cuba are clearly the only states seen as perfect
or nearly perfect examples of the type and of the two Cuba
is the best example. China is unquestionably not classified
as a dependent ally of the enemy. The most interesting
outcome is the evaluation of India. India's mean is only
4.8. This is still on the poor example side of the middle of
the scale but a good indication that there are some respondents who view India as quite hostile and close to the USSR.

98

Additionally, India's rating shows the greatest amount of threat perception for any non-communist country. As part of the non-aligned movement, India has been highly critical of the United States and to some extent of the USSR. In this sense it is more detached from the US-Soviet conflict than is Switzerland. Thus, neutrals may be viewed as quite threatening despite their non-alliance with the enemy.

In general, the results for questions 19-25 conform to the pattern that emerged in the preceding questions. There were, however, no solid examples of a dependent of the United States. This may be a result of the selection of countries in the list of eleven. The fact that some countries (Mexico and Guatemala) were given perfect ratings by some respondents indicated that the type is meaningful. An additional disturbing result of this series is the tendency to rate the allies as good examples of a dependent. This may indicate that respondents interpreted the question to mean "how dependent on the United States are the following countries?"

The most significant result of the series is the information produced concerning Mexico and the neutral image. There does seem to be a distinction between the neutral type and the others. Further, the ratings for Mexico show different images or classifications of that country. This will be important in the last part of this study.

Questions 26 and 27 in the survey concern behavioral expectations and response alternatives. It was argued in Chapter 2 that categories should have associated with them behavioral expectations and response alternatives. Questions 26 presents he respondents with six tactics and asks them to indicate which they expect from each type of state and the order in which they expect those tactics to be used. It was assumed that these responses would make it possible to gauge some behavioral expectations and to view contrasts in the behaviors expected from each type of state. The responses for behavioral expectations of the enemy, ally, neutral and dependent are shown below in Table 14. The question was clearly a difficult one for the respondents as can be seen from the drop in the number of responses after the first and second tactics have been selected.

The table shows that the first thing 50% of the respondents expect an enemy to do in a conflict with the USA is denounce it in their press. Twenty-six percent expect the enemy to initiate diplomatic exchanges first. The question of what the enemy will do next is subject to more disagreement. Thirty-nine percent of these respondents expect the

enemy to appeal to international forums as a second step.
The rest expect the enemy to use the domestic press for
rhetorical denunciations of initiate diplomatic exchanges.
Over 14% expect the enemy to threaten to use military force
as a second step in a conflict with the United States.
Twenty-six percent expect the enemy to threaten to use
military force as a third tactic. In general, the table
shows that the enemy is expected to

TABLE 14
Behavioral Expectations

Type of State	Choice	Strategies@							
		1	2	3	4	5	6	7	N
Enemy:									
	1st tactic expected	26	14	0	5	0	50	0	42
	2nd tactic expected	17	15	7	0	39	22	0	41
	3rd tactic expected	16	26	8	0	37	13	0	38
Ally:									
	1st tactic expected	86	0	0	2	0	10	2	42
	2nd tactic expected	11	0	22	5	35	27	0	37
	3rd tactic expected	0	3	17	17	30	33	0	30
Neutral:									
	1st tactic expected	55	0	0	12	14	17	2	42
	2nd tactic expected	21	0	3	8	54	15	0	39
	3rd tactic expected	12	0	18	6	27	36	0	33

(Continued)

TABLE   14 (Continued)
Behavioral Expectations

Type of State	Choice	1	2	3	Strategies@ 4	5	6	7	N
Dependent of USA:									
	1st tactic expected	60	0	0	10	0	29	2	42
	2nd tactic expected	32	0	6	6	18	38	0	34
	3rd tactic expected	4	4	8	29	29	25	0	24

@Strategies: 1 - initiate diplomatic exchanges; 2 - threaten to use military force; 3 - use economic sanctions; 4 -
do nothing; 5 - appeal to international forums; 6 - use the
domestic press for rhetorical denunciations; 7 - other (Enemy -- respondents included "sanctions against diplomats
overseas," "force," "use indirect or non-attributable pressures." Ally -- respondents included "sanctions against
diplomats overseas." Neutral -- respondents included "sanctions against diplomats overseas." Dependent of USA -- respondents included "sanctions against diplomats overseas.")

employ tactics that do not involve diplomatic exchanges in
conflicts with the United States but to use other methods of
denouncing the US. The responses seem to reflect few expectations of direct interchange. This compliments the discussion in the first part of this chapter regarding the pessimistic view of the success of diplomatic interaction with
the enemy. An additional interesting outcome is the percent
of respondents who expect the enemy to threaten to use
military force. Fourteen percent of the respondents expect
the enemy to employ this strategy as a first or second
action. More expect it to be the third action selected
(although, of course, the total number of respondents has
dropped by this point).
     Expectations concerning the behavior of an ally are
naturally quite different. A large percent, 86%, expected
the ally to initiate diplomatic exchanges as a first move in

conflicts with the United States. As a second tactic, most
expected actions 5 and 6. Neither of these are threatening
but both may be embarassing. Only 22% expect the ally to
initiate economic sanctions as a second strategy in conflicts with the USA. Threats to use military force are also
not expected from the ally, which is not surprising. In
general, expected behavior by the ally contrasts with that
expected by the enemy.

Expectations of behavior by the neutral were somewhat
different. Although a majority expected the neutral to begin
by initiating diplomatic exchanges, the percent is smaller
than for the ally. More respondents expected the neutral to
either appeal to international forums, denounce the United
States in the domestic press, or do nothing. More respondents expected these strategies as the second or third
actions in a dispute. Interestingly, no one expected the
neutral to threaten military force. This is probably reflective of Switzerland's passifism. There is no particular
reason why neutrals should be passifists yet respondents
evidently do not expect military threats from this type of
state. The dependent type is expected to respond to conflicts with diplomacy and the domestic press. The most
interesting difference between expectations for the dependent and neutral is a comparison of the extent to which
respondents expect dependents to resort to doing nothing.
More respondents expect this action by the dependent than by
the neutral. In addition, the respondents seem more conflicted as to the behavior expected from the neutral type than
by the dependent.

Question 27 in the survey asked respondents to list the
responses that the United States should make in conflicts
with each type of state. The responses were the same as
those listed in the previous question. The respondents were
asked to list the alternatives in the order in which they
should be used. The purpose of this question was to gather
information concerning the response alternatives associated
with each type and to see if significant differences would
emerge in advocated approaches to the various types of
states.

As Table 15 shows, there was quite a lot of agreement
concerning the first step the United States should take in a
conflict with the enemy type. Ninety percent chose the

TABLE 15
Response Alternative (% of respondents)

Type of State	Choice	1	2	3	Strategies@ 4	5	6	7	N
Enemy:									
	1st US tactic	91	2	2	0	2	2	0	42
	2nd US tactic	7	5	10	2	68	10	0	42
	3rd US tactic	2	5	61	2	17	10	2	41
Ally:									
	1st US tactic	100	0	0	0	0	0	0	41
	2nd US tactic	0	0	21	9	46	21	3	33
	3rd US tactic	0	0	46	23	18	9	5	22
Neutral:									
	1st US tactic	98	0	2	0	0	0	0	41
	2nd US tactic	3	0	17	6	64	8	3	36
	3rd US tactic	0	0	41	11	22	22	4	27
Dependent of USA:									
	1st US tactic	95	0	0	2	0	0	2	41
	2nd US tactic	3	0	39	7	42	10	0	31
	3rd US	0	0	50	11	11	28	0	18

(Continued)

@

Strategies: 1 - initiate diplomatic exchanges; 2 - threaten
to use military force; 3 - use economic sanctions; 4 - do
nothing; 5 - appeal to international forums; 6 - use the
domestic press for rhetorical denunciations; 7 - other (Enemy - respondents mentioned "sanctions against diplomats
overseas." Ally - respondents mentioned "sanctions against
diplomats," and "appeal to public opinion through media,
VOA, etc." Neutral - respondents mentioned the above and
"send arms to both sides." Dependent - respondents included
only "sanctions against diplomats."

---

initiation of diplomatic exchanges as the first strategy.
This is an interesting contrast to the respondents' expectations concerning the enemy's behavior. The enemy was expected to start denouncing the USA publicly rather than
initiating diplomatic exchanges. To some extent this does
conform to the argument set forth earlier that people should
associate diplomatic exchanges with the enemy type but
should have limited faith in its success. If the enemy
responds to conflict by denouncing the perceiver's state
while the perceiver's state responds by initiating diplomatic exchanges, expectations of successful conflict resolution may be limited. The next strategies advised by
respondents include an appeal to international forums followed by the use of economic sanctions. Not shown in Table
15 is the fourth strategy selected. Seventeen respondents
chose threats to use military force at this stage.

Respondents recommend a somewhat different approach
when engaged in conflicts with an ally. One hundred percent
advised using diplomatic exchanges as an initial strategy in
resolving disputes with the ally. The next most favored
response was an appeal to international forums. Interestingly, however, fewer respondents chose this as a second
strategy for dealing with an ally than chose the tactic for
use with an enemy. Respondents were split between favoring
economic sanctions and denunciations of the ally in the
press as a second response to the ally in a conflict. Fewer
people chose these as second actions to be used against an
enemy, possibly because it was assumed that they would be
ineffective. It was assumed that diplomatic exchanges would
be seen as useful in conflicts with allies and that economic
tactics would be associated with the category. The respondents were clearly willing to consider economic sanctions as
tactics associated with the image. Doing nothing was considered by some as a tactic useful against the enemy, although
it was not expected to be important from a theoretical

standpoint.

As with the ally, a high percent of the respondents chose to initiate diplomatic exchanges in conflicts with a neutral. The second strategy recommended was an appeal to international forums. More respondents favored this as a second strategy for use with a neutral than with an ally. Both of these options were expected to be associated with the category. The third strategy selected by a plurality of respondents was the use of economic sanctions, a strategy assumed to be associated with the type as selected by six respondents as a second tactic and eleven as a third. Few respondents recommended doing nothing.

The responses recommended in conflicts with the ally and neutral differ in interesting ways from those recommended for the dependent. The first response favored is, of course, diplomacy. However, 39% (twelve respondents) favored the use of economic sanctions as a second tactic, only 3% less than those favoring appeal to international forums at this stage of the hypothetical conflict. The dependent category thus differs from both the ally and neutral images in that respondents are more willing to go straight to some coercive measure to resolve conflicts with this type of state. The numerical differences are small, of course, given the small number of total respondents. However, it is noteable that twelve respondents advocated economic sanctions in step two of a conflict with the dependent type whereas only 6 and 7 advocated such steps in dealing with the neutral and ally types, respectively in step two. If one combines strategy choices two and three, one finds that 21 respondents advocated economic sanctions for the dependent whereas 17 did so for each of the ally and neutral types. In general, respondents seemed to favor stronger, more coercive, measures in conflicts with a dependent.

Question 28 asked respondents to record an event they associated with each type of state. It was argued in Chapter 2 that each type would have event scripts associated with it. The question was designed to gather information concerning the event scripts and to explore the characteristics of the scripts. The question was open-ended and respondents tended to record either specific events or descriptive adjectives.

As mentioned in the beginning of this chapter, it was expected that the enemy type would be described as having instances of aggression, suppression of dissent (reflecting the perceived monolithic nature of this type of state), and security issues associated with it. All of the responses to this question included security issues. At least 62% of the responses mention some form of explicit aggression. Suppression of dissent is also involved in many of the events cited. Of those that mention specific events rather than descriptive phrases, 34% involve the Soviet Union. Only 16% explicitly refer to World War II. As in the question asking for a perfect example of an enemy, the USSR is much more prominent than the enemies of the United States during the Second World War.

The historical events associated with the hegemonic type were expected to include instances of aggression, suppression of dissent, security and economic issues, and analogies with imperialistic conquest or colonialism. The responses were actually similar to those expected. Soviet conquest was frequently listed as an example. Other historical and current instances of aggression or conquest by a powerful state against a weaker state were listed such as the Nazi Anschluss, the Italian invasion of Abyssinia, Israeli bombings of Lebanon, and the Chinese occupation of Tibet. In addition, the descriptive terms recorded by respondents depicted suppression of dissent and economic and political imperialism. These responses indicate that at least some respondents know what a hegemonist is and see it as a stronger state that dominates weaker states politically, economically, and/or militarily.

The events associated with the dependent ally of the enemy image were also similar to those expected. Instances of threat and "aggression" by dependent allies of an enemy were widely cited. An unexpected type of event listed was aggression by the enemy against the dependent. Perceptions of governmental instability were also evident: Events such as East Germany in 1953, the Hungarian Revolution, and Soviet tanks in Czechoslovakia were cited. The issues involved were security issues. Finally, many of the events involved the interaction between the enemy and its dependent. These included instances of conflicts as well as military support from the Soviet Union and Czechoslovakia's UN voting record.

The events associated with the ally image were exactly what one would expect. They included instances of allied support for the United States, mutual defense interests and consultation. Examples included Canada's help with the hostages in Iran, NATO, the Korean War, support for the United States in the UN, and summit meetings. These rsponses were the only ones in which consultation and diplomatic interactions were consistently cited.

Neutrals were expected to be associated with events in which aggression is not prominent and there is no particular instance of governmental instability. Economic issues should be present and security issues limited to arms control rather than alliances. Finally, it was expected that neutrals would be associated with events in which mediators were important. The results for this question supported expectations. There were instances of aggression cited but only one represented a neutral engaged in armed conflict, the India-Pakistan War. Basically, the scripts had the neutral in a passive or mediating role. Some of the events depicted resistance to the policies of the United States. Some other descriptions, such as "opportunism" and "looking out for #1" were quite cynical. The responses indicate that the Third World non-aligned countries are associated with the neutral category. The events do reflect to a small extent economic issues, and to a larger extent security issues involving negotiations rather than conflict. Twenty-three percent mentioned Switzerland during World War II. Others mentioned the League of Nations, Austrian neutrality, peace, non-opposition, and UN cooperation. These examples reflect a sense of passifism associated with the image rather than simple, strict neutrality.

It was expected that the dependent type of state would be associated with aggression against the dependent, governmental instability, economic issues above security issues, and imperialism. The results show that the dependent is associated with aggressive events including both aggression against and protection of the dependent by the United States. No instances of a dependent aggressing against another were cited. The issues recorded were mainly economic in nature. Respondents mentioned "financial aid," "multinational corporations," trade imbalance," and other economic phrases. Twenty-two percent of the respondents mentioned events involving Latin America, 12% mentioned events in the Middle East, 5% mentioned the Far East, and 5% mentioned Western Europe. More specifically, respondents recalled the Alliance for Progress, the invasion of the Dominican Republic, the OAS, Camp David, trade imbalances, and adjectives such as "adolescence," "subservience," and ineffectiveness.

Both the event script expectations and the results were similar for the puppet and dependent categories. The responses for the puppet image, however, include clearer cases of US domination and direction of the puppet state's policies. The countries mentioned were also more submissive to the United States, such as the "Banana Republics of the

1920's and 1930's," South Vietnam during the war, Quemoy-
Matsu, and Taiwan. Economic issues were not as prominent as
expected. Most of the issues raised were security issues
including "war," "regional security," Guatemala-Honduras
soccer war" (actually the war was between El Salvador and
Honduras), and South Korea's defense. Descriptive adjectives
cited are also of interest and included "quiescent policies," "obedience," "unstable," "ineffective," "vassal," and
"childhood."

CONCLUSION

In general the results of the survey supported the
arguments made in Chapters 2 and 3. Five of the six categories appeared: the enemy, ally, neutral, dependent of the
USA, and dependent ally of the enemy. Several characteristics of these categories are worth review.

First, it is important to repeat that psychological
categories are not used consciously to organize the world.
Therefore, although a government may formally regard another
country as an ally (such as the Soviet Union during World
War II) that country may not be perceived as an ally below
the conscious level. It is the perception of other countries
that is examined in this chapter, not the formal relationship.

A second observation is that the neutral category
appears to incorporate both Switzerland and the non-aligned
countries. The most sympathetic of these states, Switzerland, is seen by a majority as the best example of a neutral. The category appears to be associated with benign
support for the US but is seen as more threatening than the
ally type. These characteristics are indicated by the unexpected support for the US found in Table 5, the ratings of
Switzerland, Mexico, and India as neutrals, allies, and
enemies, and by the response alternatives chosen for the
neutral. If futurist predictions that issues such as energy,
food and trade will eventually dominate international politics come true, the non-aligned, Third World developing
nations may shift out of the neutral category for many
policy makers. A new category may emerge to provide a better
organization for such a political universe.

The puppet category also requires final comment. Although the category did not appear as a separate type,
comparisons of responses to questions 18 and 2 show that
there is a tendency to group countries cited as "perfect

examples" of a puppet with the ally group. This implies that puppets are expected to support the United States as would an ally. However, it is an image that may be of little use for most respondents in organizing the world. It may also be that the survey instrument is too crude to pick up subtle distinctions among types. The term "puppet" alone may have caused respondents to refuse to consider the type.

The survey picks up some interesting patterns in behavioral expectations and response alternatives. There is disagreement concerning the expected behavior of the enemy. However, the enemy is generally seen as less likely to use diplomatic channels to resolve disputes than are other types. Also of interest is the apparent willingness to use economic sanctions against dependents more readily than neutrals or allies.

The survey showed three different views of Mexico. It was seen as either an ally, neutral, or a dependent. Given the response alternative results, one can expect the respondents with these three views to disagree on how conciliatory the United States should be in conflicts with Mexico. This point is very important in the case study in Chapters 5 and 6.

Finally, cautions regarding the interpretations of the survey results must be re-emphasized. It is well known that surveys are subject to a variety of errors that limits the reliability of their results. This is particularly important in surveys that have small sample size. Further, the survey instrument itself should be regarded as an imperfect device for data gathering in studies of non-conscious psychological processes. It is in this light that the data presented here should be viewed. It merely contributes some additional information along with the material presented in Chapter 2, supporting the argument that people divide the world into different types of states.

At this point the framework developed here has remained descriptive. In the next chapter additional psychological studies will be used to examine the effects of cognitive organization and processes upon judgments. Ultimately, several propositions concerning the effects of the political categories on political judgments will be offered. These propositions will be tested in Chapters 5 and 6.

NOTES

    1. Middle to upper GS ranks are 9-15, middle to upper FS ranks are 6-1, with 1 being the highest.

    2. The response rate is 10%. The number of respondents makes the results non-generalizable and one can properly speak only of the implications of the results of these 51 surveys. The response rate can be attributed to several factors. First, the survey is very time consuming. These respondents are very busy individuals who work long hours and would not be inclined to spend leisure time filling out a survey. Second, the surveys had to be mailed to the respondents. This meant that no personal interaction between the research and the recipients occurred that could have improved the response rate. Finally, the surveys were sent out only six months after a new administration had taken office. Government officials may have been more cautious than usual about filling out a questionnaire for a private and unknown individual.

    3. R. Cottam, Foreign Policy Motivation (Pittsburgh: University of Pittsburgh Press, 1977), p. 65.

4

Political Judgments:
Using Political Categories

Chapters 1 through 3 have been devoted to developing a framework that describes the political world view. In this chapter the effects of world view categories on judgments will be discussed. It begins with an examination of two judgment phases, the "nominal" and "ordinal" decisions, and proceeds to a review of findings concerning the effects of context on judgment. Patterns associated with adaptation to change are then examined. Finally, this psychological material is incorporated into the political framework in terms of the impact of categories on political decisions. Specific hypotheses concerning these patterns and political judgments will be offered.

The use of categories for organizing and simplifying reality begins with two judgment processes. First, nominal judgments are made in which the perceiver decides to which category an object (in this case, a state) belongs. This is an "absolute" decision in that the object either belongs to the category or it does not. A judged object is not assessed solely in terms of category membership, however. The perceiver also makes an ordinal judgment by deciding how typical a member of the category the object is in order to use the information locked in the category to predict the object's behavior. He compares category members, (below the conscious level), to assess the relative representativeness of each member. Psychologists argue that the individual uses an "implicit representation of a given stimulus dimension and will judge or 'measure' the value of further incoming stimuli in reference to the parameters of this...dimension."[1] In making this ordinal judgment, the judge evaluates information about an object by comparing it with the information and events associated with the appropriate category. "A specific act of `perceiving' or `cognizing' a given stimulus object or event is regarded as involving the projection of the stimulus onto a set of psychological dimensions, and thereby distributing to it one value from each of these dimensions."2

NOMINAL JUDGMENTS

Early studies of nominal judgments emphasized the notion that "logical rules" guide judgments.3 Today the assumption is that judgments are not the outcome of formal or logical rules.4 Several psychological models attempt to explain nominal categorical judgments. Some psychologists support a "prototype" model which assumes that category members have a family resemblance wherein members share different attributes.5 They argue that "[f]or the category as a whole, some features will be more representative of the category than others, but no feature that can serve to distinguish category members from non-members will be common to all category members. Within this framework, the typicality of an exemplar is determined by the number of characteristic features it possesses."6 New objects are judged in terms of their resemblance to a categorical prototype that seems to best represent the combination of all attributes of the category. Thus, instead of adding up categorical attributes to make a nominal judgment, the judgments are made on the basis of an assessment of the similarity of the judged object with the ideal-typical category member. Thus it is somewhat misleading to view categories with the formal definition, that is, that they are composed of attributes that define the category, for it disregards the comparisons involved in the judgment process.7

The tendency to rely upon category prototypes in making nominal judgments has been confirmed in a wide variety of psychological experiments. Posner and Keele and Reed found that even when subjects are not given clear instructions for classifying new objects, they "tend to abstract a prototype for a category and use distance from it to predict category membership."8 There are situations in which prototypes are not used to make nominal judgments. In instances in which there is a high degree of category overlap and/or substantial variability within a category, attributes will be added up to make judgments.

There is a large literature in psychology debating the question of whether or not nominal judgments are made by using prototypes or "logical rules" for combining the distinctive features of the category. Some analysts argue that although there is strong evidence supporting the prototype argument, it does not rule out the possibility that judgments or objects are based upon rules concerning distinctive features. For example, Martin and Carmazza argue that:

> The fact that Posner and Keele (1968) and many others have found evidence consistent with a prototype model for holistic stimuli does not preclude the possibility that subjects have been using a sequence of feature test for these stimuli as well...[P]rototypes are also those stimuli possessing the features most common to members of a category...Thus, correlations between reaction times and similarity to a prototype would be expected on the same basis as correlations with family resemblance, even if subjects were using a sequence of feature test to assign category membership.9

The major implication of this debate appears to be that different judgment tasks require different processing techniques. The use of prototypes and distinctive features in nominal judgments is so tightly intertwined that it is extremely difficult for psychologists to separate the processes and determine which is used in a given task. The most important outcome of the debate is the widely accepted notion that in most instances judgments of category membership are not based on the calculation of the presence or absence of formal category attributes. They are made through a comparison of the judged object and a prototypical representative of the category. This is particularly important for ill-defined categories, that is, categories in which attributes are only more or less characteristic of category members.10

Several points can now be made concerning political judgments. First, preliminary judgments of the category membership of a state will be influenced by the similarity between that state and a prototypical category member. Therefore, all the attributes discussed in Chapters 2 and 3 may define the category and may exist in the minds of the political judge, but initial nominal judgments will be made using a prototype that best represents a combination of those attributes. Thus the analyst should not expect type of state judgments to be a result of a careful, methodical examination of attributes. Instead, they are impressionistic assessments of similarities between the observed state and

an ideal-typical prototype. Decisions concerning the image
most appropriate for a particular state are not clear
decisions but subtle impressions that nevertheless affect
behavior profoundly.

Several important findings concerning prototypes should
be mentioned. First, certain attributes may be inordinately
important in depicting the category prototype. When
judgments are made people do not thoroughly review their
previous experiences for information concerning the judged
person, object, or state. Instead, the perceiver examines
only that part of his or her stored information for
knowledge which is most important and/or accessible. He then
bases his judgments upon that portion of information.11 This
suggests that certain attributes may be more distinct than
others. It will be argued later that impressions of threat
and opportunity associated with each type of state will be
very important in this regard. Second, after a prototype is
formed it is difficult to change the category's set of
attributes to an expanded set.12 Third, Kahneman and Tversky
have shown that people do not use probabilities accurately
in predicting events. Instead, people think that events that
are perceived as "representative" or "typical" occur more
frequently than they actually do. Rosch argues that this may
suggest that category prototypes are also perceived as more
common than they actually are.13

There are several additional characteristics of
categories and information that affect nominal judgments.
One is the vagueness of category boundaries. Natural
categories tend to be ill-defined. This means that "there is
no simple set of criterial features that can be used to
determine membership of all exemplars of a category."14
Determining category membership is always "a matter of more
or less, not all or nothing."15 In some cases the perceiver
is presented with information clearly indicating category
membership. Other information may not be so clear in which
case the role of the prototype is particularly important.16
Another finding indicates that the typicalness of an object
affects the amount of time needed to classify it. The more
typical the stimulus is, the less time is taken in
determining category membership.17 Third, the reliability of
nominal judgments and the confidence of the judge increases
as the object appears more similar to the prototype.18 One
should therefore expect that political decision makers will
be more certain and confident of their evaluations of other
countries when those states appear to be very close to the
ideal-typical instance.

Some studies of social judgments suggest that categories organizing the social world are likely to be ill-defined.19 Further, judgments of people may be influenced by the amount of experience the judge has had. For example, analyses of psychologists' evaluations of clients' illnesses indicate that experience provides the clinician with "anchors" or prototypical comparison models that help her to make a judgment. Bieri and his associates argue that the range of experience a judge has had with a certain type of stimuli will influence judgments of that stimuli: "If the anchor with which a given stimulus is compared is less extreme for one judge than for another, we might expect systematic differences in their judgments of that stimulus."20

This pattern may be important in political judgments in two ways. First, there may be individual, group, or institutional differences in nominal classification tendencies. For example, the experiences of individuals in the State Department with Third World countries may differ significantly from those of individuals in the Department of Energy. Second, generational differences may also emerge. For example, individuals in government who lived through World War II should have a different range of experience with the enemy type of state than those who only lived through the war in Vietnam. Those who lived through World War II may see the ideal-typical enemy as a country with which the US has had direct military conflict.

A final factor affecting nominal judgments is category accessibility. The importance of category accessibility was discussed by Jerome Bruner in 1957:

The likelihood that a sensory input will be categorized in terms of a given category is not only a matter of fit between sensory input and category specifications, it depends also on the accessibility of a category ... [G]iven a sensory input with equally good fit in nonoverlapping categories, the more accessible of the two categories would capture the input...[T]he accessibility of categories reflects the learned probabilities of occurrence of events in the person's world. The more frequently in a given context instances of a given category occur, the greater the accessibility of the category. 21

The effect of category accessibility occurs primarily at the time of nominal judgments.22

The last two patterns mentioned above indicate that political classifications will be influenced by the role of the decision maker, his experience with the particular country being judged, and the historical interaction between the two. If, for example, a state historically has been seen as an ally, that category should be most accessible when judgments of that state are made in the future.

Before proceding to the patterns associated with the ordinal judgment task, it is important to note that it is difficult for the perceiver to validate or invalidate a categorization, particularly social classifications. Information is often equivocal and, as Bruner notes, "if...one categorizes another person as dishonest, it is extremely difficult in most cases to check for the other cues that one would predict might be associated with this category."23 Ambiguous information may be distorted to confirm a categorization and even ambiguous information is not always available.

ORDINAL JUDGMENTS

Once a nominal judgment has been made a new judgment task emerges. After the state has been classified, the perceiver is less open to new information and begins to search for evidence confirming his or her categorical judgment.24 The ordinal judgment task involves a determination of how typical or "good" the judged object is as an example of the category. This is important because after the initial classification has been made the category itself begins to play a role in screening information from the environment and in supplying information upon which subsequent judgents will be made. The perceiver assesses the judged state to determine how typical of other members of the category its behavior will be. There are several perceptual patterns that emerge in this part of the judgment process.

The prototype is important in the ordinal judgment phase as well as in the nominal task. After an object is classified the prototype serves as an "anchor" for the category. People experience an "assimilation effect" in which category members shift toward the anchor so that they appear more similar to it than they are.25 Some analysts argue that there is also a "contrast effect" in which dissimilar information or category non-members shift away from the anchor and are seen as less similar to the

prototype than they are.[26] Adaptation Level theorists assume
that the anchor serves as a comparison point against which
information is judged. One's opinion on an issue is said to
serve the same anchoring function and one's Adaptation
Level, or "point of perceived neutrality," is drawn toward
that position. Therefore, people tend to see their own
positions as more neutral or moderate and consequently
better.[27] Studies in which judgments were made of statements
holding varying sentiments toward blacks demonstrate the
effects of anchors on judgments. It was found that subjects
who were very favorable toward blacks rated opinion
statements as less favorable toward blacks than did those
who had more neutral attitudes.[28]

The conclusion drawn by psychologists has been that one
of the effects of the prototype on judgments during the
ordinal judgment phase is to shift the perception of the
judged object closer to the prototype. This reduced individual differences among category members. Further, the judge
becomes more certain of his evaluation of the object since
it appears to be more like the ideal-typical example. The
perception is reinforced by a tendency to apply traits
associated with a category to the members rather than to
change the elements of the category to account for
individual members' differences.[29]

The same judgment patterns should be found in the use
of political categories. Once a state is classified, the
classification serves as a major source of information about
the state for the judge. Individual differences between
states diminish in the judge's perception. When questions
arise concerning how a particular state will behave in the
future the characteristics associated with the category are
a significant part of the answer. Allport adds that
emotional associations also come from the category. The
category "saturates all that it contains with the same
ideational and emotional flavor."[30]

A second pattern in ordinal judgments concerns missing
information. Missing information about a category member can
be supplied by the category to which it belongs. Because
categories provide a large amount of general information
about the members, they "enable the perceiver to predict the
future by specifying what events, abilities, or behaviors
have a high likelihood of occurrence."[31]

Several experiments have demonstrated this pattern in
social judgments. Studies of stereotyping have shown that
when subjects are told that a person is a member of a
minority group (a category dividing the social world)

subjects tend to over-attribute undesireable acts to that person.32 Similarly, Kahneman and Tversky found subjects willing to infer a person's occupation from a description of his personal characteristics.33

The use of categories in the judgment process can be particularly helpful for political decision makers. Necessary information is often lacking or unclear. The policy maker can "guess" about missing information by using the knowledge embedded in his categories. Thus, if a policy maker has little direct information concerning characteristics of another country's economy, the category into which that particular state has been placed provides generalized information about its economy for the policy maker. He can also infer the extent of threat or opportunity posed by the particular state from the category. Although this process permits the judge to predict the future, thus aiding in the decision making process, it can also be a liability. The perceiver may believe that he or she knows more about the country than he does and can confidently predict the country's future behavior when he cannot.

Taylor and Crocker discuss several judgment errors resulting from reliance on the category for missing information. The tendency may lead to the assumption that the category structures the environment well when it does not.34 Information may be accepted as consistent with a category when it is either neutral or inconsistent:

> This bias stems...from several different sources. First, the data base that is stored with a scheme [i.e., category] is a data base of confirming instances. Second, the criteria for a "match" to a [category] are broadly defined and admit neutral or even mildly inconsistent information. Third, disconfir- mations of a [category] lead to greater differentiation of that [category] rather than revision.35

They add that perceivers use one category and do not check indications that another category may be more suitable.36

A third judgment pattern shows that after a classification is made, subsequent evaluations of a category member are heavily influenced by traits associated with the members of the category rather than behaviors. Wyer and Carlston argue, for example that once traits are assigned to a judged person "on the basis of their association with behaviors describing him, these traits, rather than the behaviors, may come to be most easily recalled for use in describing the person."[37] Further, information that should invalidate the behavior-trait association does not automatically do so. Wyer and Srull have found that in experiments subjects will form an overall impression of a person on the basis of information supplied by the experimenter. Over time subjects forget the specific information and continue to make inferences about the judged person on the basis of the overall evaluation. The influence of the general impression increases as time passes and the original information fades from memory.[39]

These judgment findings help support the argument that categories are very important in forming a basis for predicting the behaviors of others. Policy makers are busy and inundated with events and information. The analyst should not expect to find that they can and do draw upon specific instances and traits to predict the behavior of other states. They may forget details but, knowing what type of state they are dealing with, make relatively consistent predictions about the other's behavior.[40]

Memory studies have compared the relative importance of impressions and specific information in series of judgments. The former appear to have a longer lasting impact. Specific information is difficult to store in memory, particularly for people who receive a great deal of information. But categories are a permanent part of the world view and provide a source of impressions and general information needed to make predictions. Further, studies have shown that characteristics incongruent with the overall impression were not recalled as well as congruent characteristics unless the contrast was very extreme. Relevant characteristics of a judged person were remembered more easily than irrelevant characteristics.[41] Since information that does not fit with the policy maker's image of a country will be judged incongruent, it will not be used to evaluate and predict the actions of the country in question. As will be seen in the case study in Chapters 5 and 6, this can cause important policy miscalculations.

A fourth judgment pattern involves variations in certainty and confidence in predicting another state's behavior. After a state is categorized, the judge responds to it with more speed and certainty when it is seen as being close to the categorical prototype and will overestimate the likelihood of events associated with the category.[42] This is particularly important in light of Bruner's point that people who see a category member as close to the prototype are only prepared for a narrow range of alternative events.

They will therefore respond to some situations well, but not
to others:

> If the environment is banal in the sense of containing
> only high probability events and sequences or, more
> properly, events and sequences that are strongly
> expected they will do well and perceive with a minimum
> of pause for close looking. But should the environment
> contain unexpected events, unusual sequences, then the
> result will be a marked slowdown in identification and
> categorizing. Cue search must begin again.43

All of these studies suggest that policy makers who see
another state as close to the categorical ideal-type will be
quite confident of their evaluations of issues and
predictions of the other's behavior. This, in turn, may
induce them to think of short-term remedies to issues that
arise between their state and the other. Those who are less
certain of the extent to which a state is typical of a
category may be predisposed to think of a variety of
scenarios, tactics, and strategies for meeting a variety of
possible events involving the other state in the future.
This concludes the discussion of psychological findings
regarding judgment patterns resulting from categories. The
next sections review categorical and environmental context
effect and the limits categories impose on adaptation to
change.

CONTEXT EFFECTS

Judgments are not simply the outcome of information
flowing through categories. Judgments of an object or state
are influenced by the context in which they are made and the
context created by the peculiar combination of the attributes and event scripts associated with the category in
which the state is placed. Each type of context effect will
be considered below.
It is intuitively obvious that judgments are influenced
by the circumstances in which they are made. A rock may be
judged a good table when the perceiver is hiking on a
mountain trail but not when he is preparing a gourmet meal
for his boss. A person who is known to be a good athlete but
not very bright will be more highly regarded if he is a
member of a professional baseball team than if he is a
member of a corporate board of executives. Unfortunately,

little is known about the features of a judgment context that are important influences on perception.44

Three patterns appear to be important. The first concerns category accessibility. In the earlier discussion of nominal judgments the point was made that the more accessible a category, the more likely it is that it will be used. Context plays a role here for "the more frequently in a given context instances of a given category occur, the greater the accessibility of the category."45 This may explain why people who do not think of themselves as sexists automatically assume that a nameless, faceless physician is a man. They are simply accustomed to numerical dominance of men in that particular environment. Hence, when informed that "a physician arrived on the scene" they visualize a man. The category is more accessible because it more frequently appears in that context. The same possibility exists for political judgments. If policy makers see most Third World countries as dependents and they hear that a Mexican official is coming to the United States to discuss economic issues, they may assume that he is coming to discuss loans. Economic interactions with that type of state involve US economic dominance.

A second external context effect concerns the negativity or hostility of the situation in which a judgment is made. One study found that subjects who had been introduced to a hostile environment were more influenced by that context than were subjects introduced to a kind environment. Subjects were asked to construct sentences from a series of words depicting either hostile or kind acts.46 After exposure to the context created by this task subjects evaluated characteristics of a target person.47 The results show that the second task was affected by the first. Judgments of hostility in the second task were affected by as few as six priming items. However, the effects of the kindness priming were almost negligible.48 In general, a hostile environment appears to invoke judgments of others as having hostile characteristics. Perceptions of hostility and threat are very important in the political world. The effects of hostile environmental influences coupled with the influence of category accessibility can lead to the judgment that other countries are performing hostile acts or have hostile intentions when they may be relatively benign. The Reagan Administration, for example, assumed that the purpose of the USSR's proposed European gas pipeline was to increase European dependence on the USSR rather than the more benign purpose of simply increasing Soviet revenues. The relatively stronger impact of hostile rather than kind environmental conditions may also be politically important if the response to perceived opportunity is equivalent to the response to kindness or friendly environmental conditions. If this is the case, then in situations in which policy makers are involved with both friendly and hostile states the outcome of discussions with the country seen as hostile should be given more importance even if the issue involves no threat of armed conflict. Thus cognitive factors can be used to explain why the Reagan Administration was willing to infuriate and hurt the interests of its European allies in an effort to prevent the USSR from building the gas pipeline.

A final external context effect involves the intensity of the bargaining situation. One analysis argues that during negotiations in which interaction is relatively low in intensity, the participants' view of the situation "will likely consist of a series of small pictures that relate to specific problems, with no overall integration or awareness of the inevitable contradictions implicit in the sum of these pictures."49 When procedures are intense, the view will be "simple and sharply drawn, well integrated, consistent, and unambiguous."50

Three general situational context effects on judgment have been discussed above. Less is known about the context effects resulting from the combination of characteristics of the judged object and the category in which it is placed. Many of the studies of this type of context effect are of perceptions of people. The most notable pioneer was Solomon Asch. One of his fundamental concepts was the idea that the perceiver does not see other people as composed of different units but as a whole person: "We do not experience anonymous traits the particular organization of which constitutes the identity of the person. Rather, the entire person speaks through each of his qualities, though not with the same clearness."51 When one perceives, in other words, what one sees is the whole rather than the sum of the parts. The meaning of particular traits change depending upon the context. For example, a very different impression is created of a person known to be "intelligent" when one also knows that he or she is "cruel and ruthless" rather than "intelligent, warm and caring."52

The implication is that the meaning of any given trait changes, depending upon its context. "Intelligence" in a cold, ruthless person could be threatening, potentially hostile, and destructive. In a warm, caring person, "intelligence" might be expected to contribute to empathy, to insight, and to the ability to give to another person.53

This context effect influences judgments in several ways. First, people tend to assume that good traits go together and bad traits go together. This should contribute to an overall positive or negative impression of a state and will thus influence the category into which it is placed. Second, once a state is categorized the traits associated with the category contribute to the context effect by further cementing the general impression. Finally, studies have shown that when the context in which information should be judged is unknown or unclear, subjects supply the context themselves -- they make it up.54 Once an object, event, person, or country has been classified as a category member the category becomes a source for contextual information. The category informs the perceiver of the members' traits and behaviors. The total gestalt of each country should produce a general positive or negative impression of the category members. One should therefore expect some types of states to be viewed positively and associated with opportunity more than threat (such as the dependent and puppet). Others should be associated with negative feelings and impressions of threat (such as the enemy, its dependents, and a hegemonist). The ally should be associated with an impression of friendship and positive opportunity but, as Cottam notes, it should also be associated with threat since allies are needed in conjunction with the threat from an enemy.55 The neutral should also create the impression of both threat and opportunity because its traits do not depict a state that is totally supportive of the perceiver's state. Instead, this is a type that is deter- mined to pursue its own course of action which may not be in accord with the interests of the perceiver's state.

The general implication of these psychological studies is that categories both interact with the external environ- ment and create contexts that influence judgments. Given the ease with which people incorporate hostile environmental factors into their judgments, contexts in which threat is perceived from an issue and/or the type of state category should also involve high-intensity bargaining. Although it follows that bilateral bargaining with states seen as depen- dents or puppets should be low in intensity due to the perception of opportunity and a maleable, weak opponent, it seems reasonable to expect the opportunity to achieve very highly valued goals should increase the intensity of the bargaining.56

A final task is an examination of categories and the judgment process when the environment changes. How, and how well, do people adapt to change?

ADAPTATION TO CHANGE

One point that can be made at the outset of any discussion of adaptation to change is that it is not easy. Adaptation is necessary when a judged stimulus no longer fits the category in which it is placed or when the stimulus is less representative of the category than it used to be. Failure to adapt to change can result in incorrect nominal or ordinal judgments. The perceiver either uses the wrong category to evaluate a state, assumes that the state is more representative of the category than it is (and thus incorrectly predicts the state's behavior), or uses a category that does not adequately structure the environment. (This may explain the peculiar findings in Chapter 3 concerning the puppet category. It may be inadequate for structuring the environment today.) Any of these possibilities could produce mistakes in interpreting or predicting the behavior of another state.

There are several reasons for sluggishness in adapting to change. First, categories help the perceiver predict future events and behaviors. At the same time they prompt the individual to expect these events and behaviors and this is the case even when the category is no longer appropriate.57

A second factor that contributes to slow adaptation to change is partly attributable to the ambiguous nature of social information. Boniauto has found that when people disagree in uncertain judgment situations ambiguous feedback leads them to stiffen their own position.58 Thus, people look for information confirming their expectations and become more insistent upon their position when confronted with ambiguous feedback. This is intensified when the judge has confidence and certainty in the nature of the state he is confronting. If the state is seen as a less-than-good example of the category the perceiver should be less certain of its attributes and other characteristics of the object and thus more attentive to ambiguous information. The two factors also account for the difficulty of changing a cate-

gory that does not adequately structure the environment. The
ambiguity of the social environment makes testing categories
very difficult. This also helps one understand the findings
concerning the puppet category. The whole category may be
accepted by some but rejected by others because of the
ambiguity of the political arena.

The difficulty of changing the categorization of a
state has been noted by Snyder and Diesing. They argue that
the basic image rarely changes more than marginally during a
crisis and that "[i]mmediate images and expectations often
change without effect on the underlying image."59 Unusual
and unexpected information about the behavior of the other
country is not seen as a challenge to the category in which
it is placed (that is, the "underlying image") but as a
peculiar momentary aberration. Snyder and Diesing also note
that policy makers often go to great lengths to force information to fit their expectations and to deny the
contradictory nature of information.60

A third factor in the difficulty involved in adapting
to change is that even if the perceiver does receive and
accept new information about the stimulus being judged, old
information is still considered in judgments for a time
unless it has been completely discarded. Thus, if an individual judges an object as an exemplary category member and
later received information indicating that the object is not
as good a member as previously thought, the information
contributing to the first judgment will still affect the new
judgment.61 Over time the effect of the original information
decreases.62 Adjusting judgments to new information takes
time.

A fourth factor contributing to problems in adapting to
change concerns category accessibility. Some categories may
be more accessible than others in particular contexts. When
the context changes the more accessible categories are still
used. To return to the example of male and female
physicians, presumably it will take time for the female
category to be as readily accessible as the male category
in evaluating physicians. Similarly, if one is accustomed to
thinking of Latin American countries as dependent types of
states, events will have to consistently and dramatically
demonstrate the contrary before the categorization changes.

A final point that should be made in regard to adaptation to change is that there are two basic ways of
overcoming the inappropriate use of categories. Both methods
are difficult to practice. They are explained by Jerome
Bruner:

There appear to be ...two ways of overcoming
rnappropriate perceptual readiness. The one is a re-
education of the misperceiver's expectancies concerning
the events he is to encounter. The other is the
constant close look. If the re-education succeeds in
producing a better match between internal expectancies
and external event-probabilities, the danger of misperception under hurried or substandard conditions of
perceiving is lessened. But the matter of re-educating
perceptual expectancies is complex. For where
consequences are grave, expectancy concerning what may
be encountered does not change easily, even with
continued opportunity to test the environment.63

Bruner goes on to say that careful, long-term scrutiny of
information, the "constant close look," is also no guarantee
against perceptual error:

There are some objects whose cues to identity are
sufficiently equivocal so that no such resolution can be
achieved: these are mostly in the sphere of so-called
interpersonal perception: perceiving the states of other
people, their characteristics, intentions, and so forth
on the basis of external signs. And since this is the
domain where misperception can have the most chronic if
not the most acute consequences, it is doubtful whether
a therapeutic regimen of close looking will aid the
misperceiver much in dealing with more complex cue patterns. But the greatest difficulty rests in the fact
that the cost of close looks is generally too high under
the conditions of speed, risk, and limited capacity
imposed upon organisms by their environment or their
constitutions. The ability to use minimal cues quickly
in categorizing the events of the environment is what
gives the organism its lead time in adjusting to events.
Pause and close inspection inevitably cut down on this
precious interval for adjustment.64

POLITICAL DECISION MAKING: THE USE OF POLITICAL CATEGORIES

In the preceding discussion the use of categories in
the judgment process was discussed through an examination of
psychological studies. In the next section each element of
the process, nominal judgments, ordinal judgments, context
effects, and adaptation to change, will be reviewed with
specific reference to patterns of political judgments. In

the final section of the chapter, the use of categories in judgments will be discussed with reference to the use of political categories, the dependent and neutral types of states.

Political Judgments: The Nominal Phase

Categorizations of other states will not be based upon a careful examination and analysis of their specific characteristics but upon a general impressionistic comparison of that state with category prototypes. Some category attributes may be more important than others in defining the prototype and thus in nominal judgments. The most important type of state attributes should include those such as military capacity and economic potential that are indicative of the potential threat and opportunity a type holds for the perceiver's state. As will be seen in the case study in Chapters 5 and 6, cultural comparisons may be inordinately important because they inform the perceiver of the potential for interaction on the diplomatic, economic, technological, and military planes and they inform about the potential for exploiting opportunities. It should also be mentioned that context effects will interact with the salience of particular attributes. For example, if two nations are involved in discussions of an economic nature, perceptions of the military attributes of the two should not be particularly important. The psychological studies also indicate that the more accustomed people are to classifying a state in a given category, the more accessible that category is and the more likely it will be used in the future to evaluate the state. Finally, the closer the individual state is seen to be to the categorical prototype, the more confident the policy maker will be of his categorization and his predictions regarding that state's behavior.

Political Judgments: The Ordinal Phase

The ordinal aspect of political judgments is also quite complicated. Once a state is classified, it loses some of its individuality and is seen as more similar to other members of the category. The original information contributing to the classification gradually fades from memory to some extent and the category becomes a source of information for predicting behavior. The category also

128

supplies missing information about the state for the
perceiver. This tendency can lead to assumptions that a
state is more representative of the category than it is.
When a state is seen as a better example of a category than
it is behavioral expectations can be incorrect. When the
state is perceived as close to the ideal representative of
the category, policy makers' confidence will lead to support
for short-term, issue-specific tactics in bargaining. The
more uncertain the policy makers is of the
representativeness of the state, the more he will be
predisposed to search for long-term strategies that satisfy
a variety of possible scenarios. The intensity of the
bargaining situation should contribute to this pattern. Low
intensity bargaining produces the first effect, high
intensity bargaining the second.

The traits and behaviors associated with a category may
not include information concerning what should not be associated with a member. Therefore, information may be seen as
consistent with a state's categorization when in fact it is
either neutral or mildly inconsistent. Other information
that is irrelevant or inconsistent with the category plays a
small role in ordinal judgments and predictions of behavior
because it is not well-recalled unless it is strikingly
incongruent. This is one of the drawbacks of the need for
cognitive categories. They are necessary to screen out irrelevant and incorrect information but in the process they
may block information that may be important.

Political Judgments: Context Effects

As the psychological literature suggests, judgments do
not take place in a vacuum. The use of political categories
will be influenced by the context created by the environment, the context created by the elements composing the
category, and the interaction of the two. The gestalt
created by the combination of each category's characteristics produce general impressions of threat and/or
opportunity associated with each type of state. The enemy,
its dependent state, and the hegemonist should be associated
with threat. The ally and neutral types should be associated
with both opportunity for the advancement of the perceiver's
state's goals and with threat. The neutral type offers
little direct threat but by not offering the prospect of
support it maybe associated with some perception of general
threat. The findings discussed in Chapter 3 regarding the

relative assessments of India and Switzerland contribute to this point. The more hostile the context in which judgments are made, the more likely a category associated with threat will be used to classify another state. The reverse is true for friendly of opportune environments. If a state has already been classified in a category that contributes to a friendly and/or opportune impression of the state, hostile actions by the state should be ignored unless they are in striking contrast to the state's normal behavior. If the hostile acts continue and become more dramatic the perceiver should begin to recognize negative traits and push the state farther away from the ideal example of the category or shift the state to a new category.

Political Judgments: Adaptation to Change

The psychological studies also suggest some interesting patterns concerning the problems policy-makers will have in adapting to change in another country given the role categories play in judgments. Those who are most resistant to new information indicating that a change in perception of a state is necessary are those who place the state close to the prototype of the category. Challenges produced by conflicting information are minimized by the category and may even produce stronger adherence to earlier judgments. Lyndon Johnson's conduct of the war in Vietnam up through 1968 is an example of this refusal to change an image of another political actor and subsequent rejection of information indicating that the actor will behave differently than expected.65

Political actors do not always fail to adapt to change. Nevertheless, even after the perceiver accepts and adjusts to new information about a state the old information may have a lingering effect. Information associated with a category may be slow to fade from memory if it is not completely discredited. Thus, changing the image of a state does not necessarily produce an immediate complete transformation of all judgments. Moreover, existing policies toward a state are even less likely to be completely revised all at once. When change in another state demonstrates to a policy maker that the old image of a state is no longer appropriate the policies that follow still may be influenced by old information and on-going policies. After the Second World War, for example, West Germany shifted from the enemy to the ally category. The strength of the ally classification must have grown throughout the implementation of the Marshall Plan and the institutionalization of a pro-United States government by 1949. Nevertheless, the memory of the Nazi regime and Germany's past maintain strong perceptions of threat and permitted only a very gradual rearming of Germany during the early 1950's.

Given the preceding discussion, it is now possible to combine the knowledge gleaned from the psychological literature with the categories of the political world view. The analytical question now becomes: given what is known about judgments and given the categories of the political world view, what testable hypotheses can be constructed concerning the effects of the type of state categories on political judgments? Several hypotheses concerning judgment patterns one should observe when policy makers bargain with states they perceive as neutral or dependent types can be constructed. A wide variety of case studies would be required to test all of the possible behavioral propositions that could be drawn from the information in this chapter concerning judgment patterns. This study limits itself to one case study in which several hypotheses are tested regarding judgments of a single state. The case study involves US policy makers' perceptions of Mexico in the late 1970's. It traces the course of efforts by American decision makers to adapt to change in Mexico. Before the specific hypotheses can be presented, however, it is necessary to review the charateristics of the neutral and dependent categories, that is, those used to classify Mexico, and to discuss the judgment patterns in terms of specific lenses produced by these two categories.

THE DEPENDENT CATEGORY

The dependent image has thus far been described as containing states perceived as economically and militarily weaker than the perceiver's state, different in domestic structure with competing policy advocates, moderately ineffective and inefficient in policy implementation. The economy, although weak, is permeable and thus presents the opportunity for economic interaction and profit for the perceiver's state. The dependent type was also characterized as an image in which the state is perceived as culturally inferior, supportive of the perceiver's state, flexible in international behavior, and as having goals compatible with those of the perceiver's state. The dependent was seen as moderately determined in the pursuit of its international goals.

In conflicts with the United States the dependent was expected to initiate several courses of action beginning with the initiation of diplomatic exchanges and proceding to the use of the domestic press for rhetorical denunciations, appealing to international forums, and doing nothing. These expectations demonstrate the perception of the dependent's fundamental weakness and lack of both leverage and determination in pursuing its own goals. In response to conflicts with the dependent the perceiver's state was expected to pursue diplomatic exchanges, economic pressure to and appeal to international forums as effective methods of dealing with the problem. Finally, historical experiences associated with the dependent type of state include events concerning Latin America, the Middle East, and economic and Cold War issues. The specific events reported were basically instances of United States domination and/or patronage such as the Alliance for Progress, aid in general, Puerto Rican elections, and the Panama Canal treaties.

In general, the dependent type is seen as weak, relatively supportive of and compliant with the perceiver's state, and a type that can be expected to submit in a dispute without attempting to inflict harm on the perceiver's state. The response of the peceiver's state quickly turns to harmful actions against the dependent type. In the survey responses, for example, almost 42% favored appeals to international forums as a second step in conflicts with a dependent. Nearly 39% favored the use of economic sanctions as a second response. The events associated with the dependent type reflect dominance and patronage. Given these attributes, behavioral expectations, and response alternatives, the dependent should be associated with favorable prospects for the realization of the perceiver's state's goals.66

Given these perceptual attributes, policy makers should expect success from policies that pursue the interests of their own state regardless of the interests of the dependent. Because the dependent is weak, flexible, and has compatible goals, the perceiver should expect the dependent to be unwilling and unable to hurt his country if the policies of his state neglect the interests of the dependent type. Further, because of the sense of cultural superiority associated with this type of state, policies pursuing the interests of the perceiver's state should be seen as both just and good for both countries. It is also important to note that context effects play a role in the importance of the attributes for each type of state. The case study that will be considered here is one involving bargaining over economic issues. Therefore, attributes relevant to the dependent type's economic condition, bargaining habits, and technological capacity will be particularly salient. The attributes describing the country's military capacity will not be important for the perceiver although in a different context (such as the question of Mexico's susceptibility to guerrilla action) those attributes would be more salient than others.

Drawing upon the psychological patterns discussed above and the description of the dependent type of state, several hypotheses can be proposed regarding policy makers' judgments of a state categorized as a dependent.

POLITICAL JUDGMENTS OF THE DEPENDENT TYPE OF STATE: CLASSIFICATION OF A STATE IN THE DEPENDENT CATEGORY

Hypothesis 1: The more accustomed policy makers are to classifying the particular state in the dependent category the more accessible that category is and the more likely it is that it will be used to classify that state in the future.

Hypothesis 2: If the dependent category is very accessible in classifying the state, then adjustments to change will require a new nominal judgment concerning the appropriateness of the dependent category for that state.

ORDINAL JUDGMENTS OF THE DEPENDENT TYPE

Hypothesis 3: Once a state is classified as a dependent it will lose some of its individual qualities and will be seen as similar to other states in the category and given the traits associated with the category. Thus, behavioral expectations for the particular state will be based upon the attributes and other characteristics associated with the category. Unique and important characteristics of the individual state will be ignored if they do not conform to the attributes depicted by the category as politically important.

Hypothesis 4: The tendency to supply missing information about individual states from the category will lead to the assumption that the state will behave as a typical representative of the category despite its individual differences.

Hypothesis 5: Because categories screen incoming information, neutral and inconsistent information will be ignored unless it is dramatically inconsistent. Therefore, information indicating that the state classified as a dependent is acting in a manner not associated with that type of state will be disregarded or discounted.

Hypothesis 6: Inconsistent and irrelevant information about the behaviors and traits of a state classified as a dependent will not be recalled as well as congruent information unless it is strikingly inconsistent. Therefore, information about inconsistent behavior received in the past will have relatively little effect on judgments of that state's future behavior.

Hypothesis 7: The closer the particular state is seen to be to the dependent prototype, the more confident the policy maker will be in his predictions and the more predisposed to support short-term, issue-specific strategies. The more uncertain the policy maker, the more he or she will be predisposed to search for long-term, multi-issue strategies.

CONTEXT EFFECTS AND THE DEPENDENT CATEGORY

Hypothesis 8: The context in which most bilateral issues arise between a dependent and the perceiver's state are cordial or friendly. Context effects should produce a general impression of friendship and opportunity. Thus, information indicating strain or hostility will be overshadowed and diminished in importance by the general context. The gestalt produced by the combination of attributes contribute to the impression of positive opportunity. Thus, the context effects as a whole should contribute to an emphasis on information predicting success in achieving US goals.

ADAPTATION TO CHANGE IN A STATE CLASSIFIED AS A DEPENDENT

Hypothesis 9: Those who are most resistant to information indicating a need for change in the categorization of policies toward a dependent will be those who see the individual state as a prototypical dependent. Further, the challenge of conflicting information is minimized by the category and may produce a stronger adherence to the categorical (and hence policy) judgment.

Hypothesis 10: Even after the policy maker begins to accept and use new information in making judgments and after a shift in categorization begins, old knowledge about the state has a lingering effect and will continue to influence judgments until forgotten or discredited.

The case study used here involves both the dependent and neutral categories. Hypotheses 1-10 concern perceptions of the dependent. The fundamental thrust of these hypotheses is that when a country is categorized as a dependent it will be treated as one. Policy makers' interpretation of information, predictions of future behavior, and subsequent policy recommendations will be based on that image. The rest of the hypotheses concern the transformation in perception of Mexico from a dependent to a neutral and the change in behavioral predictions that result. Therefore, a discussion of the neutral category and the types of behaviors expected of the neutral is necessary.

The neutral image is of a type of state that is different, but not radically so, from the dependent. The neutral state is also a state that is seen as militarily inferior to the United States, moderately similar to the US in form of government, and as containing domestic groups attempting to influence foreign policy. The neutral differs from the dependent in that it is seen as more effective in implementing policy, closer to the United States in economic strength and less economically penetrable than the dependent. Further, the neutral is seen as equal in culture to the US, making it more advanced than the dependent. Although like the dependent the neutral is seen as flexible in international bargaining, it is also seen as much less supportive of the international policies of the United States than is the dependent, more determined in pursuing its own international goals, and less compatible in its international goals. In general, therefore, the neutral type is still seen as weaker than the United States and as holding the opportunity for the achievement of US goals, but it is seen as more independent of and less compatible with the United States.

In terms of behavior, the neutral type is seen as most likely to respond to conflicts with the United States by first initiating diplomatic procedures, then appealing to international forums, denouncing the US in its domestic press, and either doing nothing or using economic sanctions. Although the neutral is not expected to threaten the United States, its attributes indicate that it is not expected to be as compatible with the United States in general when compared to the dependent. In turn, the United States was seen as responding approriately to the neutral when it used diplomatic exchanges, appealed to international forums, and initiated economic sanctions. However, the survey results indicated that more people advocated the use of economic sanctions sooner with the dependent than with the neutral. Forceful tactics are apparently seen as less appropriate in conflicts with the neutral type.

The historical events associated with the neutral are quite different from those associated with the dependent type. In the former case the historical instances depict situations in which the type of state has acted to achieve international peace by either opposing war, refusing to participate in the Cold War, or promoting international cooperation. The historical instances associated with the dependent depict situations of domination and patronage. The neutral's event scripts are not associated with such events.

The categorization of a state as a neutral should affect judgments of the state in several ways. The following hypotheses concern those patterns:

ORDINAL JUDGMENTS OF THE NEUTRAL

Hypothesis 11: The tendency to supply missing information about the individual state from the neutral category will lead to expectations that the state will behave as a typical representative of the category despite its individual differences.

Hypothesis 12: The context in which most issues arise with the neutral type should be relatively benign, neither hostile nor extremely friendly. The effects produced by the combination of the neutral's traits and the situations in which issues arise should produce a relatively neutral context. Therefore, the perceiver should be equally receptive to information that his state's goals will or will not be achieved.

ADAPTATION TO CHANGE

Hypothesis 13: The more accustomed policy makers are to classifying a particular state as a neutral, the more accessible that category is and the more likely that it will be used to classify the state in the future. However, as was mentioned in Hypothesis 11, even after policy makers begin the process of accepting a new category and thus new information, old information and knowledge linger. If the old information and knowledge is not dramatically rejected, the old information and knowledge facilitate a shift back to an earlier category.

CONCLUSION

One of the most basic points in the discussion of the judgment process in this chapter is that different behaviors will be expected of states classified as neutrals and those classified as dependents. It has been argued that the use of cognitive categories is largely non-conscious. Policy makers are not aware that they are organizing and simplifying the political world. The categories used in the world view cause errors in judgment but they are necessary and generally serve their purpose well. Therefore, different traits should be associated with these two types of states and different behaviors should be expected of them. While neither type is seen as concertedly and completely independent of the US and able to pursue a totally self-interested course of action, there are differences in the expected behaviors. Given the weakness and maleability of the dependent image, policy makers should expect the dependent to back down to US pressure in bargaining situations. It is seen as incapable of carrying out actions that require strength, independence, and an ability to perform effectively. The dependent is associated with events in which the United States has been either patronizing or dominating. Predictions of future interactions should expect the same type of relationship. The image should be reinforced by general context effects.

The neutral type is different. While it too is seen as weak in many ways, it is not expected to be universally supportive of the United States and is seen as more likely to pursue its own interests in bargaining situations. Its international policies will be expected to be less supportive of the United States, particularly in regard to the Cold War and other hostilities that do not involve that particular country. Therefore, in bargaining situations, the neutral should be expected to be a stronger foe, more able and willing to stand up to the United States.

The particular case used here is a study of response to change as well as judgments of a state classified as a dependent by some and a neutral by others. It will be argued that Mexico was classified as a dependent by most policy makers in the 1960's and 1970's but that it underwent considerable non-revolutionary change in the 1970's. These changes, discussed in the next two chapters, resulted in new policies, policies more closely reflecting those of a neutral rather than a dependent type of state. Therefore, several hypotheses were presented above concerning the processes involved in adapting to change and shifting a state to a different perceptual category. It has been argued that countries classifed as dependents will be expected to behave in a particular fashion. Those who saw the individual state, Mexico, as an ideal example of a dependent should have been most resistant to information indicating that Mexico would not behave as expected but as a neutral. This tendency should be particularly strong because the behaviors expected of a neutral are not dramatically inconsistent with those expected of the dependent.

Finally, it was argued that old information and knowledge linger in the perceptual milieu. Those individuals who do place Mexico in a different category after witnessing the inadequacy of the dependent category in predicting Mexican behavior should still be influenced by old information until it is completely discarded. Thus one should expect uncertainty about a new classification until time and several events show that the new classification is more appropriate for that particular state.

The next chapter traces the perceptual and historical background in US-Mexico relations. The image of Mexico from the 1960's through the 1970's is discussed. Mexican foreign policies and US policies toward Mexico are examined and analyzed in terms of world view categories. In Chapter 6 the effects of both the dependent and neutral classifications of Mexico on bargaining positions advocated by US policy makers are discussed.

138

NOTES

1. J. Bieri, Clinical and Social Judgment: The Discrimination of Behavioral Information (New York: John Wiley and Sons, Inc., 1966), p. 29.

2. R.B. Zajonc, "Cognitive Theories in Social Psychology," in G. Lindsey and E. Aronson (eds.), The Handbook of Social Psychology, vol. 1, 2nd ed. (Reading, Massachusetts: Addison-Wesley, 1968), p. 238.

3. J.S. Bruner, J.J. Goodnow, and G.A. Austin, A Study of Thinking (New York: John Wiley, 1956) is a major example.

4. R.C. Martin and A. Carmazza, "Classification in Well-Defined and Ill-Defined Categories: Evidence for Common Processing Strategies," Journal of Experimental Psychology 109 (1980): 321.

5. See E. Rosch, "Cognitive Representation of Semantic categories," Journal of Experimental Psychology: General 104 (1975): 192-233; E. Rosch and C. mervis, "Family Resemblances: Studies in the Internal Structure of Categories," Cognitive Psychology 7 (1975): 573-705; and M. McCloskey and S Glucksberg, "Decision Processes in Verifying Class Inclusive Statements: Implication for Models of Semantic Memory," Cognitive Psychology 11 (1979): 1-37, all cited in martin and Carmazza.

6. Ibid., p. 324.

7. Her point is expressed as follows:

In the first place, the attributes which define an instance as a category member and the attributes which define it as a good or less good member may be different. Attributes which are `noisy' with respect to category membership (such as size or color) may contribute to the exemplariness of an instance... Where criterial attributes can vary in `amount,' good examples of the category may require a particular amount, much narrower in its extent, than the amount acceptable for general category membership...

Formal and psychological aspects of categories are also separable to the extent that, in many cognitive tasks, categories may be processed in terms of their internal structure rather than in terms of the attributes of their formal definition." See E. Rosch, "On the Internal Structure of Perceptual and Semantic Categories," in T.E. Moore (ed.), Cognitive Developments and the Acquisition of Language (New York: Academic Press, 1973), p. 141-142.

8. Martin and Carmazza, p. 322.

9. Ibid., p. 352.

10. Ibid., p. 321.

11. R. Wyer and T.K. Srull, "Category Accessibility: Some Theoretical and Empirical Issues Concerning the Processing of Social Stimulus Information," in E.T. Higgins, C.P. Herman, and M.P.Zanna (eds.), Social Cognition: The Ontario Symposium, vol. 1 (Hillsdale, New Jersey: Lawrence Erlbaum, 1981), p. 163.

12. E. Rosch, "Universals and Cultural Specifics in Human Categorization," in R. Brislin, S. Bochner, and W. Lonner (eds.), Cross-Cultural Perspectives on Learning (New York: Halstead Press, 1975), p. 194.

13. Ibid.

14. Martin and Carmazza, p. 321.

15. G.A. Miller, "Practical and Lexical Knowledge," in E. Rosch and B. Lloyd (eds.), Cognition and Categorization (Hillsdale, New Jersey: Lawrence Erlbaum, 1978), p. 308.

16. M.I. Posner, R. Goldsmith, and K.E. Welton, "Perceived Distance and the Classification of Distorted Patterns," Journal of Experimental Psychology 73 (1967): 28-28; and S.K. Reed, "Pattern Recognition and Categorization," Cognitive Psychology 3 (1972): 382-407; all cited in Martin and Caramazza.

17. Ibid., p. 324.

18. Bieri, p. 121.

19. R.S. Wyer and D.E. Carlston, Social Cognition, Inference, and Attribution (Hillsdale, New Jersey: Lawrence Erlbaum, 1979), p. 90.

20. Bieri, p. 40.

21. J.S. Bruner, "On Perceptual Readiness," in J.M. Anglin and J.S. Bruner (eds.), Beyond the Information Given (New York: W.W.Norton, 1973), p. 17-18.

22. Wyer and Srull, p. 194.

23. Bruner, p. 31-32.

24. Ibid., p. 16-17.

25. R.J. Eiser and W. Stroebe, Categorization and Social Judgment (New York: Academic Press, 1972), p. 42.

26. J.L. Freedman, D.O. Sears, and L.M. Carlsmith, Social Psychology, 3rd ed. (Englewood Cliffs, New Jersey: Presntice-Hall, 1978), p. 311.

27. Eiser and Stroebe, p. 166-167.

28. H.S. Upshaw, "Own Attitude as an Anchor in Equal-Appearing Intervals," Journal of Abnormal and Social Psychology 64 (1962): 85-96.

29. Wyer and Carlston, p. 90.

140

30. G. Allport, The Nature of Prejudice (Garden City: Doubleday, 1954), p. 21.

31. S.E.Taylor and J. Crocker, "Schematic Bases of Social Information Processing," in E.T. Higgins, C.P.Herman, and M.P. Zanna (eds.), Social Cognition: The Ontario Symposium, vol. 1 (Hillsdale, New Jersey: Lawrence Erlbaum, 1981), p. 114. Note that Taylor and Crocker use the term "schema" rather than "category." The definition is basically the same.

32. D.L. Hamilton, "A Cognitive Attributional Analysis of Stereotyping,"in L. Berkowitz (ed.), Advances in Experimental Social Psychology, vol. 12 (New York: Academic Press, 1979).

33. D. Kahneman and A. Tversky, "On the Psychology of Prediction," Psychological Review 80 (1973): 237-251.

34. Taylor and Crocker, p. 118.

35. Ibid.

36. Ibid.

37. Wyer and Carlston, p. 92.

38. Ibid.

39. Wyer and Srull, p. 176.

40. One analyst working in this theoretical area reports an interesting occurrence that is a good example of the memory problem. In an effort to examine differences in underlying assumptions concerning the Middle East, the analyst attempted to discuss the October Declaration and Camp David with a high ranking State Department official. In reply to the analyst's questions, the official said "Remind me again what the October Declaration said." See Richard Cottam, "The October Declaration and Camp David: Competing Strategic Probes" (Unpublished paper).

41. R. Hastie, "Schematic Principles in Human Memory," in E.T. Higgins, C.P.Herman, and M.P. Zanna (eds.), Social Cognition: The Ontario Symposium, vol. 1 (Hillsdale, New Jersey: Lawrence Erlbaum, 1981), p. 62-70.

42. Taylor and Crocker, p. 111.

43. Bruner, p. 33.

44. Eiser and Stroebe, p. 2.

45. Bruner, p. 18.

46. Wyer and Srull, p. 181-182.

47. Ibid., p. 182.

48. Ibid., p. 183.

49. R. Cottam and G. Galluci, The Rehabilitation of Power in International Relations: A Working Paper (Pittsburgh: Center for International Studies, University of Pittsburgh, 1978), p. 46.

50. Ibid.
51. S.Asch, "Forming Impressions of Personality," Journal of Abnormal and Social Psychology 41 (1946): 284.
52. Freedman, Sears, and Carlsmith, p. 77.
53. Ibid. Norman Anderson and others argue that the psychological mechanism behind the context effect is a generalized halo effect. This is discussed om N.H. Anderson, "Applicability of Linear-Serial Model to a Personality Impression Task Using Special Presentation," Journal of Personality and Social Psychology 10 (1968): 354-362. Wyer, however, argues that the "change of meaning" and the "halo effect" arguments are not mutually exclusive in R.S. Wyer Jr., Cognitive Organization and Change: An Information Processing Approach (Potomac, Maryland: Lawrence Erlbaum, 1974).
54. Wyer and Carlston, p. 50.
55. R. Cottam, Foreign Policy Motivation (Pittsburgh: University of Pittsburgh Press, 1977), p. 62-65.
56. Upshaw argues that the range of alternative responses also narrows when highly valued goals are involved in an issue. See H.S. Upshaw,"Judgments and Change in Social Attitudes," in M.F. Kaplan and S. Schwartz (eds.), Human Judgment and Decision Processes in Applied Settings (New York: Academic Press, 1977), p. 210.
57. Taylor and Crocker, p. 114.
58. G.B. Boniauto, "The Feedback Problem: Cognitive Change in Conditions of Exact and Ambiguous Outcome Information,"in L. Rappaport and D.A. Summers (eds.), Human Judgment and Social Interaction (New York: Holt, Rinehart and Winston, Inc., 1973), p. 222.
59. G. Snyder and P. Diesing, Conflict Among Nations (Princeton: Princeton University Press, 1977), p. 329.
60. Ibid., p. 331.
61. Wyer and Srull, p. 172.
62. Ibid.
63. Bruner, p. 29.
64. Ibid., p. 30.
65. For a complete discussion of the impact of Lyndon Johnson's image of the Vietcong on his expectations of their behavior, see R. Cottam, Chapter 6.

5

Images of Mexico: Historical and Perceptual Background

In 1977 discussions began regarding the importation of natural gas from Mexico to the United States. The negotiations resulted not in an agreement but a strain in United States-Mexican relations. Disturbed by these developments, President Carter called for a major review of his administration's policy toward Mexico and a variety of alternative approaches were suggested. Another round of gas negotiations began in 1979 and a settlement was reached. In this chapter and the next it will be shown that the dominant view of Mexico throughout the 1960's and well into the 1970's was of the typical dependent type of state. However during the 1970's Mexico underwent profound change in its self-image and international policies. Because the change was evolutionary rather than revolutionary it was not recognized by the major participants in the energy negotiations until the natural gas "fiasco." In the next chapter it will be argued that the major cause of the failure to reach an agreement in 1977 was the dominant dependent view of Mexico and that the success of the 1979 negotiations can be attributed to a change in the image of Mexico to the neutral category. The new view of Mexico was brought to the bargaining table through change in some negotiators' perceptions and by the substitution of some negotiators with others with the different view of Mexico.

There are two basic tasks in the study of the effect of world views on political judgments. First, the world views of the policy makers involved must be analyzed to discover the category into which the state in question has been placed. Second, the policies advocated by these policy makers must be studied to determine if they do conform to the theoretical arguments concerning the effect of

143

144

categories on judgments. Policies, primary sources such as
government documents, newspapers, and speeches, and
secondary sources will be used for evidence concerning the
policy makers' views of Mexico. It is particularly important
that actions (that is, policies and policy recommendations)
be included in the study to help surmount the tendency of
public officials to conceal their personal opinions in
search of politically acceptable phrases (although, as the
reader will see in the next chapter, many officials were
quite frank in their evaluations of Mexico). The analysis of
American policy makers' views of Mexico must begin with a
review of the historical and perceptual relationship between
the two countries. The record is one of domination of Mexico
by the United States. Conflicts between the two frequently
have been settled through unilateral decisions by the United
States. The discussion will proceed through three steps.
First, the bilateral economic relationship will be described. Second, Mexico's foreign policies during the past
twenty years will be reviewed. Finally, the policies of the
United States toward Mexico will be discussed. As the story
unfolds, it becomes evident that until the 1970's Mexico
behaved as a country seen through the dependent image would.
It was not completely submissive to the United States but
took little initiative in forming a foreign policy that
pursued Mexican interests to the fullest extent possible. In
turn, Mexico was treated as a dependent country. The United
States conceded to Mexico only on issues of little
importance and freely used strong pressure to force Mexican
compliance. In the 1970's, however, Mexico's foreign
policies began to change as a result of a new interest in
international independence and a new relationship with the
United States in which Mexican problems receive equal
consideration with those of the United States.

THE STRUCTURAL RELATIONSHIP

Until the debt crisis of the 1980's Mexico was commonly
referred to as one of the developing countries with a bright
future. It has had decades of political stability and, until
the 1970's, impressive economic growth. Between 1935 and
1965 real gross domestic product per capita increased 2.3
times. It increased 17% between 1970 and 1979.1 Until 1970
Mexico's GNP grew at an annual rate of 6.5%.2 The
manufacturing sector grew and new investments were made to
promote agricultural development.3 Nevertheless, by 1970

Mexican officials were becoming increasingly concerned about
the state of the nation's economy. Growth had occurred but
the growth of exports was weak.4 In addition, inequalities
in income distribution remained severe; unemployment and
underemployment continued, in part due to the capital inten-
sive nature of Mexico's industrialization programs; Mexico's
foreign debt grew so that by 1969 Mexico experienced its
first deficit; and foreign investment, particularly in the
manufacturing sector, increased dramatically. 5

In response to these developments Mexican officials
embarked on several new policies in the 1970's. An increase
in exports was promoted through greater participation in the
Latin American Free Trade Association. Legislation was
passed aimed at limiting foreign participation in the
economy and increasing exports by foreign firms. The
discovery of large reserves of petroleum in the 1970's gave
Mexico more options in its development plans. The Lopez
Portillo Administration announced in the National
Industrial Development Plan and the Global Development Plan
for 1980-1982 that oil revenues would be used to finance
Mexico's economic development.6 This development plan relied
upon estimates of an annual increase in the gross domestic
product of 8% and an annual increase in the world price of
oil and gas of between 5 and 7%. Given these expectations,
it is not surprising that Mexico has suffered severe
economic dislocations due in part to an international oil
glut.

Throughout these years the United States has played an
enormous role in the Mexican economy. Two-thirds of Mexico's
foreign trade and direct foreign investment has come from
the United States.7 Mexico has been one of the major
borrowers of financial capital from the United States.8 It
relies heavily on American tourism and the United States as
a source of employment for a potentially explosive number of
unemployed workers.9

The interaction between the American and Mexican
economies is particularly important in two areas,
investments (by U.S. firms in Mexico) and trade. Foreign
investment in crucial sectors of the nation's economy (petroleum, banking, insurance, railroads, agriculture and many
mining industries) had been prohibited in Mexico since the
1940's.10 The relative importance of foreign investment has
declined since 1940 but as Dominquez points out:

[T]he composition of direct foreign investment has
been altered dramatically. The manufacturing share was

only 4.5% in 1911 at the outset of the revolution, rising to only 7.1% in 1940 at the end of the presidency of Lazaro Cardenas. It was up to 34% in 1955, 73.8% in 1970, and 77.5% in 1980. The value of US manufacturing investments in Mexico was 1271% higher in 1979 than in 1955. In 1970, the US accounted for 80% of foreign investment in industry and for 91% of foreign investment in mining...The US accounted still for 69% of accumulated direct foreign investment in 1980; it accounted for 70% of all technology transfer contracts registered in Mexico by the end of 1979. 11

In addition, foreign-owned enterprises import more than the nationally owned firms. US-based firms import three-quarters of their material needs from the United States. Foreign firms from other countries (with the exception of British-based firms) do the same.12 The firms not only import from their home country, they also export to their US parents. For example "[i]n 1960, Mexico exported only 56,000 dollars of electrical machinery, none of it to parent firms. By 1972, Mexico exported 28.5 million dollars worth of such products to the U.S., 8% of which went to the parent firm."13 This tie between parent and subsidiary firms reduced the ability of the Mexican government to set trade policy.14

Mexico's major trade partner is the United States. The nature of the products exported to the United States has changed since the 1960's. At that time, Mexico's major exports to the United States were traditional Less Developed Country items such as sugar, coffee, cotton, lead, copper, and zinc.15 In 1979, Mexico's major exports were petroleum; frozen shrimp; chemical products; cotton; automotive vehicles, parts and components; electrical and electromechanical machinery; tomatoes; and cattle.16

During the 1970's, the percent of the United States share of the Mexican market was relatively stable but the dollar amounts involved grew considerably. By mid-1980, Mexico was the third largest trading partner of the United States.17 Thus, although Mexico has a tremendous stake in continued access to the United States market, Mexico is not unimportant as a trading partner for the United States. The relationship is still highly asymmetrical in that the United States is Mexico's largest trading partner while Mexico takes a much smaller share of US exports (15% in 1979).18 Mexico has had continual trade deficits with the United States. The export of hydrocarbons gradually accounted for more and more of bilateral trade during the late 1970's and into the 1980's. In 1980 hydrocarbons accounted for approximately 70% of total Mexican exports compared with 42% in 1979. Meanwhile, non-oil exports fell in real terms in 1980. Almost 90% of Mexican oil was exported to the United States by 1979.20 Eventually, the Mexican government became concerned about the dependence on the United States market implied by the heavy export of petroleum and passed legislation limiting the amount of petroleum exported to any one country to no more than 50% of total petroleum exports. Despite the addition of petroleum and natural gas to Mexico's exports, its trade deficit continued to rise. In 1981 the deficit totaled $4 billion with imports increasing 28.7% over 1980.21

A final important aspect of the economic relationship between the United States and Mexico is Mexico's foreign debt. Historically, Mexico has gone through cycles of heavy and light foreign indebtedness. Beginning in the late 1950's, Mexico entered its latest period of heavy foreign debt. Maria Rosario Green explains the origins and consequences of the debt as follows:

> With respect to the public foreign debt, the stabilizing development strategy made the country more dependent and therefore more vulnerable. The growth achieved by the Mexican economy in the 1940's and 1950's had been mainly the result of a national effort, both public and private; by mid-1959 the country's foreign debt was only $574.8 million. The growth achieved by the Mexican economy afterward would be very much the result of foreign capital in the form of private investment, particularly in the form of foreign credits. This kind of financial dependence on foreign capital was fostered precisely by a development strategy that reflected the relative weakness of the Mexican state, both internally and externally... Externally, the state was weak in diversifying its financial contacts. In this field, as well as in that of international trade, it relied on the United States economy and was incapable of defending itself against pressures exerted by American private bankers to borrow their money to service old debts.22

The sources of Mexico's foreign debt have changed during the post-war period. Since the mid-1970's, 70% of Mexico's foreign debt has been owed to US lending institutions. Of the American sources of loans, the Eximbank was the first

and began lending to Mexico in the 1940's. AID was the
second major source but by the 1970's private American banks
supplied most of the credit.23 By 1972, "the total amount
lent to the country by American private banks was $5 bil-
lion, of which $2.75 billion (55 percent) was channeled to
the Mexican public sector, $1.65 billion (33 percent) to the
private sector, and $0.6 billion (12 percent) to Mexican
branches of American firms."24 By the end of 1976 the amount
loaned from private American banks had increased to $13
billion.25 The percent of the total provided by American
banks had decreased from 60% in 1977 to 42% in 1979.26

Mexico's development strategy during the late 1970's
relied heavily upon energy revenues as the major source of
funding for development programs. This strategy necessitated
a rapid build-up of the energy sector which, in turn,
required more loans.Although the dramatic increase in
Mexico's foreign debt during the late 1970's was not
entirely due to borrowing for the national oil enterprise,
PEMEX (the national petroleum agency) was responsible for
over one third of the 1977 debt increase and half of the
increase for 1978.27

In summary, the American role in the Mexican economy is
enormous. In the areas of trade, foreign investment and
debt, the Mexican economy relies heavily on continued
American activity. Nevertheless, Mexico has become the third
largest trading partner of the United States and the US has
an economic interest in continued smooth economic
interaction as well. The characteristics of the economic
relationship demonstrate, however, that the United States
has important levers that can be used if conflicts arise
between the two countries. Mexico has not been completely
subservient to the United States and the patterns of Mexican
foreign policy suggest that Mexico has taken some
independent stances internationally including some policies
not entirely pleasing to the United States. Further,
Mexico's willingness to take such policy positions has not
been dependent upon improved economic fortunes permitting
greater economic independence from the United States. As the
review of Mexican foreign policy that follows shows, Mexico
began to take a different approach to its foreign affairs
before the discoveries of large petroleum reserved suggested
that Mexico's economic future was bright. During the 1960's
Mexico behaved as a dependent country should be expected to
behave. In the 1970's Mexico changed tactics, allied itself
more closely with the Third World, and refused to comply
with US governmental decisions during some controversies.

MEXICAN FOREIGN POLICIES

Mexican foreign policies underwent a fundamental change during the 1970's, a change to which the United States has had to respond. To understand the nature of the transformation of Mexican foreign affairs, it is necessary to begin with the policies of the 1960's. Mexico's stated foreign policy principles have included support for self-determination for all nations, non-intervention in the affairs of others, independence for Mexico, collective security, and disarmament.28 During and before the 1960's Mexico's general international orientation was confined largely to the United States. Although Mexico is often described as wary of perceived American imperialist designs and therefore conscious of the need to maintain an independent stance internationally, this outlook was reflected in only a few of Mexico's foreign policies during the 1960's.

The portion of Mexican international policies in the 1960's that most clearly demonstrated the desire of Mexican leaders to be "independent" of the United States has been Mexico's disagreement with the United States position on the implications of communism and its international spread. Mexico opposed the American policy toward Arbenz in Guatemala in 1954, voted against the expulsion of Cuba from the Organization of American States in 1962, objected to the intervention of the United States in the Dominican Republic in 1965, and opposed US involvement in the war in Vietnam. Mexico's position was justified by its "nonintervention" principle.

Despite its insistence upon the rights of other states to determine their own political principles, Mexico "was not a rebel."29 None of the disagreements between the United States and Mexico on these issues reached the level of a presidential conflict. Mexico's position was moderated in several ways: it did not launch an anti-American crusade; it did not attempt to convince other govrnments to join it in its stance; and it refrained from close interactions with Cuba. Although Mexico had voted against Cuba's expulsion from the OAS, for example, it did so because the OAS charter had no rules concerning expulsion. Mexico did not join Argentina and Brazil in rejecting Cuba's expulsion because the dispute was a conflict between the United States and Cuba, not the OAS and Cuba.30 Further, Mexico did vote to

exclude Cuba from participating in several subagencies of
the OAS and it proclaimed Marxism incompatible with the
Inter-American system.31 Although Mexico was the only Latin
American state to maintain relations with Cuba, those
relations were distant during the 1960's. It was possible for
individuals to travel to and from Cuba through Mexico but
all travelers were identified and the information was made
available to the US government.32

Other than issues involving matters of judicial
principle, Mexico's foreign policies during the 1960's were
directed toward economic concerns and, in particular,
economic interaction with the United States. Mexico sought a
"special relationship" with the United States and did not
join the infant Non-Aligned Movement during the 1960's. The
notion of the "special relationship" with the United States
and the policy areas it embraced is described by Olga
Pellicer de Brody:

> Over the years, the elements that in the opinion of
> the Mexican Government should constitute the U.S. Good
> Neighbor Policy toward its southern neighbor became more
> defined. On the one hand, cooperation was sought in
> order to better confront border problems, such as the
> use of the waters of international rivers, or the status
> of Mexican braceros doing seasonal work in the United
> States. On the other hand, preferential treatment was
> sought for Mexican exports as well as a complete lifting
> of restrictions on the entry and spending of North
> American tourists in Mexico. Finally, a sustained flow
> of capital was expected from the United States in the
> form of Government loans or direct investment -- a flow
> that should obey the "rules of the game" imposed by the
> Mexican Government.33

In short, Mexican officials aimed for preferred treatment by
American policy makers for trade items from Mexico and a
close bilateral interaction to resolve problems caused by
unequal development and a large border. In the process of
setting these goals the Mexican governments of the 1960's
relegated interaction with other states to secondary
importance. Mexican leaders actively sought US investment
and an intensification of trade relations. As will be seen
during the discussion below of US policies toward Mexico
during the 1960's, Mexico's appeals for trade concessions
were not favorably answered.

Several factors contributed to the gradual transforma-

tion in Mexico's foreign policies during the 1970s. Luis
Echeverria became president in 1970 and was the initiator of
many of the policy changes. Among the major sources of
change was the realization that Mexico's economy was not
developing in a balanced fashion and was becoming more and
more dependent upon the whims of American-owned businesses.
There was also a growing suspicion that the "special
relationship" with the United States was not working.
Another related factor was the need to placate the political
left in Mexico. Echeverria's legacy of responsibility for
the assault upon student demonstrators in 1968 which left
many casualties, and his reputation as a CIA informant gave
him few followers in the left. By setting forth on a new,
more Third World oriented foreign policy Echeverria
apparently hoped to satisfy and build support among the
reformist elements in the Mexican political arena. It is
also probable that Echeverria's personal beliefs did not
conflict with the policies he chose. Those policies contained some continuity with the past. The basic principle of
self-determination and non-intervention (with one major
exception) remained important.34

There were several important elements in the
transformation of Mexican foreign policies in the 1970's.
The first was the end of the notion that Mexican-United
States relations could be based upon a "special" bilateral
relationship. There was a consequent shift to a
diversification of Mexico's international concerns with a
strong emphasis on Mexico-Third World interaction.35 A
second element was a renewed effort to restrict and control
foreign investment without alienating foreign investors.

Mexico's diversification of its international involvement was multi-pronged. It included the expansion of
diplomatic insitutitons, a more active role promoting not
only Latin American but also Third World demands, and a
search for more trade partners. Although Mexico still did
not become a member of the Non-Aligned Movement, Echeverria
supported numerous NAM positions and Mexico began to send an
observer to the NAM summit meetings. Shapira argues that the
"simgle most important foreign policy initiative under
Echeverria was the promotion of the Charter of States'
Economic Rights and Duties, purporting to reorganize and
codify a new international economic order."36 Echeverria
presented the Charter at the Third UNCTAD meeting in 1972.
It was adopted in late 1974 by the UN General Assembly. The
Charter suggested general, redistributive reforms of the
international economic order. It emphasized the duty of

industrialized states to aid the poor nations. Although the explanation for the state of the international economic order was a radical one, Echeverria's prescriptions were reformist.37 The document supports the:

> unfettered right of all nations to dispose of their natural resources; the right of all nations to define the responsibilities of private property before the public interest; the renunciation of armed or economic coercion against sovereign states; submission of foreign capital to the laws of the host nation; prohibition against multinational corporations from intervening in the internal affairs of nations; abolition of discriminatory trade practices against poor nations; earning proportional to levels of development; agreements providing for fair and stable prices for basic products; low cost tranferral of technology to underdeveloped nations and low interest, untied financing for the development of dependent nations.38

Although the Charter, like other UNCTAD resolutions, has done little if anything to alleviate the conditions of the poorest nations, it was a very important symbol of Echeverria's efforts to move Mexico away from a foreign policy aimed primarily at the United States and toward a policy tying Mexico with the rest of the Third World.

A second aspect of Echeverria's internationalization of Mexico's foreign policy involved several initiatives in the Organization of American States and other Latin American regional organizations. In the OAS Mexico pushed for democratization of the organization by promoting principles such as "ideological pluralism" and a simple majority vote procedure as part of the OAS charter.39 Mexico had been a member of the Latin American Free Trade Association (LAFTA) since its inception in 1960 but Echeverria was more assertive in his interest in LAFTA than were any of his predecessors.40 Further, Echeverria initiated policies promoting new regional institutions. He, and Mexico, led the movement to form the Sistema Economico Latino-Americano (SELA) and the Naviera Multinacional del Caribe (NAMUCAR), both of which are economic organizaions designed to promote Latin American interests in competition with the United States and other developed countries. SELA excludes the United States and includes Cuba. Its purpose is to improve planning in sectors crucial to economic development such as energy and agriculture. NAMUCAR came out of SELA and was a

Caribbean shipping business.[41]

A third component of the move to expand Mexico's involvement and role in the Third World took the form of an augmentation of Mexico's diplomatic corps. In 1972 Mexico established diplomatic ties with the People's Republic of China. In 1973 diplomatic ties were established with six nations, in 1974 with five more, and in 1975 with thirty-three additional states.[42] The 1975 expansion was particularly large and significant in that the majority of the new embassies were opened in African, Arab, and Asian countries. Mexico's relations with Cuba also became warmer in 1975.

A final characteristic of the expanding Mexican international role involved Echeverria's aggressive and vocal critique of imperialism. He made numerous trips in Latin America and elsewhere to promote his Charter. From Argentina, Brazil, Venezuela, and Peru he criticized the industrialized nations for preventing the weak from achieving independence and growth.[43] Further, Echeverria made one departure from the traditional Mexican principle of non-intervention in the affairs of others when he broke relations with the military government in Chile after the 1973 coup. The refusal to maintain relations with the Chilean military was followed by a repudiation of Franco's Spain, South Africa, and Rhodesia.[44] A final act placing Mexico in the Third World camp and in opposition to the United States was Mexico's support for the "Zionism is Racism" resolution in the United Nations in 1975. Through these actions Echeverria attempted to become a leader of the Third World and a major spokesman of its principles and positions.

Along with the diversification and Third World orientation of Mexican international policies, the government also passed legislation designed to restrict foreign control of the Mexican economy. There were two major acts: the Law on the Transfer of Technology and a foreign investment law. The transfer of technology law requires firms to use domestic technology and is intended to help correct the balance of payments deficit.[45] The foreign investment law is designed to protect and promote Mexican industry. Foreign investment may not constitute more than 49% of the capital and foreign investors may not constitute more than 49% of the firm's management. Further:

foreign investment should promote Mexico's development, complement national investment (not displace it), help

Mexico's balance of payments, create jobs, train Mexican
nationals, use national goods in manufacturing, finance
its operations from abroad, diversify investment assist
regional integration, help backward regions of the nation, avoid monopolistic practices, contribute to research, respect national values, identify with Mexican
interests as well as a few other things.46

The law was not intended to prevent foreign investment and
is ambiguous enough to give the Mexican government
considerable flexibility in interpretation.

Luis Echeverria's policies were significant departures
from traditional Mexican foreign policies in several respects. His major contributions included the expansion of
Mexican international activities, an initial effort to
decrease economic dependence upon the United States and the
establishment of a closer bond with the Third World. His
policies were new but not radical. They did not
fundamentally change the economic realities of United
States-Mexico relations. The most important characteristic
of the new policies was their symbolism for they represented
a new outlook that may or may not have indicated a sympathy
for, empathy with and concern about the conditions of the
poor nations of the Third World, but surely demonstrated a
change in Mexico's self-image in regard to its relationship
with the US. The transformation goes beyond domestic ideological competition and Echeverria's efforts to placate
domestic reformists. The policies were carried on by
Echeverria's more conservative successor, Jose Lopez
Portillo, and have become tied with a concern for treatment
"as an equal" by the United States. To some extent, the
change in Mexican self-image from a country needing and
wanting a "special relationship" with the United States to a
country capable of an independent and important
international role, perhaps including leadership of the
Third World and certainly including equality with the United
States, has been due to the promise seen in oil. The policies of Echeverria may not have succeeded in making Mexico
either independent or a leader of the Third World, but they
were important reflections of the perceptions of the Mexican
elite in the 1970's.

Lopez Portillo's policies did not depart significantly
from his predecessor's. He inherited immense domestic
problems, some of which were due to Echeverria's policies.
He also inherited strained relations with the United States
caused by Echeverria's occasional insults and the continued

heavy economic dependence upon the US. Lopez Portillo sustained the policies of involvement in the Third World, particularly Latin American regional organizations. He participated in the transformation of the Latin American Free Trade Association into the Asociacion Latinoamericana de Integracion (ALADI). Lopez Portillo continued Mexico's involvement in SELA and worked with Venezuela to establish the Caribbean Basin oil facility., This organization "converts part of the purchase price of petroleum into low cost loans for development."47 Mexico has been involved in other Third World organizations such as UNCTAD, the International Labor Organization, the World Health Organization, and the conferences on the Law of the Sea.48 Also consistent with the Third World outlook was Mexico's growing involvement in Central American and the Caribbean under Lopez Portillo. In its current position on Central American matters, developed by Lopez Portillo, Mexico has advocated an interpretation of the situation opposite of that of the United States. McShane described Lopez Portillo's policy as follows:

Mexico's current Caribbean basin policy has three discernible orientations. They are: (1) diplomatic and material support of reformist, even revolutionary, opposition movements and de jure governments where Mexican policy makers feel that they represent a progressive force moving the particular country toward a more democratic and socially responsive position; (2) continued economic collaboration and normal diplomatic relations even with those countries, including the United States, which which Mexican policy increasingly conflicts; and (3) the pursuit of regional stability via the strengthening of multilateral organizations, growing intra-regional economic cooperation, and the provision of economic and technical assistance. 49

In accordance with these positions, Mexico continued the break from tradition signified by Echeverria's active support of the Chilean Revolution under Allende and opposition to the coup-imposed military government that replaced him. Lopez Portillo openly supported the anti-Somoza forces in the Nicaraguan revolution. Mexico broke relations with Somoza in 1979 and opposed the suggestion by the United States than an Inter-American peacekeeping force be sent to Nicaragua.50 Mexico's government also objected to US aid to the government forces in El Salvador. McShane

argues that Mexico's Caribbean policy is antipathetic to the
United States position and purposely so. Mexico is
interested in reducing US influence in the area and has
carried its disagreement with the United States beyond the
question of "ideological pluralism" in the region to issues
such as fishing rights and territorial waters.51 Further,
Riding argued that Mexico's policy under Lopez Portillo was
its first concerted and clear policy toward Central America.
He quotes Lopez Portillo's response to a question concerning
possible damage to United States-Mexican relations resulting
from Mexico's Central American policy:

> Mexico has its own foreign policy. It takes its
> decisions independently and it expresses them in a world
> in which, fortunately, Mexico's voice is being heard and
> will be heard more and more.52

At the same time, Mexico's relations with Cuba improved
throughout the Lopez Portillo administration. His reception
of Fidel Castro in May, 1979, was particularly noteworthy
for its warmth and harmony. Lopez Portillo's relations with
other communist countries also demonstrated the independent
thrust of recent Mexican international policies. He took a
fifteen-day trip to Eastern Europe in May, 1978, and discussed the possibility of supplying oil to Cuba in exchange for
Russian shipments to Spain.53

Despite this interest in Third World affairs, under
Lopez Portillo Mexico maintained the same insistence upon
freedom from commitments giving other governments influence
in determining its policies that was evident during the
Echeverria administration. For example, Echeverria decided
that Mexico would not join OPEC. Lopez Portillo retained
this policy and in addition refused to join GATT in 1980
despite US pressure to do so. The prospect of joining OPEC
is political dynamite in Mexico where national control of
the petroleum industry is embedded in the national revolutionary myth and is a symbol of national independence. The
GATT issue in 1980 was also a subject of hot domestic political dispute partly inspired by nationalism. Whether Lopez
Portillo favored or opposed GATT membership he was open to
domestic criticism.54

During the Lopez Portillo administration the search for
new trading partners continued. In accordance with the
general strategy of increasing Mexico's economic options and
decreasing the economic role of the United States in the
Mexican economy through the diversification of trade

partners, Mexico restricted the sale of its most crucial export item during the late 1970's, petroleum. In November, 1980, the decision was made to prohibit any single country from purchasing more than 50% of Mexico's petroleum exports. By expanding its customers to include France, West Germany and Japan, Mexico hoped to enhance its ability "to obtain investment commitments and pay lower prices for the technology it purchases from these countries."55

The promise of oil was one of the most significant elements in the transformation of the Mexican image of Mexico. Petroleum has been part of Mexico's revolutionary mystique since the nationalization acts of 1938. Petroleum and the state's petroleum company, PEMEX, have "symbolized the essences of nationalism; national dignity, economic independence, and state sovereignty...Pemex is regarded as a standard-bearer of Mexico's struggles for economic independence. Its creation as a major institution of the Revolution is closely linked to the establishment of respect for state sovereignty within Mexico."56 The discoveries of enormous new petroleum fields in 1976 and PEMEX's increasing technological expertise giving it the ability to extract the petroleum and by-products have given Mexico the capacity to produce enough hydrocarbon energy to satisfy domestic needs and to become a major exporter. Petroleum was initially seen as the basis for Mexican developmental programs but the abundant energy sources coupled with the nationalistic significance of petroleum has fueled internal debate concerning the export of petroleum resources, particularly to the United States. Lopez Portillo and other officials justified the use of petroleum revenues for resolving developmental problems that came to a crisis point in 1976 by arguing that petroleum offered Mexico its best and perhaps last chance to achieve socioeconomic development. To fail to use petroleum for this purpose, he argued, could be considered unpatriotic.57

A logical corollary to the notion that petroleum would provide Mexico with its best chance for development was the idea that it would also provide Mexico with a powerful lever with which to gain independence from the United States. Ronfeldt, Nehring, and Gandara explain the thinking as follows:

Mexico's political leaders and policy intellectuals have been especially alert to matters affecting state sovereignty. They believe that the state is still not strong enough, that it stands at a critical stage in its development, and that it represents the only real bulwark against pressures from the United States. In their public debates, issues involving the United States are frequently interpreted more in terms of the risks for Mexico's sovereignty and freedom of action than in terms of the possible benefits for Mexico's economic growth--which is where Americans normally put the emphasis.58

The Mexican policy making elite thus strives for independence and self-determination. Petroleum, always a nationalistic symbol, became the key to these goals for Mexico in the 1970's. As Mexican confidence in the size of the reserves grew there arose an increased emphasis on the need for a new relationship with the United States in which Mexico was treated as an equal and with respect. These concerns were fueled by the natural gas controversy discussed in the next chapter which occurred during the first years in office of both Lopez Portillo and Jimmy Carter. Lopez Portillo stated in 1978 that the discovery of oil reserves in Mexico had enabled him "to demonstrate to Mexicans and foreigners alike that Mexico was not a bankrupt country, that it had people who knew how to work and who were capable of identifying the country's problems, using its own resources to solve them, and maintaining political and economic independence without hostilities or isolationism."59 Lopez Portillo clearly saw petroleum as an opening through which the world would be shown that Mexicans are responsible and capable citizens equal to those in other countries. Mexican officials have also expressed the opinion that Mexican hydrocarbons "can represent a pressure of worldwide significance" and that therefore Mexican hydrocarbons must be given their true value.60 A final component of the transformation of the Mexican self-image was a stress on a recognition of Mexican equality by the United States. Thus, Lopez Portillo complained that "`Mexico is neither on a list of United States priorities nor even on that of United States respect.'"61 He also announced that future relations between the United States and Mexico must lead to a "balanced, fair, respectful, and dignified relationship between two neighbors."62

The transformation of Mexican self-image and foreign policies is apparent in the actions and words of Mexican leaders. The record of the 1970s shows great emphasis on independence from the United States, diversified ties with other states, and a movement toward Third World positions on

international issues. Mexico's new foreign policies began
before the discovery of large hydrocarbon reserves and the
prospects for economic growth they offered. The fact that
Mexico remained tightly tied to the United States in economic matters did not alter the willingness of Mexico's
leaders to establish a new foreign policy direction. It also
did not alter the desire to be treated "as an equal." Both
the record of actions and the statements of American policy
makers, however, indicate that Mexico was seen and treated
as a dependent type of state as that psychological image has
been described above. This means that United States policies
reflected the assumptions associated with that particular
psychological category. Thus, Mexico was expected to support
the United States internationally, to be economically permeable, flexible in its international positions, culturally
less advanced than the American society, to have goals
relatively compatible with those of the United States, to be
only moderately determined in pursuing its own goals, and to
give in to diplomatic and/or economic pressure without
attempting to inflict retribution on the United States.

UNITED STATES POLICIES TOWARD MEXICO: 1960-1976

A review of US policies toward Mexico is necessary for
two reasons: First, to set forth the historical record, a
record which indicates that the prevailing and policy-
dominant view of Mexico was of a dependent type of state;
and second, to set the scene in which the 1977 and 1979
negotiations on the importation of natural gas took place.

In the 1960's, Mexico was not a high-technology industrialized nation. It was poor, it exported mainly primarly
products to the United States, and it was dominated economically by the United States. Given these conditions, the
dependent image would seem to be an appropriate one for
Mexico. The record of American policies toward Mexico indicates that the dependent image did dominate perceptions of
Mexico and that this type of state image did adequately
structure the environment during the 1960's. The United
States achieved most of its goals regarding Mexico during
this era. When Mexico began to change in the 1970's,
however, the dependent image produced policies that were
counter-productive.

The prevailing view of Mexico during the 1960's may not
have been as contemptuous as that of William J. Bryant in
1908 when he announced that "[b]efore twenty years, North

America will have swallowed Mexico. The absorption of that country by ours is necessary and inevitable..." but American actions still evinced a view of Mexico as a dependent.63

There were relatively few conflicts between the two countries but when disputes did erupt the response of the United States was often a unilateral decision pronouncing a solution with the expectation that Mexico would comply. The general post-war policy of the United States toward Mexico reflected a concern for continued political and economic stabilty in Mexico and the maintenance of Mexican support for the United States in the Cold War. American policy makers appear to have recognized the existence of competing political groups in Mexico and to have assumed that the elite, having interests essentially compatible with those of the United States, could control these competing groups. Thus, American policy makers were not concerned about Mexico's refusal to support the expulsion of Cuba from the OAS in the early 1960's because Mexico did not translate that into general support for Cuba and gave no indication that it would oppose US interests in the Western hemisphere or criticize US Cold War policies in general. Mexico's position was interpreted as a necessary, symbolically independent foreign policy which "contributed to political stability and the strength of the regime in Mexico."64

> Mexican independence fostered the image of a ruling party committed to its revolutionary heritage, an image that was a major source of the Partido Revolutionario Institucional's grip on the Mexican people, and thus of the stability so appreciated by American officials. For the Mexicans, it was a classic case of liberalism abroad in the service of conservatism at home...[T]he agreement among policy makers in the U.S. and Mexico to disagree about Cold War policies in the Western Hemisphere prevented high-level diplomatic conflicts over such issues as U.S. policies toward Guatemala, Cuba, and the Dominican Republic.65

As Wyman describes this view of the issue it reflects the essentially patronizing approach to a state classified as a dependent. Although the political society is seen in a manner complex enough to recognize the existence of competing policy advocates, it is not assumed that they have a legitimate voice in their own polities nor are they seen as capable of recognizing and resentng patronizing behavior by the United States. As Wyman argues, Mexican support of

Cuba was not interpreted as a rejection of the American view of the Soviet Union.66 The fact that the Mexican support for Cuba was actually very constrained could only have lent support to this view among US policy makers.

In bilateral conflicts btween Mexico and the United States the position of the United States government during the 1960's and the early 1970's was to pursue the narrowest interests of the United States. Donald Wyman has constructed a summary of presidential level conflicts between the two states for the period after the Mexican Revolution through 1971. The pattern of outcomes since World War II shows that of fifteen post-war conflicts, five have had results closer to Mexico's position, eight closer to the United States position, and two were equally favorable in outcome.67 More interesting than the simple number of wins and losses is the nature of the resolutions. In seven of the conflicts with outcomes favorable to the United States, the United states did not compromise its position. Mexico, however, compromised on all but one of the issues resolved in its favor. Further, the issue in which Mexico refused to compromise and was victorious was not one resulting in an agreement of great benefit to Mexico. This particular case occurred in 1947. Mexico had adopted protectionist trade measures which violated a trade agreement between the United States and Mexico. As a result, the United States requested a renegotiation of the treaty: Mexico refused and the treaty simply died.

Of the disputes during the 1960's and early 1970's in which some sort of settlement was reached, seven favored the United States and three favored Mexico. Four of the conflicts were settled through compromise and three of these were among those settled in Mexico's favor. Of the issues settled in the interest if the United States, only the Coastal Fisheries issue was settled through compromise. In this conflict, Mexico wanted to exclude US fishermen from Mexican-claimed waters. The United States government refused to recognize Mexico's claim and in 1967 a compromise was reached permitting both countries to fish in the coastal waters claimed by the other.

Four of the major conflicts between Mexico and the United States during the 1960's involved trade issues, specifically the question of restrictions on Mexican imports to the United States. Mexico sought reductions in US limits on agricultural commodities and in duties on Mexican manufactured exports to the US. The US refused.68 During the 1950's and 1960's, Mexico sought a change in the decision by the United States government to subsidize exports of cotton. The United States agreed to set up a consultative mechanism but did not change its policy. In the 1960's Mexico attempted to prevent a reduction in its sugar quota but was unsuccessful. Finally, from 1957 through 1965 Mexico attempted to convince the United States to remove restrictions on the import of lead and zinc from Mexico without success. The issues in which Mexico's objectives were attained included the Colorado River Salinity controversy, settled in 1973 when the United States agreed to decrease the salinity of the river (for which the United States was responsible in the first place); the dispute over jurisdiction of a portion of land that had been relocated by the shift of the Colorado River; and the end of the Bracero Program in 1964. In the latter issue Mexico obtained an extention of the legal authority for the program in the face of increasing domestic pressure in the United States for an end to the program.

A final major controversy resulting in Mexican compliance with the wishes of the US involved efforts by the US to convince Mexico to increase its drug control policing at the border. Mexico was unwilling to comply so the United States began Operation Intercept in which border agents slowly searched for drugs at the border crossings. The effect was to clog traffic thereby sharply reducing tourism to Mexico, a very important source of income. Mexico quickly agreed to a joint drug control program.

The record of conflict resolution between the United States and Mexico during the 1960's indicates that the notion of a "special relationship" never described the interaction between these two neighbors. As Wyman points out, the issues in which Mexico's interests were victorious were issues with little importance or cost to the United States. In the area of trade policy, Mexican problems and need for access to the United States market were not important considerations for US decision makers. Apparently, American officials were unwilling to sustain any domestic political costs in exchange for granting Mexico trade concessions that were important for Mexican growth and stability. Concessions and compromise were not seen as necessary since United States-Mexican affairs continued amicably even after a decision was made against Mexico. As will be seen in the next chapter, by the late 1970's when the image of Mexico had changed for many policy makers, American officials became more willing to accept political costs in exchange for the broader interests involved in

United States-Mexican relations.

More important that the preference for solutions not requiring a domestic political sacrifice by American policy makers is the rarity of compromise and the tendency to take unilateral steps leaving Mexico with few options but to accept the decision or risk a costly struggle. By the mid-1970's Mexico had become more resistant to this form of conflict resolution but American tactics remained basically the same until the natural gas controvery of 1977 and its aftermath prompted a change.

Of the major disputes between Mexico and the United States during the first half of the 1970's, two stand out as particularly important. The first concerns the import surcharge of 1971. Mexico requested an exemption from the 10% import surcharge instituted by the Nixon Administration in its efforts to restructure US foreign economic policies in 1971. The US refused to grant Mexico an exemption: so much for the "special relationship." The pattern continued with the United States' decision in 1974 that Mexico (and all other states) could not belong to a cartel such as OPEC and also be eligible for General System of Preferences benefits. This position was interpreted by Mexico as conflicting with the Charter of Economic Rights and Duties of Nations.70 Mexico initially resisted the GSP system but did participate in a limited fashion in 1976 and increased its activity substantially by 1977.71 As in the 1960's, Mexico had been handed decisions by the United States with little choice but to comply or take an ill-afforded and costly positions in opposition to the United States.

The record of United States actions in issues involving Mexico sketched above is, of course, incomplete. The purpose of this section was not to present a concise and full history of United States-Mexican relations up to the gas negotiations but to take a panoramic overview of the general pattern. Some of the major issues that arose between the two countries were discussed, issues that are exemplary of the conduct of US policy toward Mexico. In general, the pattern indicates that Mexico was seen as and acted as a dependent type of state. Mexico's international support for the United States was so secure that no real concern arose about Mexico's Cuba policy. Economic interaction with Mexico flourished despite the consistent refusal of the United States to grant trade concessions to Mexico for agricultural items, Mexico's primary export. In conflicts with Mexico, US officials frequently doggedly pursued the basic interests of the United States and usually achieved their goals with

164

Mexican compliance. When Mexico did win a victory at the bargaining table in a conflict with the United States it usually occurred after Mexican officals agreed to a compromise. This must have supported the American perception of Mexican flexibility.

The next chapter examines change in the Mexican self-image and the response of United States policy makers. It is evident that the dominant view of Mexico in 1977 was an image of a dependent. A minority saw Mexico as a neutral type of state by that time. The majority, however, expected the typical dependent type of state behavior when natural gas negotiations began in 1977. When the behavior was not what was expected, the image of Mexico began to change for many policy makers, but not all. The two views of Mexico correspond to two very different policy positions concerning access to Mexico's energy resources. The adaptation of American policy makers to the Mexico of the 1970's is the topic of the next chapter.

NOTES

1. J.I. Dominguez, "Introduction," in J.I. Dominguez, (ed.), Mexico's Political Economy: Challenges at Home and Abroad (Beverly Hills: Sage, 1982), p. 12.
2. O. Pellicer de Brody, "Mexico in the 1970's and Itselations
Relations with the United States," in J. Cotler and R. Fagen (eds.), Latin America and the United States: The Changing Political Realities (Stanford: Stanford University Press, 1974), p. 320.
3. Dominguez, p. 12.
4. de Brody, p. 321.
5. Dominguez, p. 12-13 and de Brody, p. 321.
6. L.R. Randall, "Mexican Development and Its Effects Upon United States Trade," in R. McBride (ed.), Mexico and the United States (Englewood Cliffs, New Jersey: Prentice-Hall, 1981), p. 53.
7. R. Villareal and R. de Villreal, "Mexico's Development Strategy," in S.K. Purcell (ed.), Mexico-United States Relations (New York: Academy of Political Science, 1981), p. 98.
8. C. W. Reynolds, "The Structure of the Economic Relationship," in S. K. Purcell (ed.), Mexico-United States

Relations (New York: Academy of Political Science, 1981), p. 125.

9. W.B. Cobb, "Tourism as a Positive Factor in the Mexican Economy and in Mexican Foreign Relations," in R. McBride (ed.), Mexico and the United States (Englewood Cliffs, New Jersey: Prentice-Hall, 1981), p. 179.

10. J.I. Dominguez, "International Reverberations of a Dynamic Political Economy," in J.I. Dominguez (ed.), Mexico's Political Economy: Challenges at Home and Abroad (Beverly Hills: Sage, 1982), p. 180.

11. Ibid., p. 179-180.

12. Ibid., p. 181.

13. Ibid.

14. Ibid., p. 182.

15. A. Wichtrich, "Mexican-American Commercial Relations," in R. McBride (ed.), Mexico and the United States (Englewood Cliffs, New Jersey: Prentice-Hall, 1981), p. 85.

16. Ibid.

17. Ibid., p. 81.

18. S. Weintraub, "Organizing the U.S.-Mexican Relationship," in R.D. Erb and S.R. Ross (eds.), United States Relations with Mexico (Washington, D.C.: American Enterprise Institute for Public Policy Research, 1981).

19. World Business Weekly January 26, 1981.

20. B.C. Netschert, "Mexican Energy Resources and U.S. Energy Requirements," in J.R. Ladman, D.J. Baldwin, and E. Bergman (eds.), U.S.-Mexican Energy Relationships (Lexington, Massachusetts: Lexington Books, 1981), p. 137.

21. Banamex Cultural Foundation, U.S. Views on Mexico, 2nd quarter, 1982, p. 97.

22. M. del Rosario Green, "Mexico's Economic Dependence," in S.K. Purcell (ed.), Mexico-United States Relations (New York: Academy of Political Science, 1981), p. 107.

23. Ibid., p. 110-111.

24. Ibid., p. 111.

25. Ibid.

26. Ibid.

27. Dominguez, "International Reverberations," p. 176.

28. G.E. Poitras, "Mexico's 'New' Foreign Policy," Inter-American Economic Affairs 28 (1974): 60.

29. Ibid., p. 61.

30. C.A. Astiz (ed.), Latin American International Politics (Notre Dame, Indiana: University of Notre Dame Press, 1969), p. 84.

31. D.L. Wyman, "Dependence and Conflict in U.S.-Mexican Relations, 1920-1975," in R. Paarlberg (ed.), Diplomatic Dispute: U.S. Conflict with Iran, Japan, and Mexico (Cambridge, Massachusetts: Harvard University Prss, 1978), p. 105.

32. Astiz, p. 82.

33. de Brody, p. 318.

34. For a full discussion of the influences on Echeverria's foreign policies see G. Poitras, p. 67.

35. Y. Shapira, "Mexico's Foreign Policy under Echeverria: A Retrospect," Inter-American Economic Affairs 31 (1978): p. 33.

36. Ibid., p. 48.

37. Poitras, p. 67.

38. Ibid., p. 68.

39. Shapira, p. 49.

40. W.H. Hamilton, "Mexico's 'New' Foreign Policy: A Re-examination," Inter-American Economic Affairs 29 (1975): 55.

41. G. Poitras, "Mexico's Foreign Policy in an Age of Inter-dependence," in E.G. Ferris and J.K. Lincoln (eds.), Latin American Foreign Policies: Global and Regional Dimensions (Boulder: Westview Press, 1981), p. 107.

42. Shapira, p. 50.

43. Poitras, "Mexico's 'New' Foreign Policy," p. 71-73.

44. Shapira, p. 52.

45. Poitras, "Mexico's 'New' Foreign Policy," p. 69.

46. Ibid.

47. S.K. Purcell, "The Mexico-U.S. Relationship," Foreign Affairs 60 (1981-82): 384.

48. Poitras, "Mexico's Foreign Policy in an Age of Inter-dependence," p. 112-113.

49. J.F. McShane, "Emerging Regional Power: Mexico's Role in the Caribbean Basin," in E.G. Ferris and J.K. Lincoln (eds.), Latin American Foreign Policies: Global and Regional Dimensions (Boulder: Westview Press, 1981), p. 197.

50. The New York Times, April 24, 1980.

51. McShane, p. 197.

52. A. Riding, "Mexico, Braced by Oil, Steps Out in Foreign Affairs," The New York Times, April 24, 1980.

53. Los Angeles Times, May 28, 1978.

54. For a discussion of the GATT issue during this time see The New York Times, June 9, 1979. On the decision not to join OPEC see G. Grayson, The Politics of Mexican Oil (Pittsburgh: Pittsburgh University Press, 1980).

55. Purcell, "The Mexico-U.S. Relationship," p. 384.

56. D. Ronfeldt, R. Nehring, and A. Gandara, Mexico's Petroleum and U.S. Policy: Implications for the 1980s (Santa Monica, California: Rand Corporation, 1980), p. vii.

57. Ibid., p. 57.

58. Ibid., p. 59.

59. United States, National Security Council, Presidential Review Memorandum 41: Summary Report. This report is unpublished and was released under the Freedom of Information Act in 1982, p. 4-5.

60. Lopez Portillo was quoted in The Journal of Commerce, September 6, 1978.

61. G.W. McGee, "A U.S. Perspective," in S.R. Ross and R.D. Erb (eds.), U.S. Policies toward Mexico: Perceptions and Perspectives (Washington, D.C.: American Enterprise Institute, 1979), p. 41.

62. A. Riding, "Mexico Angry at U.S. as Carter Visit Nears," The New York Times, February 11, 1979.

63. Quoted in M.R. Millor, Mexico's Oil: Catalyst for a New Relationship with the U.S. (Boulder, Colorado: Westview Press, 1982), p. 17.

64. Wyman, p. 105.

65. Ibid.

66. Ibid.

67. See table in Wyman, p. 100-103.

68. Ibid., p. 102.

69. Ibid., p. 103.

70. Wichtrich, p. 78.

71. Ibid., p. 91.

6

The Effects of Psychological Categories on Political Decision Making: The Case of US-Mexican Natural Gas Negotiations

An examination of bargaining between the US and Mexico presents the opportunity to return to the hypotheses presented in Chapter 4 and to evaluate the impact of images on behavior. This chapter proceeds through several steps. First, it will be argued that two views of Mexico existed in 1977. The argument is supported through a detailed examination of the statements and policy proposals made by government officials. The policy areas rviewed include immigration, trade, and energy, thereby demonstrating that the assumptions behind each image are consistent across several policy domains and are not solely associated with energy. Throughout this review it is clear that policy makers differed in their evaluations of Mexico in exactly those areas wherein the dependent and neutral images differ. They had different perceptions of Mexican culture, support for the United States, flexibility, compatibility with US goals, and economic strength.

After the two psychological images are discussed, the chapter turns to the gas negotiations. The dominance of the dependent image of Mexico is apparent through the policies advocated by American negotiators and the information they accepted as true. It is argued that policy makers with a neutral image of Mexico dominated the 1979 negotiations having different goals and using very different bargaining tactics.

Several cautions must be presented before proceding. First, there is no argument here that one group of policy makers was right and one wrong. The thrust of this argument is simple: that policy makers make evaluations and predictions because of their perceptions. The decision makers in both sets of gas negotiations approached the issue

170

in a way that they thought would produce an agreement. While one approach worked well and the other did not, the purpose of this study is not to attempt to describe what the negotiators who failed should have done to achieve success. The purpose of this project is to give a psychological explanation for the actions of both sets of negotiators. A second purpose is to examine the process involved in adapting to change. It is also important to note that this study concerns only American perceptions of Mexico and does not examine the difficulties created by Mexican negotiators. Many of the officials and former officials who were interviewed for this study clearly felt that the United States negotiators were unfairly cast as the "bad guys" in the press reports of this story and the Mexicans were given the "good guy" role without deserving it. If this study appears to do the same it is only because the Mexican perceptions and actions are not analyzed with the same scrutiny applied to American perceptions. Although there may be bigots and ego-maniacs in the government, these psychological phenomena are not being studied here. This is an examination of the inescapable need to organize and simplify political reality and the painful process of adapting to change in that reality.

Finally, a note about the explanatory claims made here. In this case a very strong correlation exists between the psychological category in which Mexico was placed and US bargaining behavior. This study does not claim to prove cause and effect: It merely makes an argument suggesting that that relationship is very possible. In addition, the claim is made in the conclusion that a psychological explanation is undoubtedly the strongest explanation for this case.

TWO VIEWS OF MEXICO

As the gas negotiations began in 1977 the dominant view of Mexico in the United States government was that of a dependent type of state. Although not universally held, this view seemed particularly pervasive in the Departments of Energy, Commerce, Treasury, Immigration and Naturalization, and some segments of the State Department such as the Bureau of Economic and Business Affairs. The view was also held by many members of Congress. The minority view of Mexico, the neutral image, appears to have been most evident in the Latin American Bureau and, in particular, the Mexican Desk, of the State Department. It was also evident among some members of Congress including Senators Church and Kennedy and Representative Manuel Lujan, and in the National Security Council. The nautral gas business community's image of Mexico was interesting. They either shared the neutral view or saw Mexico as so far removed from the ideal-typical dependent that it could not be expected to behave as a dependent on the natural gas issue. Their arguments essentially reflect the neutral image.

As has been stated, the dependent view is an image of another state depicting it as economically weak, culturally inferior, flexible in foreign policy formation, supportive of and compatible with the goals of the United States, and basically harmless. The types of policy proposals that correspond to this view are proposals that advocate pursuing the interests of the perceiver's state without particular concern for the interests of the dependent because the dependent will not harm the perceiver's state; because it will be flexible, maleable, and submissive; and because, given the perception of cultural inferiority, the dependent is expected to benefit from the policies designed by the perceiver's state anyway. The interests of the perceiver's state should be pursued vigorously, using economic coercion if necessary.

The dependent view of Mexico was dominant in 1977 and resulted in a policy approach that was described by current and former officials as a "hardline" or "globalist" position that extended through the trade, immigration, and energy issues. The advocates of his position were labeled "hardliners" or "globalists" because they argued that the United States should not concede to Mexican demands, particularly when those demands conflicted with the global policies of the US. As will be seen in the sketch below of their trade, immigration and energy positions, these individuals not only assumed that the dependent state would do as the United States desired but that by following US wishes, the dependent would also benefit. This, in turn, reflects the paternalism of the dependent image wherein the people of the other society are seen as rather childlike and in need of guidance. Although this view was held by individuals who varied greatly in their experience with and knowledge of Mexico--ranging from bureaucrats and representatives who spent little time on Mexican affairs to members of the United States Embassy in Mexico--those who were experts on Mexico tended in general to have the neutral view. This reflects the argument presented in Chapter 4 that ranges of experience affect judges' relative perceptions of the same object.

The dominance of the dependent view of Mexico was clear in Congress in 1977 and it heavily influenced trade matters.1 Agreements between the United States and Mexico in 1977 reflected the image in several ways. The United States, for example, initially refused continuing Mexican requests for reduced barriers against their agricultural and manufactured foods and imposed new restraints on lending to Mexico by private American banks.2 In accordance with the notion that Mexico should receive no concessions that conflict with US global policies, the United States insisted that any reduction in trade barriers would have to be matched by a Mexican quid pro quo. After two years of negotiations, an agreement was reached in which the US reduced tariffs on some fruits and vegetables in exchange for a quid pro quo reduction in Mexican trade barriers. This is by no means an equal exchange since the cost to Mexico in reducing trade barriers are much greater than the costs to the United States. Mexico's agreement to the United States position was important for it signified a break by Mexico from the Third World position that the less developed countries should offer no concessions in return for improved trading conditions with the developed countries.3 Hearings before the Joint Economic Committee in January, 1977, frankly expressed the power of this resistance to concessions for Mexico in the United States political arena. The president of the American Chamber of Commerce in Mexico told the committee that the position was an inescapable political reality in the United States but that "with serious study you can find areas in which both sides, both economies, can mutually benefit from these types of agreements."4 The implication is that the demand for trade concessions by Mexico would continue despite the inequality of quid pro quo conditions. Trade agreements that were mutually beneficial would not be offered.

If trade policy gives some indication of the presence of the dependent image of Mexico, the complementary outlook on the illegal immigration issue present in the American political scene is even more clearly demonstrative of that image. Explanations for the cause of illegal immigration by those who hold the image is particularly interesting. Wayne Cornelius describes this view as follows:

Proponents of this argument tend to place most or all of the blame for illegal immigration upon Mexico, citing

particularly its failure (until lately) to control population growth and its failure to invest public resources
in ways that would increase employment. They
conveniently neglect the past and continuing role of the
United States in fomenting labor migration from
Mexico...To those who prefer to blame the contemporary
immigration problem on "irresponsible" Mexican decision
makers, the history of U.S. involvement in Mexican
development is irrelevant, or simply inconvenient. Their
basic position is that "the U.S., doesn't owe Mexico
anything," and certainly nothing to the Mexican
political elite. The tendency is to see Mexico as a
spoiled child -- a petulant, ungrateful one, at that! --
who has already gotten away with too much and must be
"disciplined" by tough U.S. law enforcement efforts if
it is ever to mend its ways.5

As Cornelius described this view, it holds many of the
major characteristics that are part of the dependent image.
The state and its elite are seen as childlike, or inferior,
ineffective, incapable of resolving their own problems, and
responsive only to tough ("but fair") actions by the perceiver's state that is supposed to set them on the correct
course. In the immigration issue, the people who hold this
view argue for tough control of the United States-Mexican
border as a method of cutting down on immigration and increasing Mexico's incentives to provide jobs for the poor.
This is the essence of the Carter Administration's proposals
of August, 1977. At that time Carter, without consulting
Mexico, announced a proprosal for a new immigration policy.
He advocated giving "full amnesty" to illegal residents
living in the United States for at least seven years. Those
living in the US before January, 1977, but less than seven
years, would be able to stay in the United States to work.
Control of the border would be tightened dramatically.
Carter requested 260 additional Immigration and
Naturalization inspectors and two thousand addition border
enforcement officers.6 Finally, the proposal called for
"forge-proof" social security cards and fines for employers
of undocumented workers.7

The evaluation of the Immigration issue produced by the
dependent image was evident in many segments of American
society during the 1970's. National newspapers had numerous
editorials decrying the employment of undocumented workers
when Americans were jobless but ignoring information
indicating that US employment firgures were not affected by

illegal immigration.[8] The dislike of poor Mexicans employed in an uncontrolled fashion in the United States generally reflects the cultural contempt of the dependent image. The distain for Mexican culture and, of course, the people, can be seen in numerous statements by government officials concerning the immigration issue. They range from the desires of Representative James Scheuer (D-New York) to seal the border, strengthen deportation laws, and "work with" the Mexican government to establish more effective birth control programs in Mexico to the statment of the Secretary of Labor in August 1977 complaining that although "illegal aliens work cheaply, their children might agitate for better living conditions and become the `civil rights problem of the 1980s.'"[9]

The dependent image of Mexico was also very evident in the reasoning behind the dominant evaluation of United States-Mexican relations in the energy area. The entire energy issue will be discussed in great length in the next section. However, a brief sketch of this particular outlook on Mexican energy is important in developing the basic dependent view. The dependent image of Mexico appeared among the top level members of the Department of Energy, the State Department's Bureau of Economic and Business Affairs, and many members of Congress. Several assumptions were made by these people regarding Mexican energy resources, the United States' interest in Mexican energy resources, and the policies that should be followed by the United States. First, they assumed that the United States was, and is, the only market for Mexican hydrocarbons, particularly natural gas. It was believed that Mexico could not find other buyers for its gas due to the technological skill and financial costs involved in doing so.[10] Further, the estimation of US interests resulted in the opinion that the United States should press for easy access to large amounts of Mexican hydrocarbons at the lowest possible price.[11] Mexican gas and petroleum were viewed as a potential alternative to OPEC expected to portend a "salutary effect on energy prices."[12] Finally, Mexican hydrocarbons were expected to offer the United States the opportunity to increase its own exports and thus alleviate its deficit to some extent.[13]

These policy approaches and expectations reflect the dependent image of Mexico in several ways. First, there is a sense that Mexico is incapable of finding either the technology needed to diversify its markets for hydrocarbons or competitive buyers. Mexico is seen as unsophisticated in terms of both technology and financial and business skill.

While even the most nationalistic Mexican would probably agree that the United states is the most profitable market for Mexican energy resources, those Americans with the dependent view of Mexico assumed that Mexico could not create alternative markets. These policy makers were familiar with OPEC countries, particularly those that had had to undertake very costly and technologically complex projects such as building natural gas liquification plants. They were aware of the historical record in which other poor countries had managed to find technology, supplies, and markets for their energy resources. Nevertheless, they continued to believe that Mexico could not do the same. The assumption that Mexico had no choice but to sell its hydrocarbons to the United States became very important as an information selecting screen in the 1977 negotiations.

A second indication that these expectations come from the dependent image is the assumption that gas and oil from Mexico would be inexpensive and would thus alleviate the financial strain caused by OPEC's prices. During 1977 American policy makers repeatedly stated that they were willing to pay Mexico a "fair" price for its gas and petroleum. What is interesting is the definition of a "fair" price. A "fair" price for Mexican natural gas was seen by some policy makers to be no higher than the price paid to Canada for its natural gas. A more extreme definition of a "fair" price floating around government circles during 1977 was the price the government permitted for domestic producers (who were regulated) to charge, a price much lower than that paid for Canadian gas. Neither definition of a "fair" price permitted Mexico the opportunity to set a price that the market would bear. The advocates of this position believed that Mexico was being "unreasonable" when its officials took a stand on the pricing of the energy resources that was based on the price that the Mexican officials believed the market would bear and that would not necessarily give the United States a cheap supply.14 As in the assessment of the immigration and trade issues, the position reflects the assumption that the United States can best decide what is fair and beneficial for both parties. The decision is one that actually promotes the interests of the United States to the neglect of Mexico's.

A final aspect of this evaluation of the enegy issue that reflects the dependent image of Mexico is the idea that by importing natural gas from Mexico the US would have the opportunity to reduce its own trade deficit. The notion demonstrates indifference to the complexities of the econo-

176

mic situation in the dependent country and the single-minded pursuit of the interests of the perceiver's state. Before the United States had settled on a natural gas importation agreement with Mexico, for example, a US delegation to Mexico led by Secretary of State Vance began to press for trade concessions from Mexico. One of the delegation's officials remarked, "We are encouraging them to stop thinking like a developing country" and to lower their trade barriers to allow more imports from the United States.15 Not only does this statement and the whole conception of trade with Mexico reflect the paternalism of the dependent image, it is an unabashed demonstration of the pursuit of the interests of the United States to the neglect of Mexico's. It is difficult to imagine an American offical making an equivalent statement about Great Britain or assuming that trade agreements with Great Britain could be so one-sided in benefits. The assumptions concerning access to Mexico's hydrocarbons also reflect the perception of a very permeable and maleable economy in that it is accompanied by the belief that Mexico would continue to permit domination by the United States in trade by lowering trade barriers to offset the improvement in the balance of trade resulting from Mexican energy exports.

The dependent image can be found across numerous issues areas and it is accompanied by consistent assumptions that the United States can and will continue to dominate. The statement below by Senator Lloyd Bentsen is an example of this evaluation of United States-Mexican relations:

[T]here are a number of disparate areas where trade-offs can be made between our two countries which will entail scant sacrifice by each government, but which can reap important mutual benefits.

Mexico should modify its unfair fishing agreement with the United States to allow continued U.S. access to rich Mexican shrimping grounds. Mexico should agree to provide the United States with an assured supply of Mexican oil at reasonable prices to allow us to reduce our dependence on politically unstable Arab oil; Mexico should cooperate fully with the U.S. Drug Enforcement Agency officials to combat the illegal drug traffic which is the source of 90 percent of the heroin in the United States today and Mexico should move to reduce its spiralling rate of population growth in order to stem the tide of illegal immigration into United States.

In return, the United States should provide Mexico

with the expertise to diversify its manufacturing sector
and expand employment opportunities at home, the United
States should move to enforce more stringently its own
drug abuse laws and dry up the market for Mexican heroin
and the United States should move to control the
dangerous flow of automatic weapons to Mexican drug
peddlers and anti-government groups.

Beyond that, the United States can be of great
assistance in the area of agricultural insect control...

Both sides should avoid hurdling useless comments
against the other.

Instead, we should offer Mexico our moral, political,
and technological support for developing solutions to
the serious inequalities riddling that nation.

Mexico should demonstrate its interest in smoothing
the waters of United States-Mexican relations by doing
its won fair share to resolve bilateral problems.16

Bentsen's statement is a good example of the evaluation of
bilateral relations with Mexico made by those with the
ideal-typical dependent image of Mexico. Mexico, in this
view, should give the United States everything it needs from
cheap energy to access to Mexican fishing grounds, in
exchange for the "moral, political, and technological
support" of the United States. Not only does he advocate
that Mexico provide the United States with open access to
its hydrocarbons, he also argues that Mexico should stop the
flow of drugs into the United States which the United
States, for its part, makes an effort to enforce its own
laws. In this statement one can see the sense of cultural
superiority, the sense of US economic domination, and the
expectation that Mexico will naturally be supportive of US
goals, all of which are part of the dependent image.

The view of Mexico reflected in Bentsen's statement and
its concomitant policy proposals dominated the horizons in
the United States in 1977 when the first gas negotiations
took place. Nevertheless, the neutral view was also apparent
at that time and reflected an understanding of the change in
Mexico's self-perceptions and foreign policies. Those who
saw Mexico through the neutral image differed in their
evaluations of that country and US interests in precisely
the areas in which the neutral image differs from the dependent image.

The basic policy stance of those who held this view of
Mexico was that the interests of the United States lie in
long-term stability and amicable relations with Mexico

rather than victory on individual issues. Economic or dollar interests are not of primary importance. Instead, it was argued, it is essential that the United States have good relations with Mexico even if it loses on some specific issues. The United States should take Mexican interests into account in policy proposals.17 Those who viewed Mexico as a neutral also argued that Mexican nationalism is a constant and extremely important factor in any bargaining situation and must be taken into account if mutually satisfactory agreements are to be obtained. They recognized the cultural differences between the United States and Mexico and argued that if American policy makers do not give credence to the cultural fact of Mexican nationalism they can expect diffi- cult and ineffectual bargaining. The evaluation of United States interests in regard to Mexico reflects the behavioral expectations associated with the neutral image. These policy advocates argued that bargaining results cannot always favor the economic interests of the United States because the goals of the US and Mexico are not always compatible. There- fore, there is a basis for fearing serious ruptures in bilateral relations. Mexican officials cannot be counted upon for unquestioning support for and compliance with the United States, particularly if American policy makers insist on pressing for agreements completely favorable to the United States. As with the dependent view, the elements of the neutral image of Mexico can be seen in specific policy positions across the trade, immigration, and energy issues.

An early discussion of the policy implications of the neutral view in the area of trade can be found in the debate among two academics and two businessmen in hearings before the Subcommittee on Inter-American Economic Relationships of the Joint Economic Committee of Congress. The witnesses delivered a complex analysis of the Mexican political scene and advocated trade policies that accounted for Mexican interests as well as those of the United States. A representative of the business community, for example, des- cribed Mexico as a "different" and proud country with a complicated political system. He argued that Mexico's national plans and long-range goals should be understood as should its commitment to the Third World and independence of the United States.18 He further argued that American investors have found Mexican restrictions on foreign investment tolerable and that "reasonable profits can be made in spite of controls and restrictions."19 Good relations between the United States and Mexico were seen as contingent upon the United States' ability to respect

"Mexico's desire for economic and cultural independence.'"20 The witnesses at the hearings recommended that the United States pursue its long-range interests of stability in Mexico and amicable relations with Mexico by not insisting upon a quid pro quo in trade concessions.21 Rather than attempting to pressure Mexico to accept policies favorable to the US, it was argued that the United States should accept some risks for its domestic concerns in exchange for the promotion of long range interests of both countries. Although there was disagreement among the witnesses concerning the feasibility of these policy proposals, the essential idea was agreed to by all.22 In later forumlations of this line of reasoning it was argued that the US should be aware of and take into account Mexican interests when making decisions on trade matters that affect Mexico. In short, American policy makers should be aware of the potential impact of American economic strength on the Mexican economy and strive for policies that do not hurt Mexican developmental efforts.23

This trade policy argument reflects the neutral image in several ways. First, it is not assumed that the interests and goals of the two countries are compatible but that differences will arise and must be accounted for in policy formulation. Further, it is suggested that trade arrangements can be satisfactory for both countries even if they do not conform to US preferences. Thus, the best policy is not one imposed by the US but one that combines important decisions by both countries. These evaluations of the issue give equal importance to Mexican goals, warn against attempting to force Mexico to accept policies that conflict with these goals, and assume that Mexican policies can adequately deal with Mexico's interests. This evaluation is in contrast to that made by those with a dependent image who assume that Mexico will benefit from US decisions. There is also an obvious difference in cultural assessments since those with the neutral image see Mexican culture as different but equal to that of the United States.

As in trade, the neutral image is accompanied by a different policy position in the immigration area. There was widespread objection to the Carter immigration proposals of August, 1977, and these proposals were never acted upon in legislation. The position of those who saw Mexico as a neutral was that the fact of large numbers of illegal immigrants to the United States constituted a safety valve through which Mexico could release some of its unemployed. It helped alleviate poverty, particularly in the rural areas. Again, the real interest of the United States was seen to lie in long-run stability in Mexico and therefore it was not in the United States interests to block immigration from Mexico. The position is expressed by Edward Kennedy:

> [O]ur real concern should be with Mexico's economic and social development over the long term...Over the long run, only a Mexican economy which is sound and a Mexican society which is prosperous and peaceful will settle the immigration issue.We thus have the highest interest in jobs in Mexico...
>
> It becomes crucial that the excess revenues generated by oil and gas be invested in activities which are heavily labor-intensive particularly tourism, rural development, and small business. The Mexican Government intends to make such investments and the United States should offer every assistance it can render -- for example, in agriculture and fishing -- whenever called upon. In trade negotiations, the United States should recognize the role it can play in creating a large number of jobs, understanding where Mexico needs access to U.S. markets and avoiding the promotion of labor-saving machines for an economy which is labor-rich. 24

The more specific "solution" to the immigration problem came in the form of a proposal for more research into the causes and consequences of immigration from Mexico. As was mentioned above, there was great protest after Carter publicized his immigration proposals. In October 1978, Carter signed a bill establishing a select commission to study immigration from Mexico. The bill was "part of a larger bill that made minor revisions in the U.S. Immigration and Nationality Act" pushed through the Senate by Senator Kennedy.25 The argument behind the bill was that proposals for changing the immigration pattern at the border were useless until the nation's entire immigration policy was reviewed and updated. The bill was supported by others in Congress as well as the commissioner of immigration, Leonel Castillo. In essence, the bill indicates a recognition of the role of the United States as a "push" factor in illegal immigration and as out of date in its immigration laws. Thus, unlike those with the dependent view of Mexico, Mexico is not seen as entirely responsible for the problem by this group. Further, advocates of this view recognize the extremely sensitive nature of the immigration issue for the Mexican government.

The image of Mexico manifested by this group of policy makers was different from the first group's image in several ways. First, there is an understanding that the immigration issue is not a problem caused by Mexico and inflicted upon the United States. Instead, it is seen as a complex problem produced by factors on both sides of the border. Further, the methods for resolving the issue do not constitute forcing the other side to take action in response to unilateral decisions by the perceiver's state. In the proposals mentioned by Kennedy, for example, the United States was urged to render assistance "when called upon" and not by fiat. These recommendations are reflective of the neutral view in that they demonstrate the assumption that Mexico is capable of tackling its own problems, that the United States cannot dictate solutions, and that Mexico must be treated as an equal. An additional aspect of this position on immigration is its recognition of the embarrassment the flow of workers in search of employment causes Mexican officials. The offense to Mexican nationalism caused by this reality is understood and taken as a serious factor in any effort to form agreements on programs to control the problem.

The alternative view of the energy issue in 1977 also indicated the presence of a neutral image of Mexico. During the summers of 1981 and 1982 individuals who were either involved in the gas negotiations of 1977 or were in government and closely following those negotiations were interviewed. There was a consensus among the interviewees that the second view of the energy question in 1977 argued that United States interests lay in Mexico's long-term development. The United States should, it was thought, strive for stable prices and stable access to Mexican energy resources in amounts most appropriate for the Mexican economy. These policy advocates were described as having a "broader" view of the energy issue [26] and as advocating that Mexico be treated as an equal.27 It was also argued that given the importance of petroleum as a symbol of Mexican nationalism, for American officials to expect and announce publicly that Mexico will provide the United States with easy access to and cheap supplies of energy resources is to produce exactly the opposite result. A public demonstration of such an outlook, they argued, would be political dynamite in Mexico and would arouse and increase Mexican suspicions that the United States has imperialistic designs on Mexican petroleum. Finally, advocates of the position argued in 1977 that Mexico should be willing to pay a premium price for Mexican

energy resources because of the crucial role they would play
in Mexican development and economic growth. It was argued
that it is in the best interest of the United States to pay
a higher price for Mexican gas and petroleum as a method of
promoting economic growth and thus stability in Mexico.29

   Once again, the characteristics of the neutral view of
Mexico can be seen in this approach to the energy issue.
First, there is the familiar assumption that an energy deal
would have to serve the needs and requirements of both
countries. Second, there is a recognition that Mexico will
not necessarily be flexible and grant the United States all
the oil ad gas it wants at a low price. Instead, it is
expected that Mexico will pursue its own interests in determining price and supply. Third, there is the recognition of
the political importance of Mexican nationalism, the primary
cultural factor affecting bilateral relations. Finally,
there is a recognition that the goals of the United States,
easy access to cheap energy supplies and decreasing dependence upon OPEC, may not be compatible with those of Mexico,
to get as high a price as possible for its energy resources.
Table 16 summarizes the positions taken by those with the
neutral or dependent image of Mexico in the three issue
areas. Having set forth an outline of the two images in
general,it is now possible to turn to the 1977 negotiations.

THE NATURAL GAS NEGOTIATIONS OF 1977

Background and Context: Mexico

   In 1976 Mexico elected Jose Lopez Portillo as
President. He inherited a recently devalued peso, a public
debt that had increased fivefold to $20 billion during his
predecessor's administration, and interest payments for the
debt of $1.07 billion for an economy with an annual Gross
Domestic Product of only $79 billion.30 Shortly after his
inauguration, Lopez Portillo announced major new estimates
of Mexico's "proven" crude oil, natural gas, and natural
gas liquids reserves. The estimates were increased from
6,338 million to 11,160 million barrels of petroleum.31
After Lopez Portillo's ascent to the presidency he appointed
Jorge Diaz Serrano as director of PEMEX. Before the Lopez
Portillo administration began, PEMEX was dominated by the
"Generation of 1938," a group of nationalistic
conservationists opposed to exporting petroluem,
particularly to the United States.32 Lopez Portillo had

doubts about the reserve estimates of the state oil monopoly

TABLE 16

Dependent and Neutral Image Positions on Three Issues

Issue	Dependent Image	Neutral Image
Trade:	No trade concessions on matters potentially detrimental to US.In other area, no concessions without a quid pro quo. No advantages for Mexico contrary to US international policies.	Mexican and US economic interests differ. US should not demand quid pro quo and should accept some political costs in exchange for Mexican growth and stability.
Immigration:	Stop illegal immigration. US bears no responsibility US should increase border patrols, encourage Mexican birth control and efforts to control flow of people.	Illegal immigration to US is an important but embarrassing safety valve for Mexico. US should not block access to US lest Mexican stability be threatened. Study causes, consequences, review US laws.
Energy:	Obtain as large a supply hydrocarbons as possible. Use Mexican resources to improve US balance of payments and counteract OPEC. Pay Mexico no more than Canada. Mexico will have to sell to US.	Major US interest lies in stable access and prices for Mexican hyrocarbons. Petroleum is an important symbol of Mexican independence. Any attempt to pressure Mexico for lower prices may backfire. Prices should be determined by the international market.

during the Echeverria administration. The new PEMEX director set out to varify his new estimates of Mexico's proven reserves and to transform PEMEX from a "bloated" and corrupt bureaucracy into an efficient modern agency in order to expand Mexico's energy production.33 PEMEX hired the American consulting firm of DeGoyler and McNaughton to verify the reserve estimates. It verified and increased the estimates which improved international confidence in Mexico's future and interest in its hydrcarbons.34 On October 26, 1977, Diaz Serrano announced a "potential" reserve estimate of 120 billion barrels of petroleum.35 Lopez Portillo planned to use oil as a solution to Mexico's short-run economic difficulties and as an engine for future development. Mexico was to become energy self-sufficient at home and a net hydrocarbon exporter. Tables 17 through 19 show the PEMEX estimates of crude oil, liquid gas, and natural gas from 1970 through 1978. Note the jump in estimates of proved reserves between 1975 and 1977. (It is important to note that these are "proved" reserves. "Proved" reserves are known recoverable resources from wells that have already been drilled or have already proven successful.36 "Probable"

TABLE 17

Proved Reserves of Crude Oil in Mexico by Region, 1970-1978
(millions of barrels)

Area	1970	1971	1972	1973	1974	1975	1976	1977	1978
Northern Zone	407	389	375	330	304	305	540	543	478
Chicontepec	--	--	--	--	--	--	--	--	10,960
Poza Rica	1,109	1,689	1,639	1,592	1,556	1,579	5,652	1,609	1,530
Angnostura	2	2	1	1	4	22	63	101	97
Southern Zone	762	758	818	924	1,222	1,524	4,181	6,833	12,549
Total	2,880	2,837	2,833	2,847	3,087	3,431	6,436	9,086	25,615

Source: Petroleos Mexicanos, Memoria de Labores, Mexico City (annual). Cited in D. Ronfeldt, R. Nehring, and A. Gandara,
(Continued)

Mexico's Petroleum and U.S. Policy: Implications for the
1980s (Santa Monica: Rand Corporation, 1980), p. 5.

TABLE 18

Proved Reserves of Natural Gas in Mexico by Region, 1970-
1978 (in billions of cubic feet)

Area	1970	1971	1972	1973	1974	1975	1976	1977	1978
Northern Zone	3,448	3,526	3,509	3,590	3,775	3,889	7,924	11,260	13,519
Chicontepec	-	-	-	-	-	-	-	-	-
Poza Rica	2,956	2,903	2,847	2,786	2,744	2,791	2,861	2,833	2,761
Angostura	120	115	104	109	106	390	758	814	979
Southern Zone	4,871	4,425	4,292	4,327	3,560	4,854	7,866	12,960	14,901

Total:
1970: 11,396; 1971: 10,969; 1972: 10,752; 1973: 10,812;
1974: 11,185; 1975: 11,924; 1976: 19,410; 1977: 27,868
1978: 58,935

Source: Petroleos Mexicanos, Memoria de Labores, Mexico City
(annual). Cited in D. Ronfeldt, R. Nehring, and A. Gandara,
Mexico's Petroleum and U.S. Policy: Implications for the
1980's (Santa Monica: Rand Corporation, 1980), p. 5.

reserves are "estimated recoverable resources from known
productive fields that have not yet been developed,
including new discoveries lacking development wells and
estimated additional reserves from planned secondary
recovery projects that are being installed or are yet to be
installed."37 Finally, "potential" reserves are all ultimately exploitable reserves including "cumulative
production, proved and probable reserves, additional
recovery from known fields, and undiscovered resources."38
After the 1976 and subsequent announcements of Mexico's new
oil reserves, estimates of Mexico's future role as an oil
producer ranged from comparisons with Saudi Arabia with 200
billion barrels of oil to pronouncements that Mexico would

become another Middle East with 700 billion barrels. In part, this confusion was due to mixing estimates of proved, probable, and potential reserves.39)

TABLE 19

Proved Reserves of Natural Gas Liquids in Mexico by Region, 1970-1978 (in millions of barrels)

Area	1970	1971	1972	1973	1974	1975	1976	1977	1978
Northern Zone	80	78	94	107	115	126	228	278	323
Chicontepec	---	---	---	---	---	---	---	---	1,325
Poza Rica	137	134	132	129	127	129	135	132	128
Agnostura	---	---	---	*	*	19	41	45	57
Southern Zone	193	185	179	186	207	248	440	888	960
Total:	409	397	405	423	450	522	843	1,342	2,792

Source: Petroleos Mexicanos, Memoria de Labores, Mexico City (annual). Cited in D. Ronfeldt, R. Nehring, and A. Gandara, Mexico's Petroleum and U.S. Policy: Implications for the 1980's (Santa Monica: Rand Corporation), p. 5.

Given the important role that hydrocarbons were to play in Mexico's economic recovery, Lopez Portillo naturally planned for massive investments in PEMEX to increase production. In the six-year program announced after Lopez Portillo took office it was proclaimed that production would increase from 894,219 barrels per day (bpd) in 1976 to 2.25 million in 1982. Natural gas production would also increase to 3.6 billion cubic feet per day, twice its 1976 rate.40 The program required $15.5 billion with which to finance 3,476 new wells, to increase offshore drilling efforts, to fund rapid geological and seismological production, and to improve refining capacity, and petro-chemical production.41

The six-year plan has been modified several times since it was first presented to account for surpassed production targets (PEMEX daily output reached its 1982 goals by 1980) and to account for additional investment fund requirements.42

The decision to become an energy exporter was by no means uncontroversial in Mexico. Political forces from both the left and right opposed the decision for conservationist and nationalistic reasons. The decision to export petroleum and natural gas, and particularly the decision to build a pipeline through which natural gas would flow to the United States, fueled criticism that Mexico was becoming more, not less, dependent upon the United States by increasing its attachment to the United States energy market. In addition, the government was accused of "offending the goals of the revolution as a result of amendments to the Constitution, secured in 1977, to permit automatic expropriation of lands required for such Pemex operations."43 These lands included the territory needed to build the pipeline to the United States.

Energy production would also be limited because Lopez Portillo was determined not to neglect conservation by exploiting Mexico's energy resources leaving little for future generations. The administration was concerned not only with the preservation of the nation's most important heritage but also with the effects of vast amounts of oil revenues on the economy. The government was quoted frequently as intending to create an "economy with oil" not an "oil economy as occurred in Iran and Venezuela.44

Along with self-imposed limitations on production such as those inspired by nationalism and a desire to control the impact of petroleum revenues on the country's economy, ex-ploitation of energy resources was constrained by various technical and geological factors. For example, Mexico suf-fered from a shortage of oil rigs which made it impossible to sink as many wells as planned. PEMEX sought to solve this problem by contracting with foreign and domestic private companies for equipment and technicians.45 PEMEX production was also limited by a lack of modern port and storage faci-lities.46 By 1980, however, modernization and expansion programs were underway.47 Transportation problems caused by poor roads also caused bottlenecks.

One major geological factor that has been important in determining production levels and was crucial in the decision to build a natural gas pipeline to the United States was the fact that Mexican petroleum has large volumes of natural gas associated with it. Grayson explains it below:

To produce 2 million bpd of oil, the company [Pemex] will have to handle approximately 3.5 billion cfd [cubic

feet per day] of gas, large amounts of which require
"sweetening" -- i.e., the removal of hydrogen sulfide,
carbon dioxide, and other corrosive chemicals. The gas
must also be "stripped" of liquid hydrocarbons.
Absorption plants and cyrogenic units now have a
capacity ... far above the level of domestic
consumption. 48

Mexican petroleum production, therefore, implies the
production of large amounts of natural gas. In order to
increase petroleum extraction Mexico had the options of
either exporting the natural gas, using it domestically, or
flaring and thus wasting it. When the decision was made to
expand petroleum production Mexico could not consume
domestically the resulting natural gas. Therefore, early in
1977 considerations of export plans were undertaken.49
    There were two options available for natural gas ex-
ploitation. The gas could be sent over land through pipelines to its market or it could be liquified. Liquification
involves a process of supercooling the gas, shipping the
liquified gas through specifically constructed tankers, and
regassifying the liquid when it arrives at its import desti-
nation.50 The liquification process is expensive and
dangerous and while some countries, such as Algeria and
Indonesia, have had little choice but to invest in liquification plants, Mexico had the alternative of building a
pipeline to the United States. Liquification does have the
advantage of providing a basis for continual access to
overseas markets but the disadvantages in price were
substantial compared to the pipeline option. Liquification
plant construction would have cost between 7 and 8 billion
dollars and would have required a delay in accruing badly
needed revenue.51 Further, the liquification option would
have brought a profit of 27 cents per thousand cubic feet
(mcf) whereas the pipeline to the United States would have
brought $2.20 at an asking price of $2.60 per mcf.52
Finally, the estimated cost and time of construction indicated a clear advantage in the pipeline option. The pipeline
was estimated to cost $1.5 billion and would have a
construction time of two years. In addition, the pipeline
would "begin to earn foreign exchange at the rate of $3.3
million a day at the outset."53 Fagen concludes that:

    In effect, during the first year of operation the
pipeline would bring in 1 billion dollars, a figure that
would increase each year up to a maximum of 5.2 million

dollars a day when the pipeline would have more than paid for itself, and the foreign exchange earned over its first six years would top 10 billion dollars. As a potential contributor to Mexico's balance of payments, the pipeline seemed foolproof. As a project on which foreign private and public banks might wish to lend, it could hardly have been more attractive. Few projects promise to generate a stream of foreign earnings equal to their total cost in as short a period as the first 18 months of their active life. 54

Although the pipeline seemed to offer the best solution to the question of how to export natural gas, Mexico faced major technical and financial problems that had to be overcome in order for a pipeline to be constructed. Early in 1977 talks began with the Tennessee Gas Transmission Company to develop marketing agreements for the natural gas market in the United States.55 Plans for the pipeline began in the middle of 1977. The pipeline became known as the "gasoducto."

A marketing agreement between Mexico and six gas transmission companies was finalized in August, 1977, in a "Memorandum of Intentions." PEMEX and the consortium of the six gas companies (including Texas Eastern Transmission Corporation, El Paso Natural Gas Company, Transcontinental Gas Pipeline Corporation, Southern Natural Gas Company, Florida Gas Transmission Company, and Tennessee Gas Transmission Company) agreed to import fifty million cubic feet per day initially. This would grow to 2 billion cubic feet per day by 1979 (which was 3% of US gas consumption).56 The Memorandum of Intentions had to be approved by US regulatory agencies, in particular the Department of Energy, before an operating agreement could be finalized between the gas consortium and the Mexican government.

The terms of this agreement are very important because parts of it became crucial in the negotiations between the United States and Mexican governments. The crucial aspects of the agreement were price and escalator clause. Mexico initially demanded "most favored nation status" which would have resulted in a price "equal to that paid for any gas, regardless of source, sold in the U.S. market."57 According to Jack Ray, President of the Tennessee Gas Transmission Company, company officials convinced Mexican officials to accept $2.60 per thousand cubic feet of gas. This would have been lower than the price Mexico would receive under most favored nation conditions, that is, the price paid to

Algeria and Indonesia for liquified natural gas ($3.48 per thousand cubic feet).58 The final agreement settled on a price linked with Number 2 fuel oil delivered to New York Harbor. The actual price under this plan would have been $2.60 per thousand cubic feet.59 The price could be renegotiated every six months and therefore readjusted to any increase in the price of Number 2 fuel oil. Finally, Mexico could limit its exports by choice but the gas transmission companies were obligated to purchase the agreed upon amount whether it needed the supplies or not.60 This was not a major concession by the gas companies because the companies lose money when they have a deficient supply of gas. They are concerned with maintaining an assured adequate supply.61

The link between the price of Mexican natural gas and that of Number 2 fuel oil delivered at New York Harbor was particularly important. The British Thermal Unit (BTU) equivalency formula is a method of equating the price of natural gas with petroleum.62 Number 2 fuel oil price is set at the price of OPEC oil. Therefore, using the BTU equivalency method, the cost of Mexican natural gas could increase in accordance with increases in the price of OPEC oil since the escalator clause agreed to by the gas companies was the price of Number 2 fuel oil. The formula also conceded a higher initial price for Mexican natural gas than other foreign producers with different escalator clauses received. In addition, Number 2 fuel oil is a distillate fuel oil, that is, home heating oil, which is both more expensive and of better quality than residual oil, the fuel used by industry.63 By tying its gas to a relatively expensive formula, Mexico made the gasoducto more attractive to the investors so badly needed to finance the pipeline.64 With this agreement the pipeline would pay for itself in less than two years, even with cost overruns.65

The agreement with the gas consortium was made with the assumption that the construction of the gasoducto would begin and proceed on schedule. This presented additional problems of a financial and technical nature. The financial concerns were a result of a need for $1.0 billion in loans to finance the pipeline.66 The International Monetary Fund had placed a $3 billion ceiling on Mexico's ability to borrow money as part of an austerity program resulting from the 1976 devaluation of the peso. There were fears that the IMF would not lift the restriction which would mean that Mexico would have only $2 billion borrowing leeway left under IMF rules for all of its projects. Ultimately the IMF agreed to consider funds borrowed for the gasoducto as a separate issue and not a deduction from Mexico's spending limit.67 Other private and public financial sources were eager to participate in Mexico's oil bonanza. The Export-Import Bank offered Mexico $340 million to "assist in financing the acquisition in the United States and exportation to Mexico of American goods and services" needed for the pipeline construction.68 An additional $250 million was approved for equipment needed for natural gas production and petroleum production and refining.69

Finally, in 1977, Mexico required technical assistance for the construction project. The pipeline was designed to be 48 inches in diameter and to run from the oil fields of Chiapas-Tabasco 800 miles north to the city of Reynosa (just south of the Texas border) after linking with the industrial Mexican city of Monterrey on the way. The pipeline was to be the largest in the Western Hemisphere and required steel mill capacity beyond that available in the United States. The largest pipeline existing at the time was only 42 inches in diameter.70 Further, the pipeline had to travel through some difficult terrain, had to be covered in concrete, required heavy equipment for placement and refined technology for operation and for removing sulfur and liquids before the gas could be pumped into the pipe.71 Pipeline engineering is complex and required the expertise of the American firms which had recently constructed the Alaskan pipeline and were therefore familiar with many of the technical problems faced in Mexico.72

After overcoming all of these obstacles and settling upon an agreement with the six gas companies, pipeline construction began. The letter of intent signed with the gas consortium had to be approved by the end of December, 1977, since it was to expire in January, 1978. Thus, during the months between August and December, talks ensued. The United States government and Mexico debated the issue as the Energy Department decided whether or not to approve the agreement. When the United States government in effect rejected the agreement in December, 1977, pipeline construction was well underway.

In summary, from the Mexican side of the situation the atmosphere was one in which the gas companies and PEMEX had made an agreement satisfactory to both sides. Mexico had embarked on ambitious export and development programs, and there was general international interest in the prospect of Mexico's future as a major energy producer. The gas deal was not as opportune from the United States' standpoint as will be seen through a brief sketch of the situation in the

United States at the beginning of the bargaining rounds.

Background and Context: The United States

The formation of energy policy in the United States involves many agencies and individuals. In the late 1970s the primary actors included the Department of Energy (particularly the secretary of Energy and the Office of the Assistance Secretary for International Affairs) and the State Department (including the Secretary of State, the Bureau of Economic and Business Affairs, Security Assistance, Science and Technology, Oceans and International Environmental and Scientific Affairs, the Policy Planning Staff, and the pertinent geographic bureaus). The Department of Treasury is also involved in energy matters including the offices of the Under Secretary for Monetary Affairs and the Assistant Secretaries for international Affairs, Economic Policy, and Tax Policy. Because of the importance of energy supplies for national security, the Defense Department is included in the energy policy forum. Finally, the National Security Council is included and played an important role in the construction of energy policy during the Carter Administration.73 The major international energy policy issues were considered in the executive Office, particularly the NSC, and were usually debated by an interagency task force on an ad hoc basis.74 This frequently resulted in small deliberative groups involving a "cadre of officials from key agencies and offices including DOE, State, Treasury, Defense, CIA and NSC..."75

The role of the Department of Energy in formulating US energy policy was confused. The DOE was assigned a "central role in the formulation of international energy policies" and the Secretary of Energy was supposed to be the President's principle energy advisor.76 However, the State Department still retained primary responsibility for the formation and conduct of international policy related to energy.77 The confusion concerning the power and duties of the various governmental agencies contributed to energy policy making on an ad hoc basis with separate policy issues being considered by several different departments and agencies. Energy policy in the United States both before and after the Carter Administration's efforts to create a national energy policy was so confused that by 1980 the Department of Energy still had "no inventory and/or list of U.S. international energy policies already in effect or being developed."78 Finally, along with all of these federal

193

agencies, Congress periodically becomes involved in energy policy as was the case in 1977 when it debated Carter's Energy bill.

In 1977 the bureaucratic policy making jungle responsible for energy policy tackled an extremely complex political issue. The United States had become heavily dependent upon foreign sources of energy and the Carter Administration had proposed several policies for reducing this dependence. The role of natural gas in the energy issue in 1977 is equally complex. During the period from 1956-1976 natural gas consumption in the United States grew more rapidly than the consumption of petroleum. The increase in natural gas consumption was primarily due to the decline in the price of natural gas during the preceding decade.79 Natural gas consumption rose from 12% to 33% of US energy consumption from 1945-1972.80 Among the heaviest users of natural gas were industry and the utility companies. Forty percent of natural gas consumers were residential or commercial customers. The industrial and utility consumers composed the other 60%.81

Natural gas pricing policy in the United States has been conditioned by regional differences in supplies and consumption patterns. In the 1950's the wellhead price of natural gas was regulated for interstate markets. However, intrastate markets were not regulated.82 A large portion of the residential and commercial users of natural gas were in the Northeast and Midwest, areas that were dependent upon gas piped through interstate pipelines.83 The West and Southeast were also basically non-producing areas and dependent upon piped gas. The states in the South and Southwest were producers of natural gas and consumed gas from the non-regulated intrastate market. Because of these regional geological differences, Congressional representatives from the Northeast, Midwest, Southeast and West generally preferred continued regulation of gas prices in 1977 while the representatives from the South and Southwest did not.84 The proponents of regulation demanded "gas prices at rates no higher than the 1976 level of $1.42 per Mcf whereas Congressmen from the gas-producing states in the South and Southwest have pressed the case for decontrol and market prices of about $2.50-$3.00..."85 The regional differences not only resulted in disagreements about pricing and regulation but they also made the non-producing states susceptible to severe hardships such as those of 1976-1977 when gas shortages occurred. At that time differences in price for the regulated and non-regulated markets grew in the 1970's causing more and more gas to be delivered to the more profitable unregulated intrastate markets.86 This produced a decrease in supply for the gas-importing states. Federal regulations dictated that homes, hospitals, and schools must have priority access to pipeline gas in the interstate market which made it necessary for some industrial users to shut down operations during the winter of 1976-1977.87

The Carter energy plan had to deal with these problems. The administration proposed an increase in the price of natural gas to $1.75 per Mcf for the interstate market while continuing regulation of the market and incorporating the intrastate market into the controlled system. The application of the $1.75 ceiling to the intrastate market was intended to get more gas back into the interstate pipeline.88 By late 1977 the intrastate gas was priced at $2.41 which resulted in 80% of the gas staying in the gas producing states.89 The $1.75 price would have eliminated the disparity in price thus destroying the incentive to keep the gas in the intrastate pipelines. While the administration proposed continued domestic consumer prices below the world market price, its plan called for industrial and utility natural gas users to pay a price above the world market price. In the long run, natural gas prices were to be completely deregulated. Congressional response by late 1977 was as follows:

> The House of Representatives approved the key features of the Administration's proposals for natural gas, including the $1.75 Mcf price level for high priority gas consumers. The Senate, on the other hand, approved a bill that deregulated new gas prices (for onshore gas, immediately; for offshore gas, by the end of 1982) and allocated regulated old gas to high priority customers only until the cost of new gas to low priority users equaled the reasonable cost of substitute fuel oil. In short, the Senate version ensured that low priority customers would never pay more than the substitute cost or world price equivalent for natural gas, whereas high priority customers would continue to benefit from prices below world levels only as long as old gas contracts remained in force.90

Carter resisted political groups and representatives who

called for total decontrol of natural gas prices because of
suspicions that producers of gas already discovered would
accrue "windfall profits" for gas still in the ground.91
Although there was some indication in late 1977 and early
1978 that Carter may have been willing to accept $2.00 per
Mcf for domestic producers, it was assumed that higher
prices would not increase natural gas production because the
underground supply was limited anyway.92 New natural gas
supplies were expected from the Alaskan North Slope,
however, and the price for that gas was expected to be $5.35
per Mcf as of late 1977.93

An important contextual element in 1977 was the price
paid by the United States for imported natural gas. The
largest supplier was Canada which received $2.16 per Mcf.
Further, the Department of Energy had approved in principle
an agreement to import liquified natual gas (LNG) from
Indonesia and Algeria at $3.42 per Mcf. This price was to
increase on the basis of the cost of Indonesian crude and a
fuel price index. The Department of Energy initially
objected to this escalation proposal which partially linked
the increase in prices to OPEC oil prices. (The escalation
plan proposed by Mexico also linked price increases to OPEC
prices.) However, by October, 1978, the escalation proposal
for Algerian and Indonesian LNG was approved.94 Canadian gas
prices were also set on the basis of market prices for
competitive energy commodities. The price of $2.16 per Mcf
was primarily based upon the cost of Arabian light crude
imported into eastern Canada but it also reflected the $2.25
price ceiling for emergency gas sales to the United States
during the winter of 1976-1977 as well as the cost of LNG
supplies scheduled for delivery to the US.95 Thus, imported
natural gas in 1977 was priced through a variety of calcu-
lations including the prices of OPEC crude oil and LNG
imports.

A final aspect of the context in which the natural gas
bargaining of 1977 took place was the shortage of natural
gas in the United States in the winter of 1976. The shortage
made US officals anxious for access to foreign supplies of
natural gas and a second gas shortage was feared for the
winter of 1977-1978.96

The Context: Summary

In general, the bargaining context from August 1977
until December 1977 was one in which a good opportunity for

a new energy relationship between the United States and Mexico was seen as very possible. The Mexican government had committed itself to a gas despite domestic opposition and had acquired loans for the construction of the pipeline. Mexican officals assumed that the deal would be approved and construction of the pipeline began despite the fact that the United States government had not yet approved the arrangement. The United States was involved in an effort to create a national energy plan but was interested in Mexican gas in particular given the fact that the previous winter had witnessed a frightening gas shortage and another shortage was not unexpected. Nevertheless, the price requested by Mexico and agreed to by the gas companies was not satisfactory to the Department of Energy. Mexico was told by the United States government shortly after the letter of intent was signed with the companies that the asking price would be a problem.

Having described the setting in which the negotiations began, it is now possible to turn to the position of the US officials involved in the 1977 bargaining. The examination of the 1977 effort to strike an agreement will begin with a review of the perceptual view of Mexico held by the major participants. It will proceed to an inquiry into their position on the gas issue and the reasons given for that policy position. Finally, the information used to make a decision on whether or not to accept the gas agreement will be discussed. The basic thrust of the argument is that the position of the US negotiators on the particular gas import issue on the bargaining table was a reflection of their view of Mexico as a dependent type of state. The information accepted as accurate and the subsequent expectations concerning Mexico's likely response to the US position is also a reflection of the general image of Mexico. After the 1977 decision is discussed, the analysis will turn to the aftermath, the response to a clear example of new and unexpected behavior by Mexico and the bargaining of 1979.

THE 1977 REJECTION OF MEXICO'S NATURAL GAS OFFER

The Participants' Perception of Mexico and the Gas Issue

As was mentioned above, in August of 1977 Mexico and six natural gas transmission companies signed a letter of intent in which the gas companies agreed to purchase natural

gas from Mexico at a price of $2.60 per thousand cubic feet,
a price linked to Number 2 fuel oil at New York Harbor. By
law, the agreement between the gas companies and Mexico had
to be approved by the United States regulatory agencies.
Thus, the major decision to approve or reject the agreement
fell upon the Department of Energy and Energy Secretary
James Schlesinger. The Department of Energy and the State
Department's Bureau of Economic and Business Affairs were
the major participants in the decision to approve or reject
the agreement. Other self-imposed participants in the issue
were memebers of Congress, Adlai Stevenson in particular. In
addition to these individuals some members of the State
Department participated in an unofficial capacity as confi-
dants and informal advisors to the major participants.

The dominant policy-making group, Schlesinger and other
DOE officials, Julius Katz, Secretary of the State
Department's Bureau of Economic and Business Affairs, Glen
Rase, the petroleum attache in the US Embassy in Mexico, and
others all perceived Mexico as a member of the dependent
category. Their understanding of US interests in general and
the energy issue in particular indicate a dependent view. In
the previous section it was argued that those with the
dependent view of Mexico felt that the United States should
have easy access to Mexican energy resources at a low price.
(The code words were a "fair" and "reasonable" price.) That
price estimate varied from the $2.16 per Mcf that Canada was
receiving for its natural gas to the $1.75 that the US
domestic producers would receive after the passage of the
energy bill in Congress. Information gathered from
interviews with participants in and observers of the
bargaining as well as information available from newspaper
accounts indicate that this was the position of the major
participants in 1977. One Department of Energy official
argued that both then and four years later the interests of
the United States lay in pressing for the best possible
price for Mexican energy supplies and that in 1977 the
United States government was particularly anxious for access
to Mexican natural gas.97 He also complained that the State
Department's Mexican Desk officers would pay anything for
Mexican gas and are always arguing Mexico's view that paying
a high price for gas will help that country develop and lead
to continued stability. Two State Department officials
confirmed this description of the policy advocates. One, a
member of the Bureau of Economic and Business Affairs and
former petroleum attache at the US Embassy in Mexico, argued
that their position in 1977 was that the US should not pay a

price for Mexican gas higher than the Canadian price and
certainly not as high as the price paid for liquified
natural gas.98 A second State Department official with a
different view of Mexico and a different position on the
natural gas issue confirmed that this was the dominant view
in the Economic and Business Affairs division in 1977. He
argued that the distribution of opinion toward Mexico and
Mexican gas ranged from those who wanted a low price for and
plentiful supplies of Mexican gas as an alternative to OPEC
to those who wanted a stable price and stable access to
Mexican gas even if the price must be higher in exchange for
the stability in commerce.99

Without question, the most hardline policy advocate and
the policy makers with the most classic dependent image of
Mexico was James Schlesinger, Secretary of Energy and
primary decision maker in 1977. Schlesinger's view of
Mexico's agreement with the gas companies demonstrates the
dependent image which, in turn, affected his bargaining
behavior and final decisions. Schlesinger's evaluation of
the agreement was that the price Mexico had asked for was
too high. He further agreed that Mexico should receive no
more for its natural gas than Canada received. Finally,
Schlesinger announced publicly that Mexico had neither the
technological ability to use the gas domestically nor the
marketing ability to find other customers and would
eventually have to sell to the United States.100 He believed
that Mexico would ultimately give in to the United States
position on the issue, having no choice but to do so.101
Schlesinger's general view was of a weak, flexible Mexico
that could not and would not resist US pressure and it
reflects the assumption that US interests must come before
Mexican interests. He reportedly thought that the United
States could "strong-arm" Mexico into compliance.102 As will
be seen shortly, this view contributed to a variety of
policy stances as the talks unfolded in 1977 and 1978.

The alternate view of Mexico and the energy issue in
1977 was also described by current and former government
officials.103 According to one participant in the negotiations the Mexican Desk was not involved in the discussions
of 1977 and therefore this voice was quiet in government
circles.104 However, the gas company officials loudly proclaimed their position in the press and into Congress in
late 1977. Their view reflected the neutral image. The gas
company officials essentially saw Mexico and Mexico's
position on the energy agreement as the position an equal
would take. Mexico, they argued, should be expected to act

as any other country would in pursuit of its interests. It should be expected to request the market price for its gas, not a price best suited to the interests of the United States. Florida Gas President Selby Sullivan, for example, argued that opponents of the gas deal were taking an unreasonable stance and were "`taking the position that Mexico is not entitled to as much as we are.'"105 J.L. Ketelsen, Chairman of Tenneco, Inc., claimed that "`With Mexico's economic problems, we couldn't have expected them to sell to us at below world prices. Why should they? What it all boils down to was that our politics came before their politics.'"106 He went on to say:

> Our entire relationship to Mexico is involved here. I don't understand why he didn't take a more enlightened view of this thing instead of approaching it just as an energy question. We could have been of tremendous assistance to Lopez Portillo in getting things underway, even if it was a bad price -- which it wasn't. It's certainly in our best interest to have a strong, effective, friendly neighbor to the south. 107.

Another executive based in Mexico announced that the US government's position on the gas issue was "`just another example of our particularly clod-like approach to Mexico. We seem incapable of affording them any respect.'"108 Gas company officials were also concerned that if the United States insisted on pressing Mexico for a better price Mexico could and would find other buyers for its energy resources.109

Although the gas companies should be expected to oppose the government's position for financial reasons alone, their reaction is interesting and important in other ways. Their counterarguments all stress objections to the government's view of Mexico and propose a different view. Rather than presenting the familiar "government should not interfere with business" complaint, they argue that Mexico's interests are not the same as the United States'; they object to the lack of respect accorded to Mexico; and they argue that Mexico should not be expected to settle for a worse deal than other states get. They also claim that the United States should take a broad view of the situation, attending to the importance of the entire relationship. These points are indicative of the perceptual disagreement between the dependent and neutral images. They stress the equality embodied in the neutral image and the sense that conflict of

interests do exist and can erupt into serious disputes.
Given this understanding of the potential for conflicts that
may spread from one issue into other areas and given the
rejection of the dominant image of Mexico, they emphasize a
concern for the entire relationship, not just the outcome of
the energy issue.

The United States Bargaining Position

From the United States standpoint there were two disadvantages to the agreement between the gas companies and
Mexico. The first was the asking price for Mexican gas which
was higher than that paid for Canadian gas but not as high
as that paid for LNG. The second disadvantage was the escalator clause which tied Mexican gas to expensive Number 2
fuel oil delivered in New York and committed the gas
companies to purchase the total amount agreed to. There were
therefore two issues upon which bargaining should have taken
place. However, the actual discussions never got beyond the
price issue. The first and primary concern and position of
United States officials and other opponents of the agreement
was the price.110 The bargaining focus upon price was
accompanied by a set of expectations concerning Mexican
responses to the United States typical of those with the
dependent view of another country.
    The price issue was the most important aspect of the
agreement from the perspective of the Energy Department
officials. The price was also the most important component
from the Mexican perspective since Lopez Portillo had with-
stood domestic opposition to the pipeline in part by
insisting upon a high price based upon PEMEX's
interpretation of the world market. United States officials,
however, would not concede to Mexico a price higher than
that paid Canada. Three reasons were given by DOE for their
insistence that Mexico not be granted a price higher than
Canada's. First, they claimed that if Mexico obtained a high
price Canada would then ask for a price increase when it
renegotiated its contract in 1978. Second, they argued that
the Mexican price was higher than the government would pay
domestic producers under the proposed energy bill and thus
politically damaging to the Carter Administration, particularly given the fact that the energy issue was being
debated on Capitol Hill at that time. Finally, they argued
that it was their duty to protect the domestic consumer and
that therefore they could not accept such a high price. A

closer examination of the behavior of the Energy Department officials, however, supports a different explanation of their actions. After examining the sequence of events and the response of the DOE officials, particularly Schlesinger, appears to be more a result of a psychological image of Mexico than any other factor. Mexico would not be granted a higher price because Schlesinger did not think that Mexico should get or would insist upon a higher price in the same way that other types of states would. Schlesinger clearly did not think that Mexico could or would withstand US demands for a lower price.

What behavior by US officials indicates that the perception of Mexico caused them to reject the price issue rather than other possible explanation? One major indication that the United States officials, particularly Schlesinger, were taking a position based upon their estimations of what Mexico "deserves" and certain expectations as to how Mexico would behave, is the fact that their primary focus was upon the price. The US officials informed Mexico from the beginning of the agreement that the price Mexico was asking was unacceptable. Given the enormous importance of petroleum to Mexican nationalism and the precarious position the Mexican President had taken, a refusal to accept the price as an initial bargaining stance demonstrates an inability to recognize the importance of Mexican nationalism. Negotiations could also have concentrated on the escalator clause which was a more serious problem from the American standpoint since it governed the increases in price for the gas. US policy makers chose not to discuss the escalator clause, however, until three weeks before the negotiations were ended, at which point the publicity surrounding the price issue made concessions by Mexico very difficult on any point.

A second aspect of the United States position that indicates the importance of the image of Mexico is the fact that the price of Mexican gas had to be no more than equal to the price of Canadian gas. Canada did supply a much larger portion of US natural gas than Mexico would have, at least initially, and it is not surprising that US negotiators would be concerned about the effect of an agreement with Mexico on the Canadian price. They argued that if Mexico got the price it demanded, Canada's price would also go up. Gas company officials, however, told DOE that Canada's price was going to increaseing 1978 whether an agreement was signed with Mexico or not.111 Canadian gas was scheduled to be renegotiated in 1978. At that time Canada

did increase the price of its natural gas from $2.16 per Mcf
to $2.30 and by mid-1979 the price was $2.80 per Mcf. Thus
Canada did not need Mexican inspiration to increase prices.

The interesting aspect of the DOE position is not that
they were wrong about Canadian actions but what it reveals
about the impact of the image of Mexico on the negotiators'
perceptions of the price Mexico should receive for its
natural gas. First, while ordinarily countries do compete to
receive the best possible price for their resources, US
officials were not going to let Mexico take leadership in
setting prices. When Canada increased its prices in 1978
there was no strong resistance by energy officials and there
were no complaints to the press about the price. Mexico's
request for a high price, however, was not treated in the
same manner. Further, DOE officials were inflexible about
the price they were willing to pay Mexico until the last
days of the negotiations at which time they offered Mexico a
higher price but would not pay that price for two years.
Schlesnger was particularly hardline in refusing to give
Mexico any concessions not made to Canada. In fact, he
refused to yield to Mexico the same considerations he gave
to Canada in the natural gas area. One major example
occurred shortly after the final death knell of the 1977-
1978 negotiations. The DOE was considering permitting
Alaskan prices for natural gas to be "rolled in" or averaged
in with cheaper domestically produced gas prices to reduce
the cost to industrial users. The administration was also
considering extending the "rolling in" priviledge to
Canadian gas as well. However, Schlesinger would not give
Mexico the same advantage. One newspaper reported that "Mr.
Schlesinger seemed to go out of his way to depricate the
Mexican supply."112

Finally, although the insistence that Mexico receive
the Canadian price for its gas initially gives the
appearance of equal treatment, that illusion is short lived
when one considers the fact that the Canadian pipelines were
ten years old and paid for. Mexico had borrowed $1.5 billion
to fund its pipeline and had to deduct payments for the line
from natural gas profits. Thus if Canada and Mexico received
the same price for their gas, Canada's revenues would be
greater.

Another price issue that was raised in 1977 was a
comparison between the price Mexico was asking for its gas
and the price the United States would pay for LNG from
Algeria and Indonesia. Mexican officials pointed out that
Mexican gas was not the most expensive of the foreign gas

purchased by the United States since the US was apparently willing to pay $3.42 per Mcf for LNG. This price, in combination with the publicly announced agreement with the gas companies, made it difficult for Lopez Portillo to agree to a lower price for Mexican gas. United States government officials had two replies to this point, one of which was quite interesting. The first reply was that the United States was unwilling to pay the same price for pipeline gas as it was for LNG because of the higher costs involved in LNG production and transportation.113 This response, however, did not address the Mexican point since the Mexican price was subtantially below the LNG price. The second line of reasoning was expressed by a DOE official: When asked if the refusal to consider the comparison between Mexico's price and LNG price was due to differences in production costs he replied that the United States had only agreed to purchase LNG at $3.42 per Mcf "in principle." Since the United States had not at that time actually received and paid for any LNG, Mexico's point was not considered legitimate.114 While one would expect any negotiator, regardless of his or her image of another country, to resist paying the same price for pipeline and LNG gas given the difference in production costs, this was not really the issue in 1977. Mexico's point was simply that the United States was paying more than $2.60 for foreign gas and that Mexico's price was lower than $3.42. In other words, Mexico was not asking for a price equal to LNG. US officials appear to have been closed to Mexican arguments concerning what a "fair" and "reasonable" price amounted to in 1977. Further, while the costs incurred in producng liquified natural gas were considered when agreeing to a purchase price for Algerian and Indonesian gas, the production price for constructing the Mexican pipeline was not considered when Mexico's price was supposed to be no higher than Canada's. The point is simply that Mexico was not treated as these other gas producers were.

If in bargaining Mexico was not to receive the same treatment accorded Canada, the debate concerning what price was a "fair" price for Mexican gas was even more clearly the outcome of its psychological classification. Several different accounts have been given of the price the Carter Administration was willing to pay. The Financial Times, for example, reported that Schlesinger was willing to pay only $1.70 at the time of the termination of the negotiations.115 Most accounts of the negotiations indicate that this is not accurate. The prices that American officials regarded as

acceptable ranged from $1.75 per Mcf, the price proposed for
domestic producers, to the $2.16 paid for Canadian gas, to
$2.60 to be paid two years after the gas started to flow.
The price question had its most interesting public discussion in October of 1977 when Congress became involved in the
deliberations.

One of the first major public debates of the price of
Mexican gas was initiated by Senator Adlai Stevenson in
October, 1977. Stevenson announced in the Senate that the
United States could benefit from Mexican gas in several
ways. It could increase US exports, it would gain another
energy supplier, and it would have an alternative to
OPEC.116 However, Stevenson objected to the fact that the
Export-Import Bank was financing the pipeline to the United
States given the price Mexico was asking for its natural
gas. He argued that the Ex-Im financing could set "a
dangerous precedent for prices of other U.S. energy
imports."117 Hence, Stevenson introduced a resolution stipu-
lating that financing would be withheld until the Secretary
of Energy had approved the price of imported Mexican gas. He
also argued that Mexico could receive the same price for gas
that US producers were to get, $1.75, and "still enjoy an
attractive profit."118 Stevenson introduced a letter from
the Export-Import Bank stating that if PEMEX received $1.75
for its gas Mexico would still accrue "ample funds to cover
operating costs of the pipeline and principal and interest
payments."119 The letter further pointed out that the United
States had purchased natural gas from Mexico during the
shortages of 1976-1977 at $2.25 per Mcf and would probably
have to do so in the coming year.120 Stevenson did not
attempt to get co-sponsors for his resolution. Nevertheless:

> Stevenson's actions alarmed officials at the bank which
> needed Congressional approval of a three-month extension
> of its charter in 1977 and a four-year renewal of its
> charter in 1978. On November 30, 1977, the bank
> announced a postponement of final action on the loans
> pending an "indefinite additional review." Although
> both loans were eventually approved, this blantantly
> political move raised hackles in Mexico City. 121

The most impressive aspect of Stevenson's actions was his
willingness to pronounce that the price paid to US producers
was sufficient for Mexico. Stevenson decided that at $1.75
per thousand cubic feet of gas Mexico would make an adequate
profit and in the process introduced a letter to support his

case in which it was stated that Mexico had already received
$2.25 per Mcf for its gas when it provided emergency sup-
plies to the United States. Stevenson not only set Mexico's
price at the price to be paid to regulated producers in
United States but expected Mexico to accept less than it had
been paid in the past.

Mexico was, as Fagen notes, predictably outraged. The
response of Americans involved in the situation who had a
different view of the issue and of Mexico was also strong.
Jack Ray, President of Tenneco InterAmerica, wrote the
following to Stevenson:

> It is generally agreed that the purpose of the United
> States Export-Import Bank is to foster U.S. exports by
> supplying credit to foreign customers on terms that
> match those available from other countries. The EXIM
> Bank is a successful profit-making government
> institution which paid a $50 million dividend in the
> U.S. Treasury last year... Its success has been based on
> its non-political nature and its adherence to good
> banking practices. There is no precedent whatsoever to
> support your suggestion that EXIM be used as an arm to
> regulate or negotiate energy prices ... Furthermore, the
> threat of removing EXIM credits really have no leverage
> toward obtaining lower prices for Mexican gas as PEMEX
> is not dependent on U.S. credit sources. The $600
> million in goods and services can be obtained quite
> easily from other countries, with credit terms equal to
> those of EXIM Bank. At least five countries have offered
> financing of the project. 122

Ray also pointed out that Stevenson expected Mexico to
accept a price not only below world market prices but equal
to that of a market regulated by the United States
government. He argued that "[i]f the Mexicans had but one
reason to drop the negotiations, it would be the presumption
that they are expected to price their energy below its
commodity value because the United States Government required its domestic producers to do so."123

The Department of Energy used incidents such as Stevenson's remarks to support the argument that Congressional
reaction was a concern that argued against approval of the
gas deal. However, one must consider the order of events to
place causal factors in proper perspective. The United
States government's officials had informed Mexico two months
before Stevenson's complaint that they objected to the price

in the agreement.[124] Therefore, Stevenson's speech did not convince them that opposition was necessary. Furthermore, Leslie Goldman, one of Schlesinger's top aides, consulted with Stevenson before he introduced the resolution on October 19, 1977.[125] Although the details of the meeting have not been revealed, the fact that Energy had already opposed the Mexican price and the importance Stevenson placed on DOE approval of the Mexican price in his resolution indicated that at a minimum Stevenson did not meet with Goldman to inform him that DOE should object to the price.

THE FINAL DECISION: THE USE OF INFORMATION
AND EXPECTED MEXICAN RESPONSE[126]

The primary focus upon price as the major bargaining issue changed little until November, 1977. At that time the United States offered to purchase Mexcian gas at $2.60 per Mcf in two years. In exchange, Mexico would have to agree to change the escalator factor from Number 2 fuel oil, a price linked to OPEC.[127] The offer would have been very costly both financially, given Mexico's growth plans, and politically, given the attention the issue had by this time received in the American and Mexican press. A final meeting took place before Christmas in 1977 at which time Schlesinger demanded that PEMEX accept the price of $2.35 per Mcf which was the price of residual fuel oil (Number 6).[128] This meant that he demanded that Mexico accept both a lower price and a different escalator clause. The Mexicans refused and Lopez Portillo announced on December 22, 1977, that the letter of intent with the oil companies would be permitted to expire on December 31. It has been reported that in a final gesture of contempt Schlesinger kept the Mexican officials waiting for forty-five minutes before the final meeting. He then "greeted them with his feet on his desk, casually announced his disapproval of the price and informed his visitors that, sooner or later, Mexico would have to sell its gas to the United States anyway."[129]

The dependent image of Mexico appears to have colored the bargaining pattern throughout 1977. By focusing on the price the negotiators passed up the opportunity to negotiate on the escalator clause, the more costly aspect of the agreement, and chose instead to argue about the aspect of the agreement to which Mexican nationalism would have been most sensitive. The focus that US negotiators chose to take

is important in two ways: First, it manifests the lack of
attention to the complexities of another country's culture
that is typical of the dependent image perceptual screen.
Second, it indicates that US negotiators were not really
prepared to bargain. They did not review the entire issue
and choose an approach that could slowly lead to discussion
on all of the important aspects of the agreement. Instead,
they presented Mexico with a hardline position on a very
sensitive aspect of the agreement and expected Mexico to
give in. These tactics are also those associated with the
dependent image and have been used in United States-Mexican
relations historically. Further, one must recall that these
tactics were chosen at a time when US officials feared that
the United States would face another natural gas shortage in
the coming winter. This lends more support to the argument
that they were certain that Mexico would accept their offer
and that this certainty was a result of the dependent image
of Mexico. In addition, the determination of a "fair" price
for Mexican gas demonstrated again the extent to which
Mexico was seen as a country less than equal to the United
States and to other countries such as Canada. Mexico was not
given the option to compete on the world market for the
price of its product. The next important question concerns
whether or not the dependent image affected the information
accepted as accurate and the expectation of Mexico's
behavior. In both cases the record indicates that it did.

Schlesinger and other officials based their decision to
reject the agreement between Mexico and the gas companies
upon two basic assumptions. The first was that Mexico had no
other market but the United States. Schlesinger's parting
words to the Mexican officials in December, 1977,
demonstrate the confidence with which he held that view. The
second was the assumption that Mexico could not obtain the
technology required to use the excess gas domestically.
Thus, Mexico should have had two factors pushing it to
accept the United States' price offer. Schlesinger accepted
information that indicated that his assumptions were correct.

When it became clear that Schlesinger and the
Department of Energy were strongly resisting Mexican price
requests, the Mexican government began to hint that it would
search for other buyers.130 The Mexicans also argued that if
the pipeline could not be used to send gas to the United
States due to US intransigence on the price issue, the
pipeline would be diverted and the gas would be sent to
Mexican cities. The government claimed that Mexico would

convert domestic energy sources and either use or flare the
gas before it would be sold to the United States for a price
below that available on the international market.131 After
Schlesinger's pronouncement in December, 1977, Diaz Serrano
remarked that "Americans will never have access to cheap gas
because it is not available inside or outside their
boundaries. We have no reason to accept a low price for our
gas. The price is determined by demand and supply. The price
is not the cost of production plus transportation, but what
it is worth on the free market."132

Given the dependent view of Mexico and the discussion
in Chapter 4 concerning the effects of image on interpretation of information and expectations of behavior,
Schlesinger should have found Mexico's threats unbelievable.
Schlesinger had information available to him that would
confirm either an argument that Mexico could not carry out
its threats or that Mexico could dispose of its gas without
the United States. Schlesinger chose not to accept the
information indicating that Mexico could not sell its gas
without the United States as a market. Several important
pieces of information were available at the time of the
final rejection of Mexico's asking pice. First, Mexico had
been unable to construct a pipeline without foreign financing and technology. Mexico did not have either the technology or money needed to build the pipeline alone. Second,
the CIA had reported that Mexico had "no true economic
choice" but to sell its gas to the United States.133 On the
other hand, Schlesinger also had information available indicating that Mexico could find other sources of technology
and loans and that there were other buyers eager to have
access to Mexican gas. For example, immediately after
Stevenson's denunciation of the Mexican price in Congress
and the resulting snag in Export-Import credits, Mexico
sought and obtained steel and credits from Europe and
Japan.134 Jack Ray also claims that at least five countries
had offered total financing of the pipeline.135 Further,
Mexico and Canada were considering exchanging Mexican crude
oil for Canadian technology, particularly pipeline
technology.136 Thus there was evidence that Mexico had other
sources that could finance the pipeline and provide Mexico
with steel to complete the line. In this way Mexico could
convert to natural gas consumption domestically. This was
important to potential consumers because Mexican petroleum
production is to some extent contingent upon its ability to
dispose of the associated natural gas. If all or too much of
the gas must be flared, Mexico would have to limit petroleum

209

production. But if Mexico could use the gas domestically
then petroleum production could continue. An additional
piece of information that could have influenced Schlesinger
and the DOE was Mexico's announcement that it would take two
years to convert to domestic consumption of the gas. Thus,
if they forced Mexico to set off on this path, they would
have to wait two years before knowing whether or not
Mexico's plan would work. Finally, the DOE had had warnings
from the gas company officials that Mexico would search for
other customers if the price issue was pressed too hard.137

Schlesinger's decision to reject the price in the
agreement between Mexico and the gas consortium was
apparently based upon the acceptance of and belief in the
information that indicated that Mexico could not dispose of
its gas without the United States. The evidence supporting
this analysis is diverse. Not only did Schlesinger inform
the Mexican representatves that they would end up selling to
the United States anyway but several other officials indicated that they too believed Mexico was bluffing when it
insisted that it would not sell its gas to the United States
at a lower price. The Los Angeles Times reported that Mexico
could not sell its gas to any country but the United States
in December, 1977, and The Wall Street Journal quoted
"observers" of the negotiations who claimed that Mexico was
bluffing.138 One unnamed observer was quoted as responding
to Mexico's threats to use the gas to fuel domestic industry
with the comment: "What industry?"139 Finally, in interviews
with a DOE official, the former energy attache in the United
States Embassy in Mexico, and others, the same explanation
for the decision by US negotiators was given: Schlesinger
and the negotiators thought that Mexico would give in and
sell the gas at a lower price after Schlesinger's rejection
of the $2.60 price.140 They also stated that Mexico's actual
response to Schlesinger's position came as a surprise. In
fact, there is some indication that the entire situation did
not receive careful analysis.141 Thus, Schlesinger's confidence that Mexico would accept his decision, a result of
the category in which Mexico was placed, may have contributed to a failure to carefully scrutinize information
indicating that Mexico would not behave as expected.

AFTERMATH

The Mexican government and the American gas companies
were both incensed about the failure of the gas negotia-

tions. Lopez Portillo referring to the humiliation he had suffered by the rejection of the price after his public commitment to the pipeline construction, announced that he had been left "hanging by his paintbrush" after Schlesinger knocked over his ladder.142 Talks between the United States and Mexico continued intermittently for approximately six months. The position of the US negotiators did not change. In fact, DOE officials apparently laughed at the US Ambassador when he reported that Mexican industry was actually switching to natural gas.143 Secretary of State Vance took a party to Mexico in May, 1978, where one member of the team repeated the notion that Mexico had little choice but to sell to the United States and proclaimed the United States' willingness to be "tough but fair" when negotiations began again.144 Negotiations did not begin again. By July, 1978, Mexico embarked on a program to replace residual fuel oil and liquified petroleum with natural gas in domestic industry. Consequently, PEMEX director Diaz Serrano announced that Mexico would have no gas to sell to the United States until domestic needs were satisfied: "After we have quantified [sic] domestic demand, if there is a surplus, if we have a truly interesting offer and if the Government authorizes me we could consider exporting gas."145 The pipeline's name was changed to the Troncal Nacional (National Trunk Line) and the facility was completed in March, 1979.146 The completion of the pipeline meant that Mexico had the facility to transport the gas but it did not mean that Mexico could consume domestically all that it wanted to produce.

While in progress, the 1977 negotiations received little attention outside of the DOE and the State Department's Bureau of Economic and Business Affairs. Consequently, aside from the gas company officials' complaint, few public statements were made by those with a different image of Mexico. After the 1977 decision, however, this changed quickly. The gas decision and United States-Mexican relations in general became a hot topic and a subject of some political debate. Through this debate one can observe the process of adaptation to change. Mexico's response to Schlesinger's decision was strong enough to cause some individuals to change their view of Mexico. Others, particularly Schlesinger, bolstered the dependent view through a fascinating process of mental gymnastics. A review of the debate and eventual change of policy approach toward Mexico follows:

Objections to the decision came from a variety of

sources. Once again, the objections pointed directly to the perceptions that distinguish those with the dependent image from those with a neutral view of Mexico. First, newspaper editorials widely denounced the decision. The Los Angeles Times, for example, argued that "Washington is seeking to take advantage of what it perceived to be a weakness in the Mexican bargaining position. The Mexicans can sell their gas elsewhere -- but only after making heavy investments in gas-liquification facilities."147 They further argued that Mexico was entitled to a fair price, defined as what the market will bear, and that the benefits to be gained from a low price for gas are fleeting compared to the long-term benefis to be gained from helping Mexico develop.148 Editors of The Journal of Commerce warned that"

> The arrogance with which the U.S. tried to pressure Mexico into conforming with our will only fueled the mistrust and resentment that Mexican leaders have long felt for their giant neighbor to the north.
> U.S.negotiators barely concealed their attitude that they had the Mexicans where they wanted them. "Where else can they sell their gas?" was the quote attributed to one senior official at a particularly crucial time in the negotiations...
> [W]e have an angry neighbor at a junction in history when we can ill afford bitterness in U.S.-Mexican relations Mexico desperately needs U.S. cooperation in a variety of areas, including development of jobs and a healthy export industry.149

The decision and the DOE were also criticized by other officials including Senators Javitts and Mathias who both complained about Mexico's treatment. Representative Manuel Lujan informed John Treat, Director of the DOE's Office of Producing nations that:

> There is a general feeling that over the years, that they [the Mexicans] have been dumped on, looked at as second class citizens in the world today. That is a very true feeling that they have. It was confirmed by the Department of Energy saying "We don't want your $2.60 gas," but a little later on saying we will say Canadian gas at $2.80 is perfectly all right.150

Edward Kennedy also objected to the actions of the Department of Energy and expressed his criticism through points typical of those with the neutral image of Mexico. Kennedy argued that to ignore the importance of Mexican energy sources was to damage the interests of the United States in two ways: First, it deprived the United States of a secure source of energy; and second, it ignored the "real" concern, "Mexico's economic and social development over the long term."151 The US should recognize the role that energy resources were to play in Mexican development. Thus, the United States should not encourage production beyond the absorptive capacity of the Mexican economy. Kennedy also noted that simply because the United States needed energy supplies and Mexico needed to sell energy resources, one should not expect the two countries to "suddenly become reconciled in an amalgam of modern development. We will remain richly divergent societies."152 Finally, he argued that the United States should seek a "complimentary relationship" conditioned by economic concerns but also by "an appreciation of the cultural heritage of Mexico."153 Kennedy labeled Schlesinger's claim to have acted in the interests of the American consumer an attempt to protect domestic producers.154

In each of the above examples, objections were raised concerning the "treatment" Mexico had received. The protests focus upon the points that distinguish the two images of Mexico. These include an objection to the notion that the United States and Mexico have the same fundamental interests, an evaluation of Mexico's price policy as one that should be expected of any country, and an evaluation of the decision to refuse Mexico's desire to price its gas competitively as an example of the unequal treatment that Mexico receives. Some of the statements also demonstrate the neutral image definition of US interests regarding Mexico wherein US interests are said to lie in long-term Mexican growth.

The negotiators' response to these criticisms is interesting. During 1978-1979, the negotiators insisted that they made no mistake in rejecting the gas agreement. They continued to argue that the agreement was very bad from the United States standpoint. This, of course, may or may not be the case. What is most interesting is a tendency of US negotiators to attempt to justify their actions by re-marking that Mexico was told before the letter of intent was signed that the price would be a problem, that in the end the US did agree to pay Mexico $2.60 (with a waiting period of two years) and that Lopez Portillo and Diaz Serrano ruined the agreement.155 Neither point addressed the criticism raised by some members of Congress and the news media that Mexico was not given the opportunity to bargain for a competitive price. Judging from the frequency with which the negotiators' defense was made, it appears that they believed that Lopez Portillo should not have expected to bargain for a high price since he was told before he signed the letter of intent that the price was too high. Further, the focus on the negotiators' last minute agreement to a higher price indicates that they did not recognize the importance of the public position Lopez Portillo had been pushed into by November 1977. Finally, several negotiators proclaimed that the negotiations would have succeeded had they not received so much attention in the press.156 This is also an interesting evaluation of the problem since the opponents of the price were largely responsible for the attention the press gave the issue. In fact, Jack Ray termed Schlesinger's actions an "illegal attempt to try the case in the newspapers before a contract was presented for government approval."157

The position taken by James Schlesinger after the 1978 discussion of the issue is also noteworthy. By early 1979 Schlesinger had constructed a long list of reasons for opposing the importation of Mexican energy resources that is strikingly similar to the pattern of behavior described by Jervis as an avoidance of value trade-offs. In this pattern "people who favor a policy usually believe that it is supported by many logically independent reasons."158 Schlesinger's original objection to the importation of natural gas was price. By January, 1979, however, Schlesinger argued that the price for Mexican gas was at once too high and at the same time low enough to inhibit US domestic production. The United States, according to Schlesinger, should place highest priority on developing domestic supplies.159 Mexican gas was also seen as undersireable because it would be inflationary and contribute to the trade deficit.160 (Edward Kennedy responded that half of US purchases from Mexico return in the form of future trade.161) Schlesinger also argued that although Mexican gas was priced too high, if the United States imported large quantities of Mexican gas production in Alaska would be limited. Alaskan gas was expected to cost between $5 and $6 per Mcf by the time it became available in 1985. He predicted that by the end of the century Alaskan gas would be less expensive than Mexican gas.162 While the price of Alaskan gas remained high, he argued, it could be "rolled in" with cheaper supplies so that the consumer would not

suffer. Canadian gas may receive the same treatment but
Schlesinger was unwilling to grant this advantage to Mexican
gas. Instead, Mexican gas was seen simply as a disincentive
to domestic production and the idea that Mexico offered a
solution to the possibility of an energy shortage was termed
a "form of escapism."163 (Kennedy did not let this remark
pass unnoticed either. He wrote that given the fact that
natural gas was to be decontrolled in 1985 a large supply
would protect consumers from high prices at that time. Hence
it was to the consumer's advantage to import Mexican gas and
roll-in the price in preparation for free competition in
price after deregulation.164 Schlesinger's final point was
that "it is no favor to the Mexicans" for the United States
to purchase their gas at a high price since this would limit
the market for their gas.165 In short, Schlesinger created
an argument in which the rejection of Mexico's gas offered
the best solution to everyone's problems.

Despite the initial and continuing resistance to the
criticism of the 1977 decision, there is evidence that some
of those involved in the 1977 decision did shift their image
of Mexico. This emerged, however, after the two images of
Mexico entered into an open, administration-sponsored debate
in late 1978.

THE SHIFT TO THE NEUTRAL IMAGE: PRESIDENTIAL
REVIEW MEMORANDUM 41

By August 1978, nine months after the rejection of the
gas agreement, Jimmy Carter had become sufficiently
concerned about the strain in United States-Mexican
relations to commission the National Security Council to
undertake a complete review and re-evaluation of the
bilateral situation. The resulting report was known as
Presidential Review Memorandum 41 (PRM 41). It presents a
rare opportunity to view two different policy statements by
policy makers with two different views of another country.
The Presidential Review Memorandum was designed to give
Carter several options for handling bilateral affairs. The
central objective of the review was to organize a
coordinated and integrate approach to United States-Mexican
relations.166 The topics to be dealt with were numerous,
including immigration, energy, trade, and tourism, and the
report was supposed to "identify potential tradeoffs between
issues and suggest options among comprehensive strategies

for approaching U.S.-Mexican relations."[167] Numerous agencies were involved in the study including Commerce, Treasury, CIA, Justice, State, and DOE. Each agency was given responsibility for one issue and was supposed to draw upon other agencies for necessary information.[168] The energy issue was to be handled by DOE and its office of International Affairs in particular. DOE and State agreed to share the nuclear energy issue. Other agencies were permitted to comment on the reports of the individual agencies.[169]

One of the most significant aspects of the overall review ordered by Carter is the fact that it gave those individuals with a neutral view of Mexico the opportunity to present a new policy approach to Mexico. As has been stated, these individuals could be found primarily in the Latin American Bureau and the Mexican Desk. There is also evidence suggesting that some officials had changed their image of Mexico (to be discussed shortly). The Secretary of Energy continued to promote the general approach to Mexico that he had followed in 1977. The PRM talks, it should be noted, focused upon separate issues rather than an overall approach to Mexico.[170] Nevertheless, the final report discussed general US policy toward Mexico.

Three policy options emerged when the report was completed. Two of these received serious attention. The first was supported by the Secretary of Energy and members of DOE. It called for a "globalist" policy that would treat Mexico as any other "upper tier" country with no effort to give Mexico special treatment.[171] It was essentially a continuation of US policy. It argued:

> In the MTN [Multilateral Trade Negotiations] the U.S. is offering enhanced market access for Mexican exports but only in return for meaningful (though not equivalent) trade concessions by Mexico.
> --Consistent with U.S. global economic policy and with long-term Mexican interests...are inclined to oppose even this degree of liberalization.
> --The decreased protectionism required in Mexico is not attainable soon.
> --If we reached agreement with Mexico in the MTN only at a very low level of mutual concessions, the result would be many withdrawals from the current U.S. negotiating offer.[172]

United States energy policy toward Mexico would follow the same lines and would reflect global, not bilateral,

concerns.[173] Schlesinger argued this position both in his
report to the study commission and in his public statements.
The second position advocated in PRM 41 is labeled
by one of the articipants the "special attention" approach
to bilateral affairs.[174] This approach was favored by the
members of the Latin American Bureau, several members of the
National Security Council and some members of the energy
subsection of the Bureau of Economic and Business Affairs.[175] These policy advocates argued that Mexico would
become a major new energy exporter and one unlikely to join
OPEC. They noted that "among the obstacles to improving
relations between the two countries...is that `important
elements in both societies regard the other with suspicion
and even fear.'"[176] Because Mexico is one of the United
States three most important trading partners and because of
the long border and number of border communities, Mexico
should not be considered "just another developing
country."[177] It was advised that:

> Before making decisions on issues affecting Mexico,
> decision makers would be careful to consider the Mexican
> perspective. Globalist principles would not be directly
> contradicted, but when gray areas existed, policies
> could be shaped to better take Mexican interests into
> account.
>
> Mexicans are especially sensitive to the style of
> United States behavior toward them. Under the rubric of
> special attention, United States officials would be
> careful to avoid the imperial gruffness reportedly
> accorded Mexicans by Secretary of Energy Schlesinger.
> Nor would the United States extend the barbed wire
> "tortilla curtain" along the border.[178]

The "special attention" approach to the energy issue
followed the same ideas. The United States would have to pay
particular care to avoid offending Mexican nationalism and
would have to make an agreement that reflected the interests
of both countries. It also called for a special ambassador
to coordinate US-Mexican affairs from the United States.
Mexico would therefore have two ambassadors from the United
States, one stationed in Mexico City and the other in
Washington, D.C.
The third policy option proposed in PRM 41 received
very little attention in the press and among policy makers.
This option, called "preferences," sought an "active
bilateral relationship" that would "seek to fashion new

frameworks to govern projected movements of people, commodities, energy products, and capital."179 The ultimate goal was some form of a North American Common Market. It is difficult to tell if this was a separate policy option advocated by a separate group of officials. Both available documents and interviews indicate that it was probably an extreme, long-run formulation of the "special attention" policy option. The PRM 41 summary report described this option as:

> As intensification and possible follow-on to Option Two [special attention], based on maximizing the benefits of proximity. Could include sectoral free trade agreements in agriculture, which is highly labor intensive, leading to more predictable agricultural production and trading arrangments based on comparative advantage.180

Further, interviewees suggested that this option was proposed by the Latin American Bureau, also the advocate of option two, and that those who favored option two also made these arguments.181 Although the notion of a North American Common Market ignores the problem of Mexican nationalism, a habit not found among those with a neutral view of Mexico, the idea was apparently seen as a possibility in the future.

Once again the different perceptions of Mexico are apparent in the policy proposals. Schlesinger's globalist approach continued to reflect the dependent image of Mexico through which it was argued that Mexico should be treated as all others of its kind and that its policies must conform to US interests. The other view held that Mexican interests and US interests are not the same but can, and must, be shaped into compromise agreements. With these options in hand, Carter prepared for a trip to Mexico in February, 1979. As the report was being prepared there was a certain amount of bureaucratic conflict and jockeying for Carter's favor. In January, 1979, Schlesinger gave a public address in which he pronounced his position. The newspapers immediately reported that this also Carter's position. Meanwhile, National Security Council Adviser Zbigniew Brzezinski had written to Schlesinger the previous November criticizing him for "trying to end-run the council's PRM process by going directly to the president or negotiating directly with Mexico's national oil company."182 Carter's decision as to which group and policy approach would be adopted came during the days before and after his trip to Mexico. In the energy area he chose the "special attention" approach.

Before setting off for Mexico in February 1979, Carter announced that he was not going to Mexico to negotiate a natural gas agreement. Carter did not take Schlesinger since he was widely disliked in Mexico. As one observer noted, the Mexican press was ready to "pounce on Carter" if he made the slightest mistake and "if he makes some kind of Schlesinger-type statement, the marines will have to evacuate him..."183 Despite the absence of Schlesinger, the meetings between Lopez Portillo and Carter were publicly, if not privately, strained. Carter made indecent and insulting jokes and Lopez Portillo publicly embarrassed Carter with statements such as: "Among permanent, not causal neighbors, surprise moves and sudden deceit or abuse are poisonous fruit that sooner or later have a reverse effect."184 Nevertheless, at the end of three days of talks, Mexico and the United States announced that government-to-government talks on the sale of natural gas would resume.185

One official involved in the PRM 41 re-evaluation of US-Mexican affairs reports that Carter never really made a decision about which overall policy approach to take with Mexico. Instead, the decisions were made on approaches to specific issues.186 In the energy issue Carter's decision was clear: the special attention approach was selected and orders were given that an agreement with Mexico on natural gas must be obtained.187 The 1977 gas decision was made by Schlesinger and his underlings. The 1979 negotiations were to be undertaken by a variety of different individuals. The White House (that is, the NSC) and the State Department were given a much larger role in 1979. The new participants not only had the "broader" view of Mexico and the energy issue, indicative of the neutral image, but some of the earlier negotiators appear to have changed their views of the issue in response to the failure of the 1977 negotiations.188 The change in approach and in the major actors was attributed to the strain in relations resulting from 1977 by several of the major actors.189

THE NEGOTIATIONS OF 1979

When negotiations began again in April, 1979, the American team was headed by Julius Katz of the State Department's Bureau of Economic and Business Affairs. The negotiators also included other DOE officials and members of the Latin American Bureau and the United States Embassy.190 Toward the end of the talks in September, 1979, Warren

Christopher became a crucial negotiator.[191] News paper
accounts indicate that the State Department's Economic and
Business Affairs energy section had shifted to a position
closer to that of the Latin American Bureau.[192] In 1977
their position had been similar to Schlesinger's. Katz, the
Assistant Secretary for Economic and Business Affairs, had
apparently agreed with Schlesinger's final position in
1977.[193] In 1979, he stressed the importance of recognizing
Mexican nationalism and conflicts of interest between the US
and Mexico. In Congressional hearings he stated that the
State Department was interested in finding "ways to promote
mutually beneficial cooperation between Mexico and the
United States..."[194] He pointed out that "[i]t is inevitable
that there will be problems, there will be irritations,
there will be disputes" between the two.[195]Finally, he
agreed that the United States needed a long-range plan to
strengthen relations with Mexico.[196] However, Katz repeated
his earlier view that the price Mexico requested in 1977 was
high but stressed concern about the escalator clause of the
1977 agreement. He pointed out that current market
conditions were different and that the 1979 negotiations
would reflect that difference.[197] It is impossible to tell
exactly whether or how much the officials of Economic and
Business Affairs changed their image of Mexico. The
statements by Katz and the 1979 bargaining behavior, however, appear to reflect greater sensitivity to the
importance of Mexican nationalism. Negotiations shifted to a
focus on the escalator clause and there was no set price
above which the United States would not go as in 1977. The
shift in image was also apparent among some of the lower
ranked participants in the negotiations. One member of DOE
reported that the disagreements between DOE and State were
fewer in 1979. Both were more aware of Mexican pride in the
national patrimony an took it as a serious factor in
bargaining.[198] Further, they believed that the United States
best "bargaining card" was the international market.[199]
Thus, Mexico was finally permitted to set a price, the
fairness of which would be determined by the international
market.

Several context effects had changed in the 1979 negotiations as well. First, the United States did not suffer
from or expect a shortage of natural gas when these
negotiations began. Therefore, there was no sense of urgency
among the US negotiators, in contrast to the situation in
1977.[200] The United States had a "gas bubble," that is, an
overabundance of gas, and the pressure for an agreement came

not from a need for energy but from the Administration.[201] A
second difference in 1979 was that the market had changed.
The price of OPEC petroleum had risen 24% since 1977 which
both wiped out earlier price standards and made the price of
both Number 2 and Number 6 fuel oil higher than Mexico's
1977 price. This enabled negotiators from both sides to
begin talks without reference to the 1977 price, thereby
avoiding the possibility of reigniting the nationalistic
furor of that time.202 Finally, when the meetings began in
April, 1979, PEMEX announced that the original terms of the
agreement with the gas transmission companies would have to
be changed significantly.203 Mexico announced that it could
not sell the US the two billion cubic feet it had offered in
1977. Instead, it had available only 300 million cubic feet
in the short-run and expected to be able to sell up to 800
million cubic feet per day eventually. Therefore, although
the negotiators were headed for hard bargaining, in a
general contextual sense they started with a clean slate.

The Mexican side approached the talks very cautiously
and the Americans were not in a hurry to reach an agreement
in the spring of 1979. By July, 1979, the talks picked up
speed. The US, led by Julius Katz, offered Mexico an
escalator clause that was based on a blend of Number 2 and
Number 6 fuel oils and asked that the purchase price be set
at a mutually acceptable medium.204 This new escalator
clause set prices on the basis of an average of the prices
of Arab, Algerian, North Sea, Venezuelan, and Mexican light
oils.205 In late July, the United State suggested a price of
$3.30 per thousand cubic feet. Mexico initially made no
response to the offer and then decided that the price should
be set above $4.00 per Mcf.206 By this time, some urgency
for a settlement was being felt on the American side. Lopez
Portillo was scheduled to visit Washington in September and
the administration was concerned that an impasse in the gas
talks would cause the visit to be cancelled and relations
with Mexico to deteriorate.207 To make matters worse, in
August Ambassador Patrick Lucey met with Lopez Portillo and
then mistakenly announced that an agreement had been reached
with a price set at $3.40. The another incident caused even
more strain. Carter had appointed Robert Krueger as special
ambassador to Mexico (one of the outcomes of PRM 41).
Krueger's appointment was seen by Mexicans as a political
payoff to an important Texas Democrat temporarily out of
office. When an offshore oil well, Ixtoc No. 1, blew up and
oil spilled on the Texas shore, Krueger publicly announced,
without consulting Mexico, that Mexico should pay

compensation for the spill. His reversion back to past conflict resolution techniques cause Lopez Portillo to remark:

A special Ambassador-designate in one of his first actions, and without waiting for a reply, makes a public message of this kind. It is without precedent and constitutes and attitude that is disconcerting. 208

Concern about the upcoming meeting between Carter and Lopez Portillo caused administration aides to press both DOE and State to come to an agreement with Mexico. Deputy Secretary of State Warren Christopher was sent to Mexico to clinch the deal. Christopher offered Mexico a new price, $3.50, and Mexico countered with $3.75. They agreed to split the difference and a price was set at $3.65.209 Mexico also insisted upon the right to cancel the agreement with ninety days notice. In the final agreement the cancellation rights were granted to both sides with six months notice. The price of natural gas was to be reviewed every three months.210

The final gas agreement demonstrated several important points. First, Mexico and the United States reached an agreement as a result of true negotiations and bargaining. The American approach was quite different in 1979 than in 1977. Mexico was not confronted with a "take-it-or-leave-it" package from the United States and the United States did not receive one from Mexico. The US entered the negotiations focusing upon the escalator clause rather than price. This was most important to the US since it determined future prices and the price issue was more politically sensitive to Mexico since it is publicized and can produce heated political debate. Thus the emphasis on escalator clause indicated a recognition of Mexican nationalism. Further, in the actual price negotiations the United States did not set a limit on the price equal to Canadian natural gas. By 1979 Canadian gas was selling for $2.80 per Mcf. In addition, one member of the negotiating team reported that in 1979 the US asked Canada if the price paid for Mexican gas would prompt them to raise their own prices. The Canadians said that their price would not be affected. Canada was not asked about its reaction to Mexican price in 1977.211 It should be noted, however, that the newspaper reports in 1979 claimed that Canada had said that it would raise it prices in response to the Mexican price.

A second major aspect of the 1979 agreement it that US negotiators felt satisfied that they had a better package than they would have had with the 1977 agreement (by 1979 Mexican gas would have cost $4.00 per Mcf under the 1977 agreement). However, the United States officials had reached an agreement that was the result of major concessions. Their satisfaction with the agreement indicated a very different Eiew of what the United States should expect to get from Mexico in negotiations.

A third important aspect of the 1979 agreement concerns adaptation to change. The 1977 negotiations were conducted by individuals with a dependent view of Mexico. Mexico's own self-perception had changed in general and the sensitivity to energy resources as the national partimony had if anything intensified. The dependent view of Mexico had resulted in a failure to reach an agreement and a general strain in bilateral affairs. This caused some individuals to change their image and other individuals who already had a neutral view proposed a different policy approach. The result was a different bargaining tactic, one that reflected a recognition of Mexico's nationalism, an assumption that differences in interests and goals exist and the mutually beneficial agreement could be reached but that they would require compromise by both sides, and the assumption that Mexican officials will not necessarily be flexible. This approach resulted in different bargaining foci and a willingness to compromise on price.

THE EFFECTS OF CATEGORIES ON JUDGMENT: SUMMARY

One important question remains. In Chapter 4 several hypotheses were presented concerning the effect of world view on judgments of other governments. In the discussion of the negotiations concerning natural gas from 1977 to 1979, evidence was presented concerning two images of Mexico, policy preferences connected with each view, and expectations of Mexico's behavior associated with each image. The hypotheses, however, have not been discussed and should be reviewed at this point. Hypotheses 1 through 10 pertain to the dependent image.

Hypothesis 1 argues that the more accustomed policy makers are to classifying a particular state as a dependent, the more accessible that category is and the more likely it is that it will be used to classify that state in the future. A historic case provides little evidence with which to properly test this hypothesis. A good test would require examining the ease with which individuals classified Mexico as a dependent as opposed to another type after they were accustomed to classifying it as a dependent for some time. The evidence available from this case study does offer some support for the hypothesis, however. The historical record indicates that across several policy issues and over decades of time Mexico was thought of, treated as, and behaved as a dependent type of state. When the gas issue arose, the dominant voice continued to advocate a non-bargaining approach toward Mexico typical of the dependent image. This took place despite the transformation in Mexican foreign policy during the Echeverria Administration. The classification of Mexico as a dependent appears to have been constant and automatic. Only the dramatic and public failure of the gas negotiations were profound enough to prompt a change in the image of Mexico and the emergence of vocal advocates of the neutral image.

Hypothesis 2 proposed that classifications of a country as a dependent will continue after the initial classification until it becomes apparent that change has occurred and that adjustment to change requires a new judgment concerning the applicability of the dependent category for that state. This is clearly the course of events in the Mexican gas case. Mexico was consistently evaluated as and treated as a dependent. When that approach resulted in a failure to reach an agreement on the importation of natural gas the response of the Carter Administration was to search for a complete re-evaluation of Mexico, including all important bilateral issues. What occurred was a questioning of the nominal judgment of Mexico. Some governmental officials insisted on the traditional classification and said so in their PRM 41 position in which they advocated policies toward Mexico similar to those for all other upper tier developing countries. Their point was clearly that Mexico is what it has always been and remains part of the same group. The other perceptual faction called for a new view of Mexico and a major adjustment in bargaining behavior. The failure of the gas agreement talks in 1977 and the subsequent tensions between the two countries resulted in a period of perceptual confusion as the administration sought to undertand the new Mexico.

Hypothesis 3 claims that once a state is classified as a dependent it will lose some of its individual qualities and will be seen as similar to other states in the category. This pattern was also evident in judgments of Mexico in the 1977 period. One of the most significant instances in which the unique characteristics of Mexico were ignored was the enormous importance that hydrocarbons play in Mexican nationalism. Mexico's lack of interest in OPEC, for example, was not seen as an indicator of the strength of the prohibition against giving control of Mexican energy resources to outside powers. Instead, policy makers assumed that Mexico was not in OPEC and therefore would not resist American efforts to push for a price below that demanded by OPEC countries. Thus, a very important element of Mexican politics was never acknowledged and this contributed to the 1977 fiasco. The dependent image position in PRM 41 is also supportive of this hypothesis. Those with a neutral view advocated the "special attention" approach with an opposite outlook. They claimed that the globalist approach should not be applied to Mexico because United States-Mexican relations were different from United States relations with other developing states. To some extent those advocating the "special attention" strategy argued that Mexico should be treated as a unique country given its historical relationship with the United States and its common border. It is possible that this disconfirms this hypothesis' point that individual states lose some of their unique characteristics after they are classified. It is also possible, however, that this particular position does not conform to expectations because these individuals were in the process of recognizing Mexico's change and developing new policies for Mexico and were thus forced by the perceptual ambiguity to debate Mexico's unique qualties. Since Mexico's classification was in the process of changing for many officials, the evaluation of Mexico by those with a new neutral image may not be useful in testing this hypothesis.

Hypothesis 4 concerns the effects of categories on missing information. It argues that when information is missing about a state classified as a dependent the assumption will be made that the state will behave as a better representative than it may actually be. These assumptions were made about Mexico in the predictions of Mexico's ultimate willingness to comply with the United States' position on the price of gas in 1977 and in estimates of Mexico's ability to consume its gas domestically. In both of these instances it was assumed that Mexico would behave as a typical dependent. It would give in to US pressure on price and it would not be able to find the technology and steel necessary to construct the facilities to consume the gas domestically. Those with a neutral image of Mexico made predictions about Mexican behavior consistent with that image. For example, in the 1979 negotiations they assumed that compromises would be necessary. This was a prediction of Mexican behavior consistent with that of a neutral in that Mexico was not expected to be willing to comply with demands detrimental to its own interests. They also assumed that Mexicans could understand and manipulate the international oil market. Even after Mexico's serious misinterpretation of the oil glut in 1981 Mexican energy officials were seen as increasingly "sophisticated in their understanding of the market."212

Hypothesis 5 records similar tendencies in the perceiver's recognition and use of inconsistent and neutral information regarding the dependent type of state. Except for dramatically inconsistent information, policy makers will ignore inconsistent or neutral information conflicting with their expectation. American policy makers with the dependent image did not take the transformations in Mexican foreign policies during the 1970's into account when predicting their behavior in 1977. Mexican policies during the 1970s were not dramatically inconsistent with the dependent image despite the fact that they manifested a clear shift in interest, attention, and identification toward the Third World. Mexico did nothing to demonstrate dramatically a change in policies toward the United States. The only act that received a great deal of attention was Echeverria's support for the "Zionism is Racism" resolution in the United Nations. His eventual retreat from that stance in response to boycotts of Mexico by American toursists could only have lessened the psychological impact of that act. The subtle nature of the transformation in Mexico resulted in the disregard of discrepant bits of information that could have led to different predictions of Mexico's behavior in 1977. Reports that Mexico had found non-US sources of financing and technology for the pipeline and potential customers for the gas were also undramatic. Thus it is not surprising that Schlesinger relied upon information consistent with his psychological expectations in 1977. Dramatic evidence is necessary to challenge expectations and to produce a shift in categorization.

Hypothesis 6 is closely related to Hypothesis 5. It states that inconsistent and irrelevant information about the dependent's behaviors and traits will not be recalled as well as consistent information unless it is striking. Although the evidence is limited, there is no indication that the 1977 negotiators were influenced by recollections of Echeverria's policies. The 1979 negotiators, however, were clearly aware of and sensitive to the actions of the Mexican officials after the failure of the 1977 negotiations. The actions of Mexican officials after 1977 were dramatic, public and hostile. They were "lessons" easily recalled and important in awakening negotiators to the complexities of Mexican politics.

Hypothesis 7 is a complicated on and the case study yields only ambiguous information regarding its strength. It is argued that the closer a particular state is seen to be to the dependent prototype, the more confident the policy maker will be in his predictions and the more he will be predisposed to support short-term, issue specific strategies. The more uncertain the policy makers is of the representativeness of the state, the more he or she will be predisposed to search for long-term, multi-issue, and multi-strategy options for bilateral relations. The first part if evident in the behavior of Secretary Schlesinger. He demonstrated an ideal-typical image of Mexico as a dependent and never wavered in his certainty that Mexico would give in to the US on the question of price. He showed no interest in or concern about the effects of this issue on bilateral relations in general and did not associate the energy issue with any other issues. Schlesinger consistently maintained this position on Mexico and United States-Mexican relations during the re-evaluation of bilateral affairs during late 1978. The intensity of the 1977 bargaining was low level. In Chapter 4 it was argued that low level intensity will be a contextual factor in contributing to the concentration on short-run, issue-specific bargaining.

The problem with this hypothesis lies more in the second part of the propositions than in the first. Do those who are less certain about the classification of a state demonstrate an interest in broad combinations of issues and strategies? Clearly, those who disagreed with Schlesinger on the Mexican gas issue argued for a completely different approach to Mexico in 1978. In their re-evaluation of United States-Mexican relations they argued that bilateral affairs should not be treated according to US global policies on individual issues but that the United States should take a multi-issue approach to Mexico and create policies toward Mexico that took into consideration the peculiar situation produced by the common border between the two countries. In the energy negotiations these individuals emphasized both the escalator clause and the price, offering different formulas for each with many options for negotiating a mutually satisfactory agreement. It has been argued throughout Chapter 6 that these individuals saw Mexico as a neutral. It is possible, and perhaps probable, the Mexico was not seen as the ideal-typical neutral. Given the psychological properties attached to the neutral and given Mexico's history, it is not likely that it would be seen as close to the prototype of a neutral. Thus, those who saw Mexico as a neutral may have been convinced that Mexico would not behave as it had in the past but they may not have been as certain of future Mexican behavior as the ideal-typical neutral image would permit them to be. While the available evidence does support the argument that there were two very different images of Mexico, it dos not provide strong evidence with which one can assess the degree to which Mexico was seen as a neutral in late 1978. The final factor mentioned in this hypothesis was the level of intensity context effect. The level of intensity associated with the 1979 negotiations was high. There was great concern than an agreement be achieved. This high level of intensity was accompanied, as expected, by complex, multi-issue evaluations of Mexico.

Hypothesis 8 pointed out that given the lack of hostility associated with most issues between the perceiver's state and a dependent state, information indicating strain and hostility will be overshadowed and given little importance in judgments of ongoing negotiations with the dependent. This pattern was reflected during the 1977 negotiations when warning from Mexico and the gas companied that DOE's resistance to the agreement would strain relations were ignored. Mexico's anger after Stevenson's remarks in Congress was discounted and US negotiators responded to Mexican anger with surprise after the gas deal fell through. The 1977 talks received relatively little attention in government circles and there was no suspicious that they would make a significant difference in US-Mexican relations in the short-run.213 Further, US negotiators were both surprised and annoyed when the Mexican government reacted with anger to the final 1977 episode. They argued that Mexico knew the agreement would fall through and therefore should not have reacted with such a furor. Mexican hostility was simply unexpected.214 This is an action that is not associated with the dependent image.

Hypothesis 9 described the effects of the extreme ideal-typical classification of a state upon judgments of the state. It was argued that those who have an ideal-typical view of a state as a dependent will be most resistant to conflicting information and may become even more adamant about the category to which the individual

228

state belongs. This pattern was evident in the behavior of
James Schlesinger. Other negotiators, such as Leslie Goldman
of DOE, displayed a less extreme dependent image of Mexico.
He claimed, for example, that they had become aware of the
extreme nationalistic sentiment attached to Mexico's
petroleum resources during the 1977 negotiations and would
endeavor in the future to take this factor into account in
negotiations.215 Schlesinger, however, consistently refused
to accept information indicating that Mexico would not
behave as a dependent. During the negotiations, as was
pointed out earlier, he accepted the information indicating
that Mexico could not use its gas domestically and would be
unable to find other buyers. He rejected the evidence
demonstrating interest by other energy consumers in Mexican
hydrocarbons and Mexican access to other sources of aid and
technology. Schlesinger continued to expect Mexico to accept
his price offer despite repeated statements to the contrary
and the vocal concern of the gas companies that they would
do so. Finally, Schlesinger's reaction to the Mexican gas
issue after the failure of his bargaining tactics was to
announce that Mexican gas was detrimental to the United
States anyway. He strongly resisted changing his view of
Mexico and instead bolstered it through a variety of
explanations of the undesirability of Mexican gas.

Hypothesis 10 argued that old judgments of another
state require some time before they fade sufficiently from
memory so that they no longer affect judgments. Again it is
difficult to find evidence that conclusively supports this
hypothesis but there are a couple of important and
significant events that occurred during the negotiations and
the formulation of PRM 41. While it is apparent that the
general image of Mexico shifted to a neutral view after the
failure of the 1977 negotiations, one of the policy
propositions in PRM 41 has a mixture of the elements of the
dependent and neutral views. It has been argued throughout
this study that the dependent image of a country is one that
produces both domineering and partonizing policies. They are
opposite sides of the same coin. The essential image of the
other country holds that these are people who are really
incapable of managing for themselves. When the interests of
the perceiver's state are in jeopardy they are thought of
(nonconsciously) as children who must be forcefully led back
to the correct path. At the same time, when the situation is
not threatening, patronizing behavior should come from those
with the dependent view of the other country. this is a
result of the same view of the other people as childlike,

needing guidance. The PRM 41 re-evaluation of 1978-1979 contained some elements of this patronizing approach. This is best illustrated in the policy position that advocated an extremely conciliatory approach to Mexico, one in which the US pays Mexico a premium price for its petroleum and natural gas. This is a policy that is both impossible to maintain and assumes that the Mexicans cannot bargain as equals and need special concessions to keep their country running. The price they receive will be a gift from the United States. One foreign service officer who observed the discussions of the Mexican "problem" in 1977-1979 claimed that those who advocated an extremely conciliatory approach were in some cases the same people who had earlier wanted easy access to Mexican gas at a low price. In other cases these were individuals who were concerned that the United States simply establish a stable energy relationship with Mexico. It is a position that appears to have remnants of the dependent image. It is also a position that by 1982 appears to have lost some of its support. The interviews conducted by this writer in the summer of 1982 found no officials advocating this approach to Mexico, but two government officials who reported that others in government were at the time making this type of argument.

Hypotheses 11 through 13 concern the effects of the neutral classification on perceptions of Mexico. Hypothesis 11 concerns the tendency to supply missing information about a particular state from the category in which it is classified and to base expectations about that state's behavior upon the behavior typical of the members of that category. Expectations of the neutral type of state behavior from Mexico were clearly present among the individuals involved in the 1979 bargainings. This group consistently warned against any assumption that Mexico would become a source of energy supplies that would fill all, or most, or even a large portion of US energy imports. They argued that the United States could not pressure Mexico into selling the United States natural gas at a low price or in greater quantities than the Mexican officials thought appropriate for their development strategy. They argued that Mexico could be expected to set the price for its resources at world market levels rather than at prices beneficial to US customers. Mexico's refusal to enter OPEC was not taken as an indication that Mexico would be a cheap source of energy for the United States. They also predicted that Mexico's increasing knowledge of the international energy market would result in fewer mistakes such as the August 1981 price

for petroleum that cost Mexico many of its customers.[217] In
general, these predictions of Mexico's behavior made by
individuals with a neutral view described actions that are
clearly in the interest of the Mexican economy and not
necessarily in the interest of the American consumer.

Hypothesis 12 concerns the context within which interactions between the perceiver's state and the neutral take
place. The context should be one that is relatively benign,
neither hostile nor extremely friendly. The context effect
results from both the issues and the combination of the
neutral's attributes. Those who held the neutral image do
appear to have been sensitive to both the threat and
opportunity in future US-Mexican affairs. They saw at once
the need for "special attention" to bilateral issues because
of their unique importance and because of the possibility of
resolving problems bilaterally. While Mexico was seen as a
secure source of supply for energy needs, it was also seen
as a source that will be limited and that must be
courted.218 In issue areas other than energy many policy
makers appeared to be concerned about Mexican stability but
confident that the governmental system was strong.219

Hypothesis 13 addresses the influence of previous
categorizations on perceptions after a state has been
reclassified in the process of adapting to change. It is
argued in hypothesis 11 that once a state is classified in a
category, that category becomes more accessible and more
readily invoked in future perceptions of the state. However,
when a category is newly used to classify a state the
category in which the state was previously classified is
still accessible. Time is required for the accessibility to
diminish. If the reclassification of the state is equivocal
or if new information is received that does not conform to
the new classification but is compatible with the old
category, the old information and knowledge concerning the
country facilitate a shift back to the earlier category.
Unfortunately, it is difficult to determine whether the
image of Mexico has returned to the dependent image as a
result of Mexico's economic traumas during the 1980's. On
one hand, Mexico's financial dilemma may promote the return
to that image but on the other, Mexico's leadership of the
Contadora process would further promote the accessibility of
the neutral category. Although this is speculative, it is
possible that these two aspects of Mexico's recent history
merely bolster the views of those who see Mexico as either a
dependent or a neutral. The top level of the Reagan
Administration appears to be filled with individuals who

have a dependent image of Mexico. The entire reaction to, or
rejection of the Contadora process is indicative of that
image since it is accompanied by efforts to pressure Mexico
with economic instruments and the apparent assumption that
Mexico is incapable of truly understanding the dangers of
the alleged communism in the hemisphere. Indeed, as early as
1982 there were individuals in the government who advocated
that the US use Mexico's economic weaknesses to force a
change in the Mexican economic system.220 The forcefulness
of the Reagan Administration obscures indications that those
with neutral images remain in government as advocates of
alternative policies.

OTHER EXPLANATIONS?

    In this chapter the impact of images on bargaining
tactics during the gas negotiations of 1977 and 1979 have
been used to explain the outcome of those negotiations.
There are three possible and popular alternative
explanations for the results of US negotiations with Mexico:
a power determinist explanation, a domestic politics
explanation, and a bureaucratic politics explanation. The
power determinist explanation would argue that states act
the way they do because of their power interests. The
actions a state takes are made in pursuit of the state's
national interests (defined in terms of the maintenance of
augmentation of power) and the outcome of conflicts between
the two states is the result of their relative amounts of
power. This form of analysis would evaluate United States-
Mexican natural gas negotiations using the concepts of the
pursuit of the national interest and the relative amount of
power held by the United States and Mexico. At first glance
it would seem that this approach can successfully predict
that in pursuit of the national interest, low prices for
energy supplies, the United States would refuse to pay
Mexico a high price for natural gas. A closer analysis,
however, reveals the weakness of this approach. First, the
United States did take a position against giving Mexico a
higher price for natural gas in 1977. This was a time,
however, when a shortage of natural gas as expected for the
winter of 1977-1978. Thus the national interest of the US
should have been to secure adequate amounts of gas given the
fact that the previous winter's shortage had caused people
to go without heat and industry to shut down in some parts
of the country. Further, the United States eventually

conceded a price for Mexican gas that was higher than that paid Canada during a time when natural gas was not in short supply. The course of events indicates that the national interest is either very unclear or was not pursued in either the 1977 or the 1979 negotiations. When natural gas was abundant the government accepted a high price for gas that was not needed. When natural gas was in short supply the United States took a position that made it impossible to secure additional supplies. The problem with the explanation is not so much that it is wrong but that it cannot pinpoint unequivolcally the national interest of the United States. The power determinist explanation fares no better in explaining Mexican behavior. According to this argument Mexico, being the weaker participant in the dispute no matter how one measures power, should have given in to US pressure for a lower price in 1977, both because of the greater power of the US and because Mexican statesmen should pursue the national interest of their own country. To refuse the Canadian price for natural gas was to lose badly needed revenue and to commit Mexico to the very costly projects of using gas domestically and finding foreign buyers.

The power determinist argument also expects actors to behave rationally and would argue that the price paid in the end was better than the one it would have paid had it agreed to the 1977 deal. Thus, it may be argued, Schlesinger behaved quite rationally in 1977. Again, one must question the definition of terms. Was it "rational" to ignore information indicating that Mexico would not sell below $2.60 when the US was predicting another gas shortage? Was it rational to anger and strain relations with a neighbor that shares an unguarded 2,000 mile border? The power determinist approach conveniently permits the analyst to disregard individual statesmen and to use hindsight to obscure important events. Thus they can claim rationality on Schlesinger's part despite the fact that his actions in 1977 were regarded as such a disaster that he was not involved in the 1979 negotiations. To argue that Schlesinger's actions were rational implies that he somehow knew that eventually the United States would make a deal with Mexico when in fact his behavior was based upon the assumption that Mexico would simply give in to his demands. In addition, after the negotiations ended Schlesinger decided that Mexican gas was undesireable anyway. In the long run it can only be said that the United States was very fortunate that Schlesinger did not do more harm than he did and that other negotiators were more capable than he. The fact that different negotiators with a different image of Mexico produced a satisfactory agreement points to the importance of the psychological approach rather than the power determinist approach. Schlesinger can hardly be credited with the final outcome. This is not to say that the psychological approach should be used to explain failures alone. The bargaining process is the important analytical focus and it is reasonable to view studies of successful bargaining situations to be just as important as explanations of failures.

A second very common explanation for the outcome of the gas negotiations of 1977 and 1979 is a domestic politics argument. This holds that domestic interest group pressure and fears of angering Congress made it politically impossible for the Carter Administration to accept the Mexican price offer in 1977. It is argued that there was great concern that giving Mexico its requested price would kill Carter's energy bill that was being debated in Congress. Again, this is an argument that looks good and simple initially. Congress objected to the price in the agreement in 1977 which caused a rejection of the deal. In 1979 Congress was concerned that relations with Mexico improve which caused an acceptance of the deal. However, the argument is weak in several respects. First, the Department of Energy and Schlesinger opposed the Mexican price before Congress was aware of the issue. Therefore, Congress did not have to push Schlesinger to reject the agreement. Second, only one Congressman, Stevenson, posed any threat to the gas deal and he never asked for a vote on the resolution to limit EXIM financing of the pipeline. Third, interviewees who worked in the State Department, the NSC and Congress all agreed that the negotiators were not concerned about Congressional reaction in 1977.221 One individual stated that Congress would not have threatened Carter's Energy bill over an issue such as Mexican gas because it was totally irrelevant as far as votes were concerned. Congress may have criticized the Carter Administration had it decided to accept the Mexican offer but the evidence indicates that there was no "fear" of Congress because there was no real interest in accepting the Mexican offer in the first place. Finally, there were many members of Congress who reacted negatively to the 1977 decision. Thus the argument that the gas deal was rejected due to fear of Congressional anger cannot explain why fear of Congressional anger did not cause the deal to be accepted. Congress holds the same perceptual split that was evident in the bureaucracies. These perceptions caused some members of Congress to agree with Schlesinger and other to disagree with him. Perceptions of Mexico rather than fear of Congress account for the reaction to the gas proposal.

It is also argued that powerful interest groups dominate policy-making toward Mexico and this explains the 1977 decision. In fact, this argument does not begin to explain the 1977 decision. It is argued that concern about the pressure from domestic producers who would receive much less for their gas than Mexico would have received under the terms of the contract contributed to the rejection of the agreement. However, domestic producers did not adamantly oppose the agreement because they saw high prices for foreign gas as an argument supporting their pleas for higher prices for domestic natural gas.222 Pressure from powerful interest groups also does not account for the 1977 decision. The gas companies are powerful interest groups and they lobbied Congress and the bureaucracies heavily to have their gas agreement approved.223 They failed to move Schlesinger's position. (It is worth noting that the interests of powerful pressure groups were also rejected after the change in image of Mexico. A major controversy over tomatoes, for example, was settled in Mexico's favor against the wishes of the agricultural lobby in the United States.)

A third argument often offered to explain the natural gas decisions of 1977 and 1979 is a bureaucratic politics argument. According to this view the Energy Department and the State Department's Bureau of Economic and Business Affairs have global interests and therefore sought to treat Mexico as they would any other country. Their bureaucratic tasks involve coordinating energy policy for the United States worldwide. Thus their bureaucratic interests lay in denying Mexico a high price. It is also argued that the Latin American Bureau and the Mexican Desk of the State Department should have taken a position advocating Mexico's interests since this is their bureaucratic territory and country desks are notorious for their "clientelism." The argument has several problems. First, it cannot explain the change in position of the Economic and Business Affairs Bureau between 1977 and 1979. The position of this bureau moved closer to that of the Latin American Bureau but its bureacratic responsibilities did not. Second, it cannot explain the positions of some members of the US Embassy in Mexico who advocated a very hard line in negotiations with Mexico.224 These bureaucrats did not take the client's position. Third, the argument cannot explain why the State

Department's Latin American Bureau recommended the appointment of a special ambassador who was supposed to be independent of the State Department. This was a voluntary reduction of the Latin American Bureau's power and control over bilateral relations. This should not happen if bureaucratic politics explains the results of the 1977-1979 period in US-Mexican relations.225 Fourth, it cannot explain the position of members of the NSC who advocated the special attention policy since the NSC has global rather than Mexican responsibilities. The approach cannot explain either the positions taken by members of Congress or the role some individual Congressmen may have played in the events of 1977 and 1979. Finally, even if the approach can predict the positions of some segments of the government, this does not explain the change in policy from 1977 to 1979.

In general, there are major portions of the 1977 and 1979 decisions that the three alternative theoretical approaches cannot explain. The psychological approach can explain events that stump the other such as the relative lack of influence of the gas companies as pressure groups, the change in position by members of the bureaucracies and the failure of some individuals to serve the interests of their bureaucracies. The psychological approach is well suited to an issue such as the gas negotiations between the United States and Mexico. It was a situation in which decision makers did not act in their own best interest or in the best interest of their nation. It was a situation, in fact, in which the definition of "best interest" was a subject of some debate. Finally, it was a situation in which some policy makers clearly made major miscalculations in predicting the behavior of others. Miscalculations of this sort can be best explained by examining the perceptions of the policy makers.

EPILOGUE

Perceptions of Mexico did seem to have changed by the end of 1979. The assumptions associated with the new image of Mexico carried over into other policy areas. The United States government, for example, ruled against powerful agricultural interests in finding Mexico innocent of dumping tomatoes in 1980. This was the first time in over fifteen years of tomato controversy that the United States ruled against domestic interests in favor of Mexico. The energy area also continued to demonstrate the elements of the neutral view throughout the rest of the Carter Administration. During the early years of the Reagan Administration (1981-1982) the United States had no clearly defined objectives concerning Mexican energy supplies although some officials advocated improved ties in the energy area. 226 Mexico continued to receive a high price for its gas. But, as mentioned above, the Reagan Administration appears to have brought into power individuals who have a dependent image of Mexico, for the dispute between Mexico and the United States concerning developments in Central America is reminiscent not only of the dependent image of the 1970's, but the more stereotyped extremes of the 1950's. That was an era of extremely simplified views of the politics and people of the South, and that is the perception of the Current Administration.

Two final points are in order. The study of images indicates that people do indeed see what they expect to see. The interpretation of information and predictions of the behavior of other states can be seen to be associated with images and can be seen to affect bargaining tactics. To the extent that policy makers realize this, of course, they can check and cross-check their tactics in search for potentially damaging courses of action. But it also offers insights for those who are perceived. The most important lessons seems to be that if a state's leaders want to change the perception another state's leader have of them they must act contrary to the perceiver's expectations. Unfortunately, this may mean that they may have to do something dramatic, possibly harmful to their own interests, to force a change of image. And if one can generalize at all from the Mexican case, the change in image can be difficult to maintain, particularly if a new set of leaders who did not experience the lesson from the recent past, come into office.

NOTES

1. Interview with Ed Nef, Staff Aid for Senator Baucus, formerly a Congressional Affairs Officer for Inter-American Affairs, Department of State (1978), Washington, D.C., June 30, 1982.
2. A. Riding, "Mexico and the U.S. Finding Ways to Patch Things Up," The New York Times, November 13, 1977.

3. New York Times, December 3, 1977.

4. United States, Congress, Recent Developments in Mexico and Their Economic Implications for the United States, Hearings before the Subcommittee of Inter-American Economic Relationships of the Joint Economic Committee, Congress of the United States, 95th Cong., 1st sess., January 17 and 24, 1977 (Washington, D.C.: Government Printing Office, 1977), p. 75.

5. W. Cornelius, "Immigration, Mexican Development Policy and the Future of U.S.-Mexican Relations," in R. McBride (ed.), Mexico and the United States (Englewood Cliffs, New Jersey: Prentice-Hall, 1981), p. 106-107.

6. R. Shafer and D. Mabry, Neighbors -- Mexico and the United States (Chicago: Nelson-Hall, 1981), p. 98.

7. Ibid.

8. The New York Times, April 1979.

9. See The Washington Post, December 21, 1978, and Shafer and Mabry.

10. The Wall Street Journal December 5, 1977, and Los Angeles Times, December 22, 1977.

11. Interview with Robert Hopper, Foreign Service Officer, Washington D.C., June 23, 1982.

12. United States, Congress, Congressional Record (Washington, D.C.: Government Printing Office, October 19, 1977), p. 34425.

13. Ibid.

14. Ibid.

15. The Miami Herald, May 5, 1978.

16. United States, Congress, Recent Developments in Mexico, p. 89-90.

17. Interview with Richard Feinberg, former member of th Policy Planning Staff, U.S. Department of State, Washington, D.C., July 1, 1982.

18. United States, Congress, Recent Developments in Mexico, p. 58.

19. Ibid., p. 65.

20. Ibid., p. 67.

21. Ibid., p. 73.

22. Ibid., p. 75-84.

23. R. Feinberg, "Bureaucratic Organization and United States Policy toward Mexico," in S.K. Purcell, (ed.), Mexico-United States Relations (New York: The Academy of Political Science, 1981), p. 34-35.

24. United States, Congress, Mexico's Oil and Gas Policy: An Analysis, Report prepared by the Congressional Research Service, Library of Congress, for the Committee on

238

Foreign Relations and the Joint Economic Committee, 96th Cong., 2d sess. (Washington, D.C.: Government Printing Office, 1978), p. ix-x.

25. *Los Angeles Times*, October 6, 1978.

26. Interview with Richard Feinberg, July 1, 1982.

27. Interview with Robert Pastor, former member of the National Security Council, New York City, September 4, 1981.

28. Jack Ray, letter cited in R. Fagen and H. Nau, "Mexican Gas: The Northern Connection," in R. Fagen (ed.), *Capitalism and the State in U.S.-Latin American Relations* (Stanford: Stanford University Press, 1979), p. 412.

29. Interview with Brad Botwin, Department of Energy, International Affairs Division, Washington, D.C., June 28, 1982.

30. G. Grayson, *The Politics of Mexican Oil* (Pittsburgh: Pittsburgh University Press, 1980), p. 55.

31. Ibid., p. 58.

32. R. Mancke, *Mexican Oil and Natural Gas* (New York: Praeger, 1979), p. 113.

33. Grayson, p. 59.

34. Mancke, p. 88-89.

35. Fagen and Nau, p. 392.

36. D. Ronfeldt, R. Nehring, and A. Gandara, *Mexico's Petroleum and U.S. Policy: Implications for the 1980's* (Santa Monica, California: Rand Corporation, 1980), p. 4.

37. Ibid.

38. Ibid.

39. Ibid., p. 3.

40. Grayson, p. 62.

41. Ibid.

42. Ibid., p. 63.

43. Ibid., p. 74.

44. S.K. Purcell, "The Mexico-U.S. Relationship," *Foreign Affairs* 60 (1981/82): 380.

45. Grayson, p. 76.

46. Ibid.

47. Ibid.

48. Ibid.

49. Fagen and Nau, p. 394.

50. Ibid.

51. Ibid., p. 395.

52. Ibid.

53. Ibid., p. 396.

54. Ibid.

55. Grayson, p. 187.

56. Ibid.

239

57. Ibid., p. 188.
58. Jack Ray, interviewed by George Grayson, in Ibid., p. 188.
59. Ibid., p. 187.
60. Ibid.
61. Ibid.
62. Fagen and Nau, p. 400.
63. Ibid.
64. Ibid.
65. Ibid.
66. The early cost estimates called for $1 billion in loans but later the loan requirement was set at $1.5 billion.
67. Grayson, p. 189.
68. Ibid.
69. Ibid.
70. Fagen and Nau, p. 399.
71. Ibid.
72. Ibid.
73. United States, General Accounting Office, Formulation of U.S. International Energy Policies, Report to the Congress by the Comptroller General (Washington, D.C.: Government Printing Office, 1980), p. 2-3.
74. Ibid., p. 7.
75. Ibid., p. 10.
76. Ibid., p. 13, 2.
77. Ibid., p. 15.
78. Ibid., p. 14.
79. Fagen and Nau, p. 384.
80. Ibid.
81. Ibid., p. 385.
82. Ibid.
83. Ibid.
84. Ibid., p. 410.
85. Ibid.
86. Ibid., p. 385.
87. Ibid.
88. Los Angeles Times, February 6, 1978.
89. Ibid.
90. Fagen and Nau, p. 411.
91. Los Angeles Times, February 6, 1978.
92. Los Angeles Times reported the possibility of $2.00 on February 6, 1978, and Fagen pointed out the limits of supply estimations in Fagen and Nau, p. 413.
93. Los Angeles Times, February 6, 1978.
94. The Wall Street Journal, October 13, 1978.
95. United States, Congress, Mexico's Oil and Gas

240

Policy: An Analysis, p. 48.
    96. Interview with Brad Botwin, June 28, 1982.
    97. Ibid.
    98. Interview with Glen Rase, Economic and Business Affairs, Department of State and former energy attache in the U.S. Embassy in Mexico City, Washington, D.C., July 14, 1982.
    99. Interview with Robert Hopper, June 23, 1982.
    100. Grayson, p. 195.
    101. Interview with Brad Botwin, June 28, 1982.
    102. Interview with Richard Feinberg, July 1, 1982.
    103. Ibid.
    104. Interview with Glen Rase, July 14, 1982.
    105. The Miami Herald, December 24, 1977.
    106. The Journal of Commerce, September 28, 1978.
    107. Ibid.
    108. Ibid.
    109. The Wall Street Journal, December 5, 1977.
    110. Interview with Brad Botwin, June 28, 1982.
    111. Grayson, p. 195.
    112. The Journal of Commerce, January 18, 1979.
    113. Interview with Glen Rase, July 14, 1982.
    114. Interview with Brad Botwin, June 28, 1982.
    115. The Financial Times, January 4, 1978.
    116. United States, Congress, Congressional Record, October 19, 1977, p. 34425.
    117. Quoted in Grayson, p. 192.
    118. Ibid.
    119. Letter from J.L. Moore, President of the EXIM Bank, printed in the Congressional Record, p. 34425.
    120. Ibid.
    121. Grayson, p. 192.
    122. Quoted in Fagen, p. 412.
    123. Quoted in Ibid., p. 412.
    124. See The Washington Post, February 13, 1979.
    125. The Washington Post, February 18, 1979.
    126. The term "decision" requires some explanation. Schlesinger's "decision" came in the form of his final offer to the Mexican officials. There was never a formal decision on the agreement by DOE because Lopez Portillo decided to terminate negotiations and let the letter of intent expire. Schlesinger's decision was still a decision but not a formal one. This point is often stressed by the 1977 negotiators in response to criticism of the DOE's actions. It is, however, an exercise in semantic fencing and is basically irrelevant.
    127. Grayson, p. 194.

128. Ibid.
129. P. Smith, Mexico, the Quest for a U.S. Policy (New York: Foreign Policy Association, 1980), p. 19.
130. Los Angeles Times, December 22, 1977.
131. Grayson, p. 196.
132. The New York Times, January 6, 1978.
133. The Washington Post, February 18, 1979.
134. Grayson, p. 174.
135. Reported in Fagen and Nau, p. 405.
136. The Journal of Commerce, November 30, 1977.
137. The Wall Street Journal, December 5, 1977.
138. Ibid.
139. The Journal of Commerce, November 6, 1978.
140. Interviews with Brad Botwin, June 28, 1982 and Glen Rase, July 14, 1982.
141. Interview with Robert Pastor, September 4, 1981.
142. Grayson, p. 195.
143. The Washington Post, January 14, 1979.
144. Los Angeles Times, May 8, 1978.
145. The New York Times, July 1, 1978.
146. Grayson, p. 196.
147. Los Angeles Times, June 13, 1978.
148. Ibid.
149. The Journal of Commerce, September 28, 1978.
150. United States, Congress, House, Mexican Oil and Technology Transfer, Hearings before the Subcommittee on Investigations and Oversight of the Committee on Science and Technology, U.S. House of Representatives, 96th Cong., 1st sess., July 31, August 1, 1979 (Washington, D.C.: Government Printing Office, 1979), p. 22.
151. United States, Congress, Mexico's Oil and Gas Policy: An Analysis, p. ix.
152. Ibid., p. x.
153. Ibid.
154. Ibid., p. viii.
155. Testimony of John Treat in United States, Congress, House, Mexican Oil and Technology Transfer, p. 23.
156. Interview with Glen Rase, July 14, 1982.
157. Grayson, p. 195.
158. R. Jervis, Perception and Misperception in International Politics (Princeton: Princeton University Press, 1976), p. 128.
159. The Washington Post, January 10, 1979.
160. The New York Times, January 18, 1979.
161. United States, Congress, Mexico's Oil and Gas Policy: An Analysis.

242

162. The Wall Street Journal, January 24, 1979
163. The Journal of Commerce, January 18, 1979.
164. United States, Congress, Mexico's Oil and Gas Policy: An Analysis.
165. The Wall Street Journal, January 24, 1979.
166. United States, General Accounting Office, p. 47.
167. Ibid., p. 48.
168. Ibid.
169. Ibid.
170. Interview with Richard Feinberg, July 1, 1982.
171. United States, National Security Council, Presidential Review Memorandum 41: Summary Report[1978]. This document is unpublished and was released under the Freedom of Information Act, p. 9.
172. Ibid.
173. Feinberg, p. 33.
174. Option 2 was "sanitized" from the sections of the report released to me. However, Richard Feinberg worked on the report and indicated during the interview that the three options in his article corresponded to options 1-3 listed in PRM 41. Therefore, see Feinberg, p. 34, for a discussion of Option 2.
175. This was reported in The New York Times, January 28, 1979, and in The Washington Post, December 15, 1978.
176. The Washington Post, December 15, 1978.
177. United States, National Security Council, p. 9.
178. Feinberg, p. 34.
179. Ibid., p. 35.
180. United States, National Security Council, p. 10.
181. Interview with Richard Feinberg, July 1, 1982, and Robert Hopper, June 23, 1982.
182. The Washington Post, December 15, 1979.
183. The Wall Street Journal, February 6, 1979.
184. Los Angeles Times, February 15, 1979.
185. The Washington Post, February 17, 1979.
186. Interview with Richard Feinberg, July 1, 1982.
187. Interviews with Brad Botwin, June 28, 1982, and Glen Rase, July 14, 1982.
188. Richard Feinberg reported this change in personnel to those with a "broader" view in an interview on July 1, 1982.
189. Interviews with Richard Feinberg, July 1, 1982 and Brad Botwin, June 28, 1982.
190. Interview with Richard Feinberg.
191. J. Kraft, "A Reporter at Large: The Mexican Oil Puzzle, The New Yorker, October 19, 1979.
192. The Washington Post, December 15, 1978.

243

193. Interview with Brad Botwin, June 28, 1982.
194. United States, Congress, House, Mexican Oil and Technology Transfer, Testimony of Julius Katz, p. 251.
195. Ibid., p. 262.
196. Ibid., p. 264.
197. Ibid., p. 265-266.
198. Interview with Brad Botwin, June 28, 1982.
199. Ibid.
200, Ibid.
201. Interview with Glen Rase, July 14, 1982.
202. Kraft, p. 176.
203. Ibid.
204. Interview with Glen Rase, July 14, 1982.
205. Interview with Mike Barry, Economic Office, Mexican Desk, United States Department of State, Washington, D.C., June 22, 1982.
206. Kraft, p. 176.
207. Ibid.
208. Ibid., p. 177.
209. Ibid., p. 178.
210. Ibid.
211. Interview with Robert Pastor, Sptember 4, 1981.
212. Interview with Brad Botwin, June 28, 1982.
213. Interview with Robert Pastor, September 4, 1981.
214. Interviews with Brad Botwin, June 28, 1982, and Glen Rase, July 14, 1982. It would not be most theoretically satisfying if evidence could be found indicating that those with a neutral view were not surprised by the Mexican reaction. Unfortunately, in all of the interviews conducted, I found several individuals who were sympathetic with Mexico and thought the Mexican anger justifiable but no one who remembers predicting that Mexico would call Schlesinger's bluff. Instead, one interviewee recalled that he was surprised when he learned that Schlesinger had finally caused the agreement to be cancelled. He had expected Schlesinger to approve it in the end. (This was Robert Hopper, interviewed on June 23, 1982.)
215. See Leslie Goldman's statement in United States, Congress, House, Mexican Oil and Technology Transfer.
216. Interview with Brad Botwin, June 28, 1982.
217. Ibid.
218. Interviews with Mike Barry, June 22, 1982, and Brad Botwin, June 28, 1982.
219. Interview with Mike Barry, June 22, 1982.
220. Interview with a member of the State Department who asked to remain anonymous.

244

221. Interview with Robert Pastor, September 4, 1981.
222. Fagen and Nau, p. 404.
223. Interview with Glen Rase, July 14, 1982.
224. This was the position taken by Glen Rase.
225. This point was made by Richard Feinberg in the interview of July 1, 1982.
226. Interview with Mike Barry, June 22, 1982.
227. Ibid.
228. Ibid.

Conclusions

The purpose of this study has been to develop and test the utility of a model of political judgments. The model used here is based upon both political analyses and cognitive psychology. A general world view was discussed and several patterns of behavior were expected to emerge as a result of the images used to evaluate a particular state, Mexico. It may be most useful to conclude with a brief discussion of the goals of the study and the problems and prospects of psychological studies of politics.

THE UTILITY OF THE COGNITIVE APPROACH

As the study of negotiations between the United States and Mexico demonstrates, it is possible to develop and test propositions concerning political behavior based upon cognitive psychology. This particular psychological focus permitted the construction of a framework depicting the political world view and some speculation about the impact of psychological images on judgments and predictions of another state's actions. In the particular case used here only two images were evident. The framework presented seven images. Evidence that these seven images do exist was sought through a review of scholarly analyses and through a survey distributed to foreign policy-makers. In the process, one of the images, the "puppet" category, received little support. This category may be an image that was useful in the past but no longer adequately structures a part of the political environment for American policy makers. Another category, the hegemonist, apparently caused some confusion among the respondents probably because most Americans do not use this particular category. The other five images, the enemy, the dependent of the enemy, the ally, the neutral, and the dependent of the perceiver's state, received empirical support from the survey and from other sources. The effects of the political world view categories on judgment were discussed in Chapter 4 and several hypotheses were offered concerning the behavior resulting from the psychological processes. They were tested in a bargaining case study.

In the case study the two images affecting behavior did so in ways that conformed to theoretical expectations. Different policies and bargaining strategies were proposed by individuals with different views of the country in question. The policy proposals and the general outlook of the two groups were internally consistent and conflicted with each other in the expected areas. Despite the problems of evidence, it was found that cognitive psychology can be used to develop a general model and to construct patterns of behavior that are observable in policy makers' actions in specific situations. Thus the basic theoretical goal was accomplished.

Future projects using this same approach could benefit from several steps. First, many more cases are necessary to test fully the behavioral patterns associated with the categories. This study included only two images. Not only must studies be undertaken of the behavioral effects of the other images, but additional cases are necessary for examining and re-testing the behavioral patterns found here. These same patterns should be observable repeatedly as judgments are made with the dependent and neutral categories and, of course, with the other categories as well. The case offered in this study can only be suggestive. The policy makers do appear to have acted as the model expected. However, information was limited by the passage of time and the fact that the psychological processes being studied are not evident to the policy makers themselves. This study found a strong correlation between political world view and judgments of Mexico but one case cannot "prove" anything. A variety of cases and tests are needed to verify these findings.

The study brings to the surface several interesting theoretical questions. First, it is possible that other categories exist in the political world view. Additional images should involve a different combination of the same attributes discussed in Chapter 2. Second, while psychological studies point to patterns of behavior that can be expected of those who have a prototypical view of another state, more information is needed concerning the behavior of those who view another states as far from the prototype. In this study, for example, there was a good argument that Mexico's new classification as a neutral was not at the ideal-typical center. Psychological studies offered very few behavioral patterns to look for. The variations in these ordinal judgments raise other questions. For example, do perceptions of states tend to gravitate toward the prototype? It would seem reasonable that once people experience several interactions with the government of another state they become more certain of that state's behavior. Thus, they should become more certain that the category in which the state has been placed is appropriate. Over time, therefore, they may become over-confident psychologically and push the state farther toward the prototype than they would if they maintained a constant "close look." Another interesting area of inquiry would be a study of the influence of old policies on the speed with which psychological adaptation to change occurs.

Finally, a few words about the policy implication of this study. First, although some of the evaluations of Mexico by US officials are breathtaking in their arrogance, a certain amount of sympathy is appropriate. There was no indication that policy makers set out to exploit Mexico, got caught in the act, and had to change policies. The policy makers for both sets of negotiations acted in a manner that they thought offered a good solution to the problem. There was also little indication that policy makers were aware of their underlying cognitions. Some policy makers were interested in and pointed out groups of policy advocates and conflicts between these groups regarding Mexico's leverage and probable behavior. Others were simply interested in explicating their own position on the issue. One clear policy implication, therefore, is to make policy makers more aware of their own and the other policy makers' assumptions about another country. This may at least enable them to set forth different bargaining strategies and scenarios.

One of the most disappointing aspects of this study is that it became more and more apparent that cognitive world views are so strong that it is only by observing some dramatic event such as a policy failure that policy makers change their image of another country. On the other hand, one policy makers who was watching the 1977 negotiations from the State Department but not participating reported that he was surprised when Schlesinger rejected the Mexican offer. This indicates that policy makers may not know either the positions of others or the reasoning behind those positions. Another official stated that he knew of no one who advocated that Mexico should be pushed into particular domestic and foreign policies. Two weeks later another official in the same agency reported that this opinion emanated from an office down the hall. A simple improvement in the flow of information may ultimately lead to questions within policy making groups about each others' assumptions. This may also be a useful role for non-governmental groups and individuals -- such as academics.

Appendix

AN IMPORTANT QUESTION IN STUDYING FOREIGN POLICY DECISION
MAKING IS HOW POLICY ADVOCATES ORGANIZE THE POLITICAL WORLD.
QUESTIONS 1-5 CONCERN THIS PROBLEM.

1. As an observer of international events, please judge the
following states as you usually do when considering their
general international policies. Which ones are alike in
their policies? Please group them into as many groups as
seems appropriate to you. They are arranged alphabetically
below. They may be groups by number rather than name.

1. Brazil	7. Great Britain	13. Poland
2. Canada	8. Guatemala	14. South Africa
3. China	9. India	15. South Korea
4. Czechoslovakia	10. Mexico	16. Switzerland
5. El Salvador	11. Nigeria	17. USSR
6. France	12. North Korea	18. West Germany
		19. Yugoslavia

2. What groups do they form when judged solely on the basis
of their overall policies toward the United States?

3. How would you label the groups you have created in
questions 1 and 2?

4. In general, how influential do you think each of the
following actors is in shaping international issues and
disputes? Please circle the number which best represents
your evaluation of each actor's importance.

	Unimportant				Important		
1. Multinational Corporations	1	2	3	4	5	6	7
2. United Nations Agencies	1	2	3	4	5	6	7
3. Individual state governments	1	2	3	4	5	6	7
4. Economic cartels (eg. OPEC)	1	2	3	4	5	6	7
5. Regional organizations (eg. Organization of African Unity, Organization of American States, etc.)	1	2	3	4	5	6	7
6. International judicial agencies	1	2	3	4	5	6	7
7. Terrorist groups	1	2	3	4	5	6	7

5. Of all the ways of distinguishing one state from another,
which of the following do you consider the most useful?
Please rank the alternatives from most to least useful, with
#1 being most useful.

_____ States distinguished by regional position such as
geographic location.

_____ States distinguished by their general policies
toward the US such as Enemy, Ally, Neutral,
Dependent, etc.

_____ States distinguished by their ideological stance
such as fascism, christian democracy, authoritarian
corporatism, liberal democracy, socialism, etc.

_____ states distinguished by size.

_____ Other -- do you use some other distinguishing
criteria? If so, please record those criterion
below and rank them along with the four options
provided above.

QUESTIONS 6 TO 17 DEAL WITH SEVERAL CHARACTERISTICS OF
DIFFERENT TYPES OF STATES.

Below is a list of several possible types of states and
a variety of different characteristics. Below each
characteristic is a scale which presents possible variations
of that characteristic.
Please place each type of state above the number on
each scale which best describes that characteristic for that
type of state.
(An example is provided below.)

The seven types of states are:

A) Enemy; B) Hegemonist; C) Dependent Ally of an Enemy;
D) Neutral; E) Ally; F) Dependent of the US; G) Puppet
of the US

Example:

When evaluating each type of state in terms of the
quality of fine food found in that type of state, if you
felt that fine food is frequently available in an Ally,
slightly less available in a Puppet and Dependent of your
state, moderately often available in a Hegemonist, and
basically absent in an Enemy or its Dependent Ally, you
would rate each type of state as follows:

Fine Food

Absent			Occasionally available			Frequently available	
/ A /	C	/	/ B /	D	/ G,F	/ E /	
1	2	3	4	5	6	7	

Characteristics

6. Military strength compared to that of the US

Inferior			Equal			Superior	
/	/	/	/	/	/	/	/
1	2	3	4	5	6	7	

252

7. Willingness to use military force

Very unwilling   moderately willing   Very willing
  /   /   /   /   /   /   /   /
  _____
     1   2   3   4   5   6   7

8. Similarity to the US in form of government

Very dissimilar   Moderately similar   Very similar
  /   /   /   /   /   /   /   /
  _____
     1   2   3   4   5   6   7

9. Existence of domestic groups which actively attempt to
influence foreign policy.

                                              Present and
Absent   Moderately active   very active
  /   /   /   /   /   /   /   /
  _____
     1   2   3   4   5   6   7

10. Effectiveness in the implementation of foreign policy.

Very effective   Moderately effective   Ineffective
  /   /   /   /   /   /   /   /
  _____
     1   2   3   4   5   6   7

11. Economic strength in comparison to that of the USA

Superior   About equal   Inferior
  /   /   /   /   /   /   /   /
  _____
     1   2   3   4   5   6   7

12. Economically penetrable, permitting economic interaction
with other states.

Highly penetrable   Moderately penetrable   Impenetrable
  /   /   /   /   /   /   /   /
  _____
     1   2   3   4   5   6   7

13. Culture in comparison to the USA

Less advanced   Equal   More advanced
  /   /   /   /   /   /   /   /
_____
  1   2   3   4   5   6   7

14. Degree of support for the international policies of USA

Highly   Moderately   Completely
supportive   supportive   unsupportive
  /   /   /   /   /   /   /   /
_____
  1   2   3   4   5   6   7

15. Flexibility in international bargaining

Inflexible   Moderately flexible   Highly flexible
  /   /   /   /   /   /   /   /
_____
  1   2   3   4   5   6   7

16. Degree of determination and will in pursuing general
international goals

Vigorous   Moderate exertion   Passive
  /   /   /   /   /   /   /   /
_____
  1   2   3   4   5   6   7

17. Compatibility of each type of state's general
international goals with those of the USA

Highly compatible   Moderately compatible   Incompatible
  /   /   /   /   /   /   /   /
_____
  1   2   3   4   5   6   7

18. From the perspective of the USA, please list those
modern or historical state which you consider to be perfect
examples of:

a. Enemy _____ b. Neutral _____
C. Hegemonist _____ d. Puppet of the USA _____
e. Dependent Ally of the Enemy _____
f. Dependent of the US _____ g. Ally _____

THE NEXT FEW QUESTIONS DEAL WITH THE JUDGMENTS FOREIGN
POLICY OBSERVERS MAKE ABOUT PARTICULAR STATES.

Below is a list of states:

A) USSR; B) Great Britain; C) China; D) Mexico; E) Poland;
F)Canada; G) Cuba; H) West Germany; I) Switzerland; J)
India; K) Guatemala

Please consider each state's general international policies
toward the USA during the last decade.

19. As an example of an Enemy, how would you rate each state
above on the scale below?

Terrible example   Perfect example
 /   /   /   /   /   /   /   /

───
    1   2   3   4   5   6   7

20. As an example of a Hegemonist, how would you rate each
state above on the scale below?

Perfect example   Terrible example
 /   /   /   /   /   /   /   /

───
    1   2   3   4   5   6   7

21. As an example of an Ally, how would you rate each state
above on the scale below?

Terrible example   Perfect example
 /   /   /   /   /   /   /   /

───
    1   2   3   4   5   6   7

22. As an example of a Dependent Ally of an Enemy, how would
you rate each state above on the scale below?

Perfect example   Terrible example
 /   /   /   /   /   /   /   /

───
    1   2   3   4   5   6   7

23. As an example of a <u>Neutral,</u> how would you rate each state above on the scale below?

Terrible example   Perfect example
/   /   /   /   /   /   /   /
_____
   1   2   3   4   5   6   7

24. As an example of a <u>Dependent of the US,</u> how would you rate each state above on the scale below?

Perfect example   Terrible example
/   /   /   /   /   /   /   /
_____
   1   2   3   4   5   6   7

25. As an example of a <u>Puppet</u> of the US, how would you rate each state above on the scale below?

Terrible example   Perfect example
/   /   /   /   /   /   /   /
_____
   1   2   3   4   5   6   7

BELOW IS A LIST OF STRATEGIES STATES CAN USE DURING INTERNATIONAL DISPUTES:

    A. Initiate diplomatic exchanges and negotiations
    B. Threaten to use military force
    C. Use economic sanctions
    D. Do nothing
    E. Appeal to international forums
    F. Use the domestic press for rhetorical denunciations
    G. Other (Please indicate the strategy) _____

26. Please consider the usual disputes the USA has with each type of state below. Which strategies do you <u>expect each type of state to use</u> during a dispute with the USA? List the strategies (by letter) in the oerder in which you expect them to be used by that type of state.

Enemy _____   Hegemonist _____
Dependent Ally of the Enemy _____
Ally _____   Neutral _____
Dependent of USA _____   Puppet of USA _____

256

27. Please consider again the usual disputes the USA has with each type of state. In what sequence <u>should</u> <u>the</u> <u>USA</u> <u>apply</u> the strategies mentioned above to each type of state listed below?

Enemy _____ Hegemonist _____
Dependent Ally of an Enemy _____
Ally _____ Neutral _____
Dependent of USA _____ Puppet of USA _____

28. What specific historical events do you associate with the following types of states? Please place one phrase or word that best describes the historical events you associate with each type of state.

Enemy _____
Hegemonist _____
Dependent Ally of an Enemy _____
Ally _____
Neutral _____
Dependent of the USA _____
Puppet of the USA _____

FINALLY, HERE ARE A FEW PERSONAL QUESTIONS. THIS INFORMATION WILL BE USED ONLY FOR COMPARATIVE ANALYSIS AND WILL NOT IDENTIFY YOU IN ANY WAY.

29. Age: _____ years
30. Sex: _____ male _____ female
31. Department or agency for which you work _____
32. How long have you been in your present position? ___
33. G.S. level of current position ____; or F.S. _____
34. What do you consider yourself a specialist in? For example, political affairs, economic analysis, communications, cultural exchange, security analysis, intelligence, research and analysis, etc.

_____

35. Politically, do you consider yourself: (circle one)

   a. Very Liberal   b. Liberal
   c. Moderate/Middle of the Road
   d. Conservative   d. Very Conservative

36. Would you like a copy of the summary results of this survey? _____ yes _____ no

Index

Adaptation Level Theory, 22, 116-117. See also Helson
Agency for International Development, 61
Alaskan North Slope, 195
Algeria, 188, 195, 202
Alliance for Progress, 106, 131
Allport, G., 22, 24, 36, 117
American Chamber of Commerce in Mexico, 172
Anderson, N., 22
Arbenz, J., 149
Argentina, 149
Asch, S. 23, 26, 122
Atlantic Alliance, 63, 65, 68, 69, 88, 89
    as ally, 92
    as dependent, 94
    as enemy, 90
Attitude(s), 5, 7, 8
Attribution Theory, 6
Axelrod, R., 18, 19

Beliefs, 8, 14, 16. See also Cognition
    information processing, 16
    definition, 11
    instrumental, 10
    motive(s) and, 15
    operational code and, 13

philosophical, 9-10
Bentsen, L. 176-177
Bieri, J., 22
Blalock, H., 8
Bolsheviks, 10, 17
Bonham, M., 18
Boniauto, G.B., 124
Brazil, 62-65, 67, 68, 149, 153
British Thermal Unit, 190
Bruner, J., 115, 116, 125, 126
Bryant, W., 159
Brzezinski, Z., 217
Bulgaria, 87
Byers, R.B., 43

Canada, 62, 63, 66, 90, 200, 202, 203, 208, 221
    as ally, 92, 93, 105
    as dependent, 95
    as neutral, 93
Capability, 48, 49
Cardenas, L., 146
Carlston, D., 118
Carter Administration, 1, 97, 143, 158, 173, 180, 192, 194, 200, 214, 221, 223, 233, 235
Castro, F., 156
Category, 23, 33-36, 46, 50, 56, 170. See also change

257

Department of Justice, 214
Department of State, 61,
214. See also State
Department
Department of Treasury, 170,
192, 214
Diesing, P. 125
Dominican Republic, 106. See
also United States
Dulles, J.F., 44

Echeverria, L., 151-155, 156,
223
Eiser, R., 35
El Salvador, 62, 63, 65, 68,
155. See also United
States policy toward
as a dependent of the USA,
83, 89
as a puppet, 88,
Energy. See Mexico, United
States, and US-Mexico
relations
Event scripts. See Category
Export-Import Bank (Ex-Im),
204, 205

Fagen, R., 205
Falkowski, L., 16
Festinger, L., 16
France, 45, 62, 63, 68
Frohock, F. M., 8

General Agreement on Tariffs
and Trade (GATT), 156
George, A., 5, 12, 13, 15
Germany,
East, as dependent ally of
the enemy, 87, 105
Nazi, 87
West, 45, 62, 63, 68,
90
as ally, 92, 93
as neutral, 93, 94
Gestalt, 23, 26, 33, 48
Goldman, L., 206

Grayson, G., 187
Great Britain, 45, 50, 62,
63, 90, 176
as ally, 87, 92, 93
as dependent, 94, 95
as neutral, 93
Green, M. R., 147
Guatemala, 62, 63, 65, 90, 98
as ally, 93
as dependent, 95
as puppet, 89, 96,
as neutral, 93, 94
Hanson, L., 43
Helson, H., 22. See also
Adapation Level Theory
Herrmann, R., 48, 49
Hitler, 74
Holsti, O., 13, 14, 17, 42,44
Honduras, 107
Hopple, G., 42, 44
Images, 13, 21, 42, 47-49,
125, 203
and information, 44
and judgment, 7, 21-22
of ally, 51, 69, 81-82
of dependent ally of the
enemy, 51, 78-79
of dependent of the per-
ceiver's state, 51, 69,
83-84, 130-134
of enemy, 47, 51, 69, 74-
76
of hegemonist, 51, 76-78
of neutral, 51, 69, 80-82
of puppet, 51, 85-86,
106, 107, 108
India, 62, 63, 65, 68,
90, 130
as ally, 92, 93
as dependent, 94, 95
as dependent of enemy, 97
as enemy, 90, 91, 93, 94,
as neutral, 87, 88, 93,94,
107
Indonesia, 188, 202
International Labor